Multithreaded Programming with Pthreads

Bil Lewis • Daniel J. Berg

Sun Microsystems Press
A Prentice Hall Title

PH
PTR

The publisher offers discounts on this book when ordered in bulk quantities. For more information, contact: Corporate Sales Department, phone: 800-382-3419; fax: 201-236-7141, email: corpsales@prenhall.com or write Corporate Sales Department, Prentice Hall PTR, One Lake Street, Upper Saddle River, NJ 07458.

Editorial/production supervision: *Craig Little*
Cover design: *Talar Agasyan*
Cover illustration: *Karen Strelecki*
Cover design director: *Jerry Votta*
Interior design: *Meg Van Arsdale*
Art Director: *Gail Cocker-Bogusz*
Manufacturing manager: *Alexis R. Heydt*
Acquisitions editor: *Gregory G. Doench*
Sun Microsystems Press publisher: *Rachel Borden*

10 9 8 7 6 5 4

ISBN 0-13-680729-1

Sun Microsystems Press
A Prentice Hall Title

Contents

Appendices

Figures

Tables

Code Examples

Preface

Today, there are three primary sets of multithreading (MT) libraries: the "standards-based" libraries (all of the UNIX® implementations and VMS, which are moving to POSIX), the OS/2® library, and the Win32 library. (The NT and OS/2 libraries are fairly similar, which should not be too surprising. NT did start life as OS/2, version 2, after all.) Although the APIs[1] and implementations differ significantly, the fundamental concepts are the same. The *ideas* in this book are valid for all three; the details of the APIs differ.

All the specific discussion in this book focuses on the POSIX multithreading model, with comparisons to OS/2 and Win32 throughout.

A frank note about our motivation is in order here. We have slaved away for countless hours on this book because we're propeller-heads who honestly believe that this technology is a superb thing and that the widespread use of it will make the world a better place for hackers like ourselves.

---

[1]"Applications Programming Interface." This is the set of standard library calls that an operating system makes available to applications programmers. For MT, this means all the threads library function calls.

Your motivations for writing MT programs? You can write your programs better and more easily, they'll run faster, and you'll get them to market more quickly, they'll have fewer bugs, you'll have happier programmers, customers, and higher sales. The only losers in this game are the competitors, who will lag behind you in application speed and quality.

MT is here today. It will soon be ubiquitous. As a professional programmer, you have an obligation to understand this technology. It may or may not be appropriate for your current project, but you must be able to make that conclusion yourself. This book will give you what you need to make that decision.

Welcome to the world of the future!

Who Should Use This Book

This book aims to give the programmer or technical manager a solid, basic understanding of threads—what they are, how they work, why they are useful, and some of the programming issues surrounding their use. As an introductory text, it does not attempt a deep, detailed analysis. (At present, there *are* no deep, detailed analyses!) After reading this book the reader should have a solid understanding of the fundamentals, be able to write credible, modestly complex, threaded programs and have the understanding necessary to analyze their own programs and determine the viability of threading them.

This book is written with the experienced C/UNIX programmer in mind. A non-UNIX programmer will find a few of the details unfamiliar, but the concepts clear. A non-C programmer will find the code fragments and API descriptions mildly challenging, though possible to decipher, while the concepts should be clear. A technically minded nonprogrammer should be able to follow most of the concepts and understand the value of threads. A nontechnical person will not get much from this book.

This book does not attempt to explain the usage of the Win32 or OS/2 APIs. It does contrast them to the POSIX API in order to give the POSIX programmer a feeling for what kind of porting issues might be involved when writing to more than one of these libraries.

How This Book Is Organized

Chapter 1, *Introduction*—In which we discuss the motivation for creating thread libraries, the advent of shared memory multiprocessors, and the interactions between threads and SMP machines.

Chapter 2, *Concepts*—In which the reader is introduced to the basic concepts of multitasking operating systems and of multithreading as it compares to other programming paradigms. The reader is shown reasons why multithreading is a valuable addition to programming paradigms, and a number of examples of successful deployment are presented.

Chapter 3, *Foundations*—In which we introduce to the underlying structures upon which threads are built, the construction of the thread itself, and the operating system support that allows an efficient implementation.

Chapter 4, *Lifecycle*—In which the reader is treated to a comprehensive explanation of the intricacies in the life of a thread—birth, life, and death. Even death by vile cancellation. A small program which illustrates all of these stages concludes the chapter.

Chapter 5, *Scheduling*—In which we explain the myriad details of the different scheduling models and the various alternative choices that could be made, describe context switching in detail, and delve into gruesome detail of the various POSIX options and parameters. There is a light at the end of the tunnel, however.

Chapter 6, *Synchronization*—In which the reader is led on a hunt for the intimidating synchronization variable and discovers that it is not actually as frightening as had been thought. Programs illustrating the basic use of the POSIX primitives are shown.

Chapter 7, *Complexities*—In which a series of more complex synchronization variables and options are presented and the trade-off between them and the simpler ones are discussed. Synchronization problems and techniques for dealing with them conclude the chapter.

Chapter 8, *TSD*—In which an explanation of thread-specific data is provided, its use and some of the implementation details. We note a few places where use of TSD could be made more efficient and a few other optimizations that can be made.

Chapter 9, *Cancellation*—In which we describe the acrimonious nature of some programs and how unwanted threads may be disposed of.

The highly complex issues surrounding bounded time termination and program correctness are also covered. A simple conclusion is drawn.

Chapter 10, *Signals*—In which we deal with the various aspects of handling asynchronous events in a multithreaded program. The definitions are given, alternative designs are discussed, and a program illustrating the most complex case is shown.

Chapter 11, *Details*—In which the details of actually writing and compiling an MT program are reviewed. The defined constants are described and methods of dealing with errors are proposed. We note which vendors have made extensions to Pthreads, and where POSIX is headed.

Chapter 12, *Libraries*—In which we explore a variety of operating systems issues that bear heavily upon the usability of the threads library in actual programs. We examine the status of library functions and the programming issues facing them. We look at some design alternatives for library functions.

Chapter 13, *Design*—In which we explore some designs for programs and library functions. Making both programs and individual functions more concurrent is a major issue in the design of these functions. We look at a variety of code examples and the trade-offs between them.

Chapter 14, *Languages*—In which the use of threads in various programming languages is considered and a few minor notes about special features and requirements are made. A number of public Pthreads libraries and some commercial products exist and are noted.

Chapter 15, *Tools*—In which we consider the kinds of new tools that a reader would want when writing a threaded program. An overview of the Solaris tool set is given, as representative of what should be looked for.

Chapter 16, *Performance*—In which we make things faster, look at general performance issues, political performance issues, and thread specific performance issues. We conclude with a discussion of the actual performance of multithreaded NFS.

Chapter 17, *Hardware*—In which we look at the various designs for SMP machines (cache architectures, interconnect topologies, atomic instructions, invalidation techniques) and consider how those designs affect our programming decisions. Some optimization possibilities are looked at.

Chapter 18, *Examples*—In which several complete programs are presented. The details and issues surrounding the way they use threads are discussed and references to other programs on the net are made.

Acknowledgments

Acknowledgments to the Threads Primer

Thanks to Matt Delcambre for his support of the book and his assistance in the review process. Thanks also to John Bost and James Hollingshead for their support and funding of the trips to California. Thanks also go to Mary Himelfarb for putting up with all the paper and time I consumed on her printer.

Special thanks to Ty "Tyrone" McKercher, for all the time in the review process and for always taking the time to listen to my wild new ideas; also for his keen insight during the many late night and weekend programming sessions where many of the examples in the book were born.

Many thanks to Tim Hayes, Jim Thompson, and Richard Robison for providing their customer testimonials and for their early adoption of threading technology in their production applications. Thanks also go to all the people who make up the POSIX committee for all their work on the pthreads draft and the threads documentation team for all their work on the quality documentation.

We owe an enormous debt to Devang Shah and Dan Stein for their constant support, answering innumerable questions, debating issues of presentation and concept. In spite of numerous barriers, we always managed to come to a consensus on the major issues— something which speaks well for the true nature of science.

Many thanks to Richard Marejka, Eric Jaeger, Adrienne Jardetzky, Richard Schaefer, and Charles Fineman for their assistance in the review process and their numerous accurate and insightful comments and suggestions; to Ron Winacott for coming all the way to Sweden to introduce me to the subject; to Chris Crenshaw for his comments and discussion; to Karin Ellison for starting us on this book and for her enormous energy in dealing with all those little problems that always seem to crawl out of the woodwork at 2 a.m. Roses to Marianne Muller who made the Web work for us and was always there with reassurance and support when things got rough.

Thanks to Bill Lindeman, Mukul Goyal, Ben Catanzaro, Morgan Herrington, Paul Lorence, Brian Kinnard, Larry Gee, Shaun Peterson, and Leif Samuelson for their help, comments, and guidance in the numerous fine points of writing, formatting, and interpretation; to my peers in Developer Engineering and the Shaysa council; to RMS who did more to shape my writing abilities than he realizes; to Manoj Goyal who was so pivotal in making the personal interactions at Sun work like they should.

Appreciation for reviewing and discussing numerous points to Carl Hauser, Tom Doeppner, Bart Smaalders, and Barry Medoff.

And for assistance on numerous points, large and small thanks to: Christopher Nicholas, Don Charles, Greg Nakhimovsky, Larry Kilgallen, David Boreham, William E. Hannon Jr., Steve Vinoski, Susan Austin, Rob Rimbold, Jeff Denham, Bill Paulsen, Mike Boucher, Dave Crowley, Bob Rushby, Ben Catanzaro, Tarmo Talts, Greg G. Doench, Burke Anderson, Michael Sebree, Susan Bryant, Timo Kunnas, Kim Albright, and Robert Demb.

A special thanks to two computer scientists whom I have always held in awe and whose writing abilities and finely tuned senses of humor I admire more than I can express, Peter van der Linden and the great Quux. How two individuals can have such depth of understanding and also be such amazing copyeditors, I don't know!

Tusan tack till alla på Sun Sverige, och kram till dej, Madelene.

Ja Tarvi, Kati, Lõvi, Tiia, Epp, Mari ja Kaur, kuna mõnikord vajab inimene sõpru rohkem kui midagi muud.

Acknowledgments to the Pthreads Primer

The first edition of this book was a rush job—we completed the manuscript in four months. After work hours. Four very *long* months. By the end of the year we could see the copious flaws and egregious omissions. "Let's just take a couple of months, change the focus to POSIX and fix a couple of those problem," we said.

Two years later, we have this book, which we think is finally a reasonable introduction to the subject. (But not great, that's for the third edition.) This book is the product of an enormous amount of thought, discussion, and experimentation. A book, even a bad book, requires an amazing amount of effort. And then to compare the fruit of our labors to a truly excellent text... It's humbling.

And we didn't even to all the work on this book! The people who helped on this book are legion. We owe debts of gratitude to:

- The roughly 3,000 people who took our different classes and presentations on threads, in the US, in Sweden, India, Finland, and Estonia, plus those who helped organize them.

- The hundreds of people who have asked questions, given answers, or just plain argued issues on the newsgroup.

- Everyone who brought issues to our attention that forced us to think deeper.

- The reviewers:
    * Dave Cortesi (SGI)
    * Dave Butenhof (Digital)
    * Mike Boucher (Dakota Scientific Software)
    * William E. Hannon, Jr. (IBM)
    * Richard Schaefer (Sun)
    * Richard Marejka (Sun, Canada)
    * Gregory Bumgardner (Rogue Wave)
    * Chary G. Tamirisa (IBM)
    * Shin Iwamoto (who both reviewed and translated!)

- The folks who helped us get information, fix mistakes, test programs, and avoid confusion: Chris Thomas, Brian Hall, Doug Schmidt, Jeremy Allison, Frank Mueller,

Christopher Provenzano, Michael T. Peterson, Xavier Leroy, Dr. Douglas Niehaus, Frank Mueller, Steve Vinoski, Pankaj Garg, Bart Smaalders, James Pitcairn-Hill, Tarik Kerroum, Sanjay Kini, Matthew Peters, Tom Barton, Bertrand Meyer, Glenn J. Allin, Stacey Carroll, Toshihiro Matsu, Chris Thomas, Ivan Soleimanipour, Bart Smaalders, Bo Sundmark, Bryan O'Sullivan, Pekka Hedqvist, Ian Emmon, John Bossom, Asad Hanif, Matt Dillon, David Holmes, Imhof Michael, Rolf Andersson, Jacqueline Proulx Farrell, Richard Marlon Stein, Ted Selker, Keith Bierman, Peter Jeffcock, Prakash Narayan, Charlie Fineman, Dan Lenoski, Wolf-Dietrich Weber, Tom Doeppner, and Scott Norton.

- The editors and staff: Gregory G. Doench, Rachel Borden, Mary Treacy, John Bortner, and Gwen Burns.
- The authors of all the other books which we perused so carefully.
- All of the folks on 1003.1c, who did such an excellent job.
- Bil's PacAir Formula which never lost a thermal, nor bonked a landing, which kept him both alive and sane.
- And: Mom.

    — *Dan Berg*   — *Bil Lewis*

To Elaine, my wife and best friend, for her encouragement and understanding during all the late nights and weekends when I should have been spending time with her. Thank You!

— Dan

A mes enfants, Caleb, Matthew, et Rebecca. "Tu deviens responsable pour toujours de ce que tu as apprivoisé"

— Bil

Introduction

In which we discuss the motivation for creating thread libraries, the advent of shared memory multiprocessors, and the interactions between threads and SMP machines.

Multithreading (MT) is a technique that allows one program to do multiple tasks concurrently. The basic concept of multithreaded programming has existed in research and development labs for several decades. Co-routine systems such as Concurrent Pascal and InterLisp's Spaghetti stacks were in use in the mid-70s and dealt with many of the same issues. Ada's tasks are a language-based construct that maps directly onto threads (so directly, in fact, that current Ada compilers implement tasks with threads). Other versions of co-routining have existed even longer.

The emergence of this concept in industry as an accepted, standardized programming paradigm is a phenomenon of the 1990s. As with many other concepts, the research and the experimental use of threads have been widespread in specific industries, universities, and research institutes, and are entering industry as a relatively well-formed whole on all fronts almost simultaneously. In 1991, no major commercial operating systems contained a robust user-level threads library. In 1997, every major player in the computer industry has one.

Some of the motivation for this emergence can be ascribed to general good sense and the recognition of a technology whose time has come. Some can be related to the unification efforts surrounding UNIX. Probably the greatest push, especially when viewed from the point of view of the independent software vendor (ISV) and the end user, is the emergence of shared memory symmetric multiprocessors (SMP). MT provides exactly the right programming paradigm to make maximal use of these new machines.

The threading models we describe are strictly software models that can be implemented on any general-purpose hardware. Much research is creating a better hardware that would be uniquely suited for threaded programming. We do not address that aspect in this book.

To those of us concerned with the theoretical underpinnings of programming paradigms and language design, the true value of multithreading is significant and obvious. It provides a far superior paradigm for constructing programs. For those others concerned with the practical details of getting real tasks done using computers, the value is significant and obvious as well. Multithreading makes it possible to obtain vastly greater performance than was ever before possible by taking advantage of multiprocessor machines.

At whatever price point, the purchasers of workstations want maximal performance from their machines. The demands of computationally intensive users are always growing, and they invariably exceed the provisions of their wallets. They might want a "Personal Cray," but they can't afford one.

One of the solutions to this demand lies in the ever-increasing performance of CPUs. Along with the obvious technique of increasing the clock speed, a wide range of other methods is used to increase the performance of individual CPUs. The use of long instruction pipelines or superscalar techniques has allowed us to produce multiple-instruction machines that can do a lot more in a single clock tick. Finer compiler optimization techniques, out-of-order execution, predictive branching, VLIW, etc., allow us to obtain better and better performance from processors. However good these methods are, they still have their limits.

One of the major limiting factors is the problem of limited bus, memory, and peripheral speeds. We can build CPUs today that operate at 600 MHz, but we can't build communications buses that operate at the same speed. RAM speeds are also falling further behind the demands of the CPUs. It is expensive to build 600 MHz CPUs, but as there are only a few in a system, it is affordable. To build memory that can keep up with these speeds would be prohibitively expensive. A great many machines today implement two-level caches to deal with this problem (single-level caches weren't enough!). Multilevel caches work effectively with well-behaved programs, where sequential data and instruction references are likely to be physically adjacent in memory. But truly random-access programs wreak havoc on this scheme, and we can point to any number of programs that run faster on slower machines that lack that second-level cache.

None of the issues addressed above play favorites with any manufacturers. Sun, Intel, HP, IBM, SGI, DEC, etc., have come up with techniques for dealing with them. Some techniques have proven to be more effective than others, but none of them avoids the fundamental limitations of physics. Nature is a harsh mistress.

This is where SMP comes into play. It is one more weapon in our arsenal for performance. Just as the above techniques have allowed us to increase our single-CPU performance, SMP allows us to increase our overall system performance. And that's what we really care about—overall system performance. As one customer put it "SMP, superscalar—buzzwords! I don't care if you have little green men inside the box! I want my program to run faster!"

We can build 64-processor machines today (e.g., the Cray CS6400) that will yield 64 times the performance of a single-processor machine (on some problems). The cost of that 64-CPU machine is a fraction of

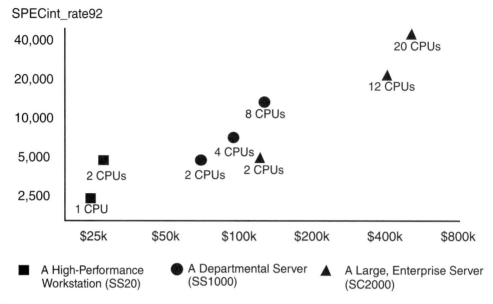

Figure 1–1   *Cost vs. Performance for SMP Workstations and Servers*

the cost of 64 single-processor machines. In a 64-way SMP machine, all 64 processors share the system costs: chassis, main memory, disks, software, etc. With 64 uniprocessors, each processor must have its own chassis, memory, etc. This fact makes SMP highly attractive for its price/performance ratio. An additional attraction of SMP is that it is also possible to purchase a machine with a small number of CPUs and add more CPUs as demands (and budgets) increase. In Figure 1–1, these advantages of SMP are clear.

The economics of purchasing an SMP machine are pretty much the same as the economics of purchasing any machine. There are some extra unknowns ("I have 600 different applications that I run from time to time; how much faster will they all run? How much time will I save in a day?"), but if we focus on the primary applications in use, we can get reasonable data upon which to make our decisions. The basic question is, "If my applications run an average of N% faster on a dual-CPU machine that costs M% more, is it worth it?"

Only you (or your customers) can answer this question, but we can give you some generalities. Here is a typical situation: The customer's major application is MARC Analysis' MARC Solver (for circuit simulation). The MARC Solver runs about 80% faster on a dual-processor SPARCstation™ 20 than it does on a single-processor SPARCstation 20. The single-processor machine costs $16,000; the dual-processor costs $18,000 (about 12% more). If the designers (who cost at least $100,000/year) are constantly waiting for the solver to complete its runs, is it worth it? Obviously, yes. You will save a lot of money on a minor investment. Indeed, MARC sells very well on SMP machines.

If you are a program developer (either in-house or an ISV), your question is going to be, "Should I spend the time to write my program so that it will take advantage of SMP machines?" (This probably means threading, although there are other possibilities.) Your answer will be related to your anticipated sales. If your program runs 50% faster on a dual-processor machine, will your customers buy SMP machines and more of your software? Or, to pose the question differently, if you don't do it, will some competitor do it instead and steal your customers?

The answer depends upon your program. If you write a simple text editor that is never CPU-bound, the answer is a clear "no." If you write a database that is always CPU-bound, it's "yes." If you write a page-layout program that is sometimes CPU-bound, the answer is "maybe." In general, if users ever have to wait for your program, you should be looking at threading and SMP.

But there is more value to threading than just SMP performance. In many instances uniprocessors will also experience a significant performance improvement. And that bit about programming paradigms? It really does count. Being able to write simpler, more readable code helps you in almost all aspects of development. Your code can be less buggy, get out there faster, and be easier to maintain.

Multithreading is not a magic bullet for all your ills,[1] and it does introduce a new set of programming issues that must be mastered, but it goes a long way toward making your work easier and your programs more efficient.

---

[1] If you have ever spent days debugging complex signal handling code, you may disagree. For asynchronous code, it *is* a magic bullet!

2

Concepts

In which the reader is introduced to the basic concepts of multitasking operating systems and of multithreading as it compares to other programming paradigms. The reader is shown reasons why multithreading is a valuable addition to programming paradigms, and a number of examples of successful deployment are presented.

Background: Traditional Operating Systems

Before we get into the details of threads, it will be useful for us to have some clear understanding of how operating systems without threads work. In the simplest operating system world of single-user, single-tasking operating systems such as DOS, everything is quite easy to understand and to use, though the functionality offered is minimal.

DOS divides the memory of a computer into two sections: the portion where the operating system itself resides (*kernel space*[1]) and the portion where the programs reside (*user space*). The division into these two spaces is done strictly by the implicit agreement of the programmers involved—meaning that nothing stops a user program from accessing data in kernel space. This lack of hardware enforcement is good, because it is simple and works well when people write perfect programs. When a user program needs some function performed for it by kernel code (such as reading a file from a disk), the program can call the DOS function directly to read that file.

Each program has some code that it runs (which is just a series of instructions, where the *program counter* points to the current instruction), some data (global and local) that it uses, and a stack where local data and return addresses are stored (the *stack pointer* designates the current active location on the stack).

Figure 2–1 illustrates the traditional DOS operating system memory layout.

Thus, the division between user space and kernel space, as shown in Figure 2–1, is a division by agreement of the programmers; there is no hardware enforcement of the policy at all. The drawbacks to this technique are significant, however. Not all programs are written flawlessly, and a programming mistake (or virus!) here can bring down the entire machine or, worse, destroy valued data. Neither can a machine run more than one program at a time, nor can more than one user log in to the machine at a time. Dealing with networks from DOS machines is somewhat awkward and limited.

In a typical multitasking operating system such as VMS, UNIX, Windows NT, etc., this dividing line between the user space and the kernel space is solid (Figure 2–2); it's enforced by the hardware. There are actually two different modes of operation for the CPUs: *user mode*, which allows normal user programs to run, and *kernel mode*, which also allows

---

[1]"Kernel space" is UNIX-lingo for this concept, but the concept is valid for all operating systems.

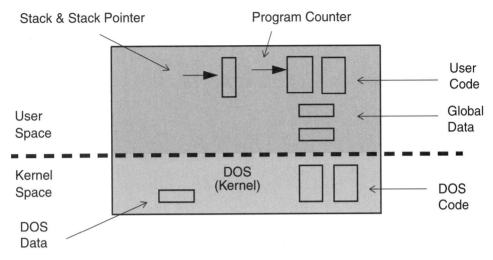

Figure 2–1   *Memory Layout for DOS-Style Operating Systems*

some special instructions to run that only the kernel can execute. These kernel-mode instructions include I/O instructions, processor interrupt instructions, instructions that control the state of the virtual memory subsystem, and, of course, the *change mode* instruction.

So, a user program can execute only user-mode instructions, and it can execute them only in user space. The data it can access and change directly is also limited to data in user space. When it needs something from the kernel (say, it wants to read a file or find out the current time), the user program must make a *system call*. This is a library function that sets up some arguments, then executes a special *trap* instruction. This instruction causes the hardware to trap into the kernel, which then takes control of the machine. The kernel figures out what the user wants (based upon the data that the system call set up), and whether the user has permission to do so. Finally the kernel performs the desired task, returning any information to the user process.

Because the operating system has complete control over I/O, memory, processors, etc., it needs to maintain data for each process it's running. The data tells the operating system what the state of that process is—what files are open, which user is running it, etc. So, the concept of *process* in the multitasking world extends into the kernel (see Figure 2–2), where this information is maintained in a *process structure*. In addition, as this is a multitasking world, more than one process can be

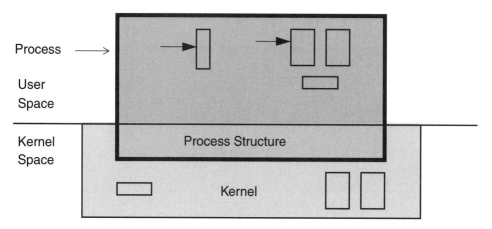

Process ⟶

User
Space

Kernel
Space

Process Structure

Kernel

Figure 2–2   *Memory Layout for Multitasking Systems*

active at the same time, and for most of these operating systems (notably neither Windows NT nor OS/2), more than one user can log in to the machine independently and run programs simultaneously.

Thus, in Figure 2–3, process P1 can be run by user Kim, while P2 and P3 are being run by user Dan, and P4 by user Bil. There is also no particular restriction on the amount of memory that a process can have. P2 might use twice as much memory as P1, for example. It is also true that no two processes can see or change each other's memory, unless they have set up a special *shared memory* segment.

For all the user programs in all the operating systems mentioned so far, each has one stack, one program counter, and one set of CPU registers per process. So, each of these programs can do only one thing at a time. They are *single threaded*.

What Is a Thread?

Just as multitasking operating systems can do more than one thing concurrently by running more than a single process, a process can do the same by running more than a single *thread*. Each thread is a different stream of control that can execute its instructions independently, allowing a multithreaded process to perform numerous tasks concurrently. One thread can run the GUI, while a second thread does some I/O, and a third performs calculations.

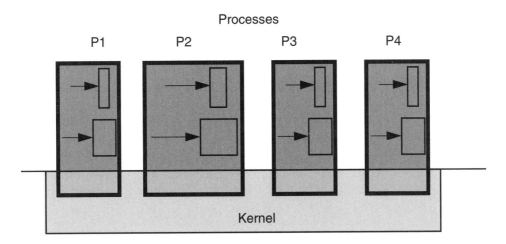

Figure 2–3 *Processes on a Multitasking System*

A thread is an abstract concept that comprises everything a computer does in executing a traditional program. It is the program state that gets scheduled on a CPU, it is the "thing" that does the work. If a process comprises data, code, kernel state, and a set of CPU registers, then a thread is embodied in the contents of those registers—the program counter, the general registers, the stack pointer, etc., and the stack. A thread, viewed at an instant of time, is the state of the computation.

"Gee," you say, "That sounds like a process!" It should. They are conceptually related. But a process is a heavy-weight, kernel-level entity and includes such things as a virtual memory map, file descriptors, user ID, etc., and each process has its own collection of these. The only way for your program to access data in the process structure, to query or change its state, is via a system call.

All parts of the process structure are in kernel space (Figure 2–4). A user program cannot touch any of that data directly. By contrast, all of the user code (functions, procedures, etc.) along with the data is in user space, and can be accessed directly.

A thread is a lightweight entity, comprising the registers, stack, and some other data. The rest of the process structure is shared by all threads: the address space, file descriptors, etc. Much (and sometimes all) of the thread structure is in user space, allowing for very fast access.

The actual code (functions, routines, signal handlers, etc.) is global and can be executed on any thread. In Figure 2–4, we show three

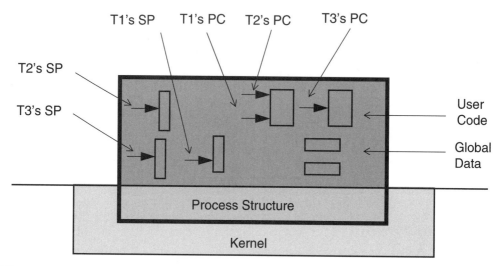

Figure 2–4   *Relationship Between a Process and Threads*

threads (T1, T2, T3), along with their stacks, stack pointers (SP), and program counters (PC). T1 and T2 are executing the same function. This is a normal situation, just as two different people can read the same road sign at the same time.

All threads in a process share the state of that process (Figure 2–5[2]). They reside in the exact same memory space, see the same functions, see the same data. When one thread alters a process variable (say, the working directory), all the others will see the change when they next access it. If one thread opens a file to read it, all the other threads can also read from it.

Let's consider a human analogy: a bank. A bank with one person working in it (traditional process) has lots of "bank stuff" such as desks and chairs, a vault, and teller stations (process tables and variables). There are lots of services that a bank provides: checking accounts, loans, savings accounts, etc. (the functions). With one person to do all the work, that person would have to know how to do everything, and could do so, but it might take a bit of extra time to switch among the various tasks. With two or more people (threads), they would share all the same "bank stuff," but they could specialize in their different functions. And if they

---

[2]From here on, we will use the squiggle shown in the figure to represent the entire thread—stack, stack pointer, program counter, thread structure, etc.

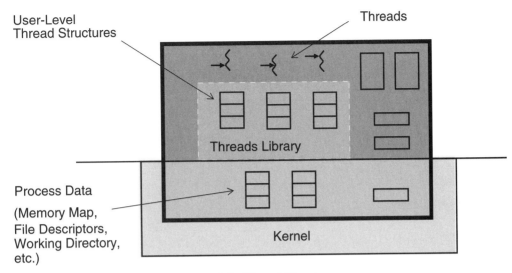

Figure 2–5   *The Process Structure and the Thread Structures*

all came in and worked on the same day, lots of customers could get serviced quickly.

To change the number of banks in town would be a big effort (creating new processes), but to hire one new employee (creating a new thread) would be very simple. Everything that happened inside the bank, including interactions among the employees there, would be fairly simple (user space operations among threads), whereas anything that involved the bank down the road would be much more involved (kernel space operations between processes).

When you write a multithreaded program, 99 percent of your programming is identical to what it was before—you spend your efforts in getting the program to do its real work. The other one percent is spent in creating threads, arranging for different threads to coordinate their activities, dealing with thread-specific data, and dealing with signal masks. Perhaps 0.1% of your code consists of calls to thread functions.

Kernel Interaction

We've now covered the basic concept of threads at the user level. As noted, the concepts and most of the implementational aspects are valid for all thread models. What's missing is the definition of the relationship

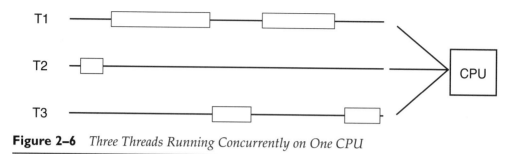

Figure 2–6   *Three Threads Running Concurrently on One CPU*

between threads and the operating systems. How do system calls work? How are signals handled? And how are threads scheduled on CPUs?

It is at this level that the various implementations differ significantly. The operating systems provide different system calls, and even identical system calls can differ widely in efficiency and robustness. The kernels are constructed differently and provide different resources and services.

Keep in mind, as we go though this implementation aspect, that 99% of your threads programming will be done above this level, and the major distinctions will be in the area of efficiency. For UNIX machines, you will be writing strictly at the user level, so as soon as all the vendors implement the POSIX standard, your program can be completely portable, requiring no more than a single TSR (Theoretical Simple Recompile) in order to move to different platforms.

Concurrency vs. Parallelism

Concurrency means that two or more threads (or traditional processes) can be in the middle of executing code at the same time; it could be the same code or it could be different code (see Figure 2–6). The threads may or may not actually be executing at the same time, but rather in the middle of it (i.e., one started executing, it was interrupted, and the other one started). Every multitasking operating system has always had numerous concurrent processes, even though only one can be on the CPU at any given time.

Parallelism means that two or more threads actually run at the same time on different CPUs (see Figure 2–7). On a multiprocessor machine, many different threads can run in parallel. They are, of course, also running concurrently.

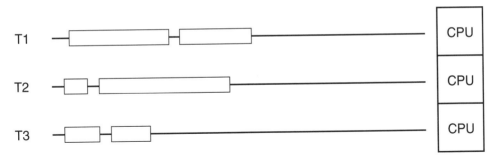

Figure 2–7 *Three Threads Running in Parallel on Three CPUs*

The vast majority of timing and synchronization issues in MT are those of concurrency, not parallelism. Indeed, the threads model was designed to avoid your ever having to be concerned with the details of parallelism. Running an MT program on a uniprocessor does not simplify your programming problems at all. Running on a multiprocessor doesn't complicate them. This is a good thing.

Let us repeat this point. If your program is correctly written on a uniprocessor, it will run correctly on a multiprocessor. The probability of running into a race condition is the same on both a UP and an MP. If it deadlocks on one, it will deadlock on the other. (There are lots of weird little exceptions to the probability part, but you'd have to try hard to make them appear.) A buggy program, however, may run as (naively) expected on a UP, and only show its problems on an MP. Happily, a static analysis tool (such as *Static Lock Analyzer* on page 246) can find all of those problems, leaving you the program logic to work on.

System Calls

A system call is basically a function that ends up trapping to routines in the kernel. These routines may do things as simple as looking up the user ID for the owner of the current process, or as complex as redefining the system's scheduling algorithm. For multithreaded programs, there is a serious issue surrounding how many threads can make system calls concurrently. For some operating systems, the answer is "one"; for others, it's "many." The most important point is that system calls run exactly as they did before, so all your old programs continue to run as they did before, with (almost) no degradation.

Signals

Signals are the UNIX kernel's way of interrupting a running process and letting it know that something of interest has happened. (Neither NT nor OS/2 have such a mechanism.) It could be that a timer has expired, or that some I/O has completed, or that some other process wants to communicate something. Signals are one of the harder aspects of multithreaded programming to understand and to use effectively. Truth be known, they are not so simple in regular UNIX programming. The primary requirement, when designing the multithreaded signal model, was to ensure that the original UNIX semantics were retained. Singlethreaded programs had to run exactly the same way as they had before, and on top of this, the multithreaded programs had to have some sort of "reasonable" semantics. The details we'll reserve until later, but the important point here is that for your old programs, nothing changes.

Synchronization

Synchronization is the method of ensuring that multiple threads coordinate their activities so that one thread doesn't accidently change data that another thread is working on. This is done by providing function calls that can limit the number of threads that can access some data concurrently.

In the simplest case (a *Mutual Exclusion Lock*—a *mutex*), only one thread at a time can execute a given piece of code. This code presumably alters some global data or performs reads or writes to a device. For example, thread T1 obtains a lock and starts to work on some global data. Thread T2 must now wait (typically it goes to sleep) until thread T1 is done before T2 can execute the same code. By using the same lock around all code that changes the data, we can ensure that the data remains consistent.

Scheduling

Scheduling is the act of placing threads onto CPUs so that they can execute, and of taking them off of those CPUs so that others can run instead. In practice, scheduling is not generally an issue because "it all works" just about the way you'd expect.

The Value of Using Threads

There is really only one reason for writing MT programs—to get better programs, more quickly. If you're an ISV, you sell more software. If you're developing software for your own in-house use, you simply have better programs to use. The reason you can write better programs is that MT gives your programs and your programmers a number of significant advantages over non-threaded programs and programming paradigms.

A point to keep in mind here is that you are not replacing simple, non-threaded programs with fancy, complex, threaded ones. You are using threads only when you need them to replace complex or slow non-threaded programs. Threads are just one more way to make your programming tasks easier.

The main benefits of writing multithreaded programs are:

- Performance gains from multiprocessing hardware (parallelism)
- Increased application throughput
- Increased application responsiveness
- Replacing process-to-process communications
- Efficient use of system resources
- Simplified realtime processing
- Simplified signal handling
- The ability to make use of the inherent concurrency of distributed objects
- There is one binary that runs well on both uniprocessors and multiprocessors
- The ability to create well-structured programs
- There can be a single source for multiple platforms

The following sections elaborate further on these benefits.

Parallelism

Computers with more than one processor offer the potential for enormous application speedups (Figure 2–8). MT is an efficient way for

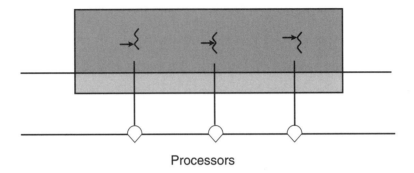

Processors

Figure 2–8   *Different Threads Running on Different Processors*

application developers to exploit the parallelism of the hardware. Different threads can run on different processors simultaneously with no special input from the user and no effort on the part of the programmer.

A good example is a process that does matrix multiplication. A thread can be created for each available processor, allowing the program to use the entire machine. The threads can then compute distinct elements of the resulting matrix by performing the appropriate vector multiplication.

Throughput

When a traditional, single-threaded program requests a service from the operating system, it must wait for that service to complete, often leaving the CPU idle. Even on a uniprocessor, multithreading allows a process to overlap computation with one or more blocking system calls (Figure 2–9). Threads provide this overlap even though each request is coded in the usual synchronous style. The thread making the request must wait, but another thread in the process can continue. Thus, a process can have numerous blocking requests outstanding, giving you the beneficial effects of doing asynchronous I/O, while still writing code in the simpler synchronous fashion.

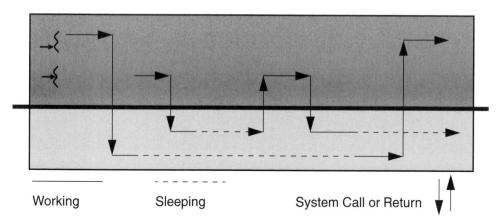

Figure 2–9 *Two Threads Making Overlapping System Calls*

Responsiveness

Blocking one part of a process need not block the whole process. Single-threaded applications that do something lengthy when a button is pressed typically display a "please wait" cursor and freeze while the operation is in progress. If such applications were multithreaded, long operations could be done by independent threads, allowing the application to remain active and making the application more responsive to the user. In Figure 2–10, one thread is waiting for I/O from the buttons, and several threads are working on the calculations.

Communications

An application that uses multiple processes to accomplish its tasks can be replaced by an application that uses multiple threads to accomplish those same tasks. Where the old program communicated among its processes through traditional interprocess communications facilities (e.g., pipes or sockets), the threaded application can communicate via the inherently shared memory of the process. The threads in the MT process can maintain separate connections while sharing data in the same address space. A classic example is a server program, which can maintain one thread for each client connection such as in Figure 2–11.

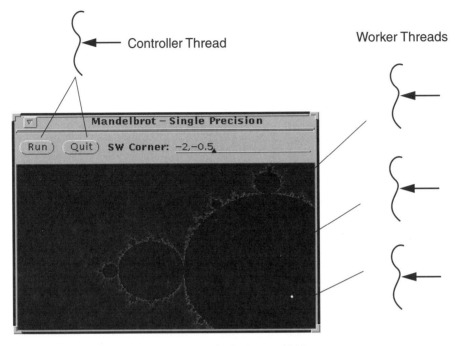

Figure 2–10   *Threads Overlapping Calculation and I/O*

This program provides excellent performance, simpler programming, and effortless scalability.

System Resources

Programs that use two or more processes to access common data through shared memory are effectively applying more than one thread of control. However, each such process must maintain a complete process structure, including a full virtual memory space and kernel state. The cost of creating and maintaining this large amount of state makes each process much more expensive, in both time and space, than a thread. In addition, the inherent separation between processes may require a major effort by the programmer to communicate among the different processes or to synchronize their actions. By using threads for this communication instead of processes, the program will be easier to debug and can run much faster.

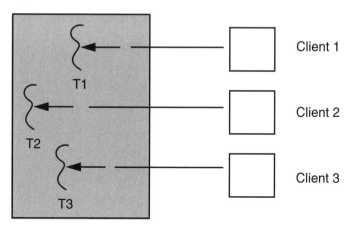

Figure 2–11   *Different Clients Being Handled by Different Threads*

An application can create hundreds or even thousands of threads, one for each synchronous task, with only minor impact on system resources. Threads use a fraction of the system resources needed by processes.

Simplified Realtime Processing

Programs that run in so-called "real time" scheduling classes have complete control over when they get to run and can easily block out other important user or system tasks inadvertently. By running only the truly time-critical sections of a program in a realtime thread, and letting the program do all the rest of its work in a normal, time-shared thread, much of the complexity of realtime programming can be avoided.

Simplified Signal Handling

The asynchronous nature of signal handling makes it very difficult to write code that can handle these asynchronous events and do anything non-trivial. By dedicating a thread to this purpose, it is possible to handle signals in a simple, synchronous fashion.

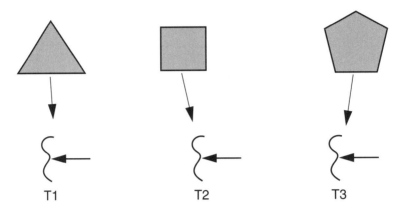

Figure 2–12 *Distributed Objects Running on Distinct Threads*

Distributed Objects

With the first releases of standardized distributed objects and object request brokers, your ability to make use of these will become increasingly important. Distributed objects are inherently multithreaded. Each time you request an object to perform some action, it executes that action in a separate threads. Object servers are an absolutely fundamental element in distributed object paradigm, and those servers are inherently multithreaded.

Although you can make a great deal of use of distributed objects without doing any MT programming, knowing what they are doing and being able to create objects that are threaded will increase the usefulness of the objects you do write.

Same Binary for Uniprocessors and Multiprocessors

In most older parallel processing schemes, it was necessary to tailor a program for the individual hardware configuration. With threads, this customization isn't required because the MT paradigm works well irrespective of the number of CPUs. A program can be compiled once, and it will run acceptably on a uniprocessor, whereas on a multiprocessor it will just run faster.

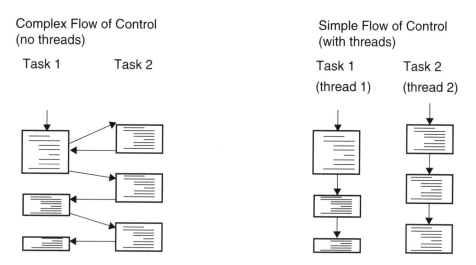

Figure 2–13 *Simplified Flow of Control in Complex Applications*

Program Structure

Many programs are more efficiently structured with threads because they are inherently concurrent. A traditional program that tries to do many different tasks is crowded with lots of complicated code to coordinate these tasks. A threaded program can do the same tasks with much less, far simpler code, as in Figure 2–13. Multithreaded programs can be more adaptive to variations in user demands than single-threaded programs can.

Single Source for Multiple Platforms

Many programs must run on numerous platforms. With the POSIX threads standard (see *Threads Standards* on page 27), it is possible to write a single source and recompile it for the different platforms. Most of the UNIX vendors have POSIX threads.

This is quite some set of claims, and a bit of healthy skepticism is called for. Sure, it sounds good when we say it, but what about when you try to use it? We cannot guarantee that you will experience the same wonderful results, but we can point out a number of cases where other folks have found MT programming to be of great advantage (see *Performance* on page 28).

What Kind of Programs to Thread?

There is a spectrum of programs that one might wish to thread. On one end, there are those that are inherently "MT-ish"—you look at the work to be done, and you think of it as several independent tasks. In the middle, there are programs where the division of work isn't obvious, but possible. On the far other end, there are those that cannot reasonably be threaded at all.

Inherently MT Programs

The inherently MT programs are ones that are easily expressed as numerous threads doing numerous things. Such programs are easier to write using threads, because they are doing different things concurrently anyway. They are generally simpler to write and understand when threaded, easier to maintain, and more robust. The fact that they may run faster is a mere pleasant side effect. For these programs, the general rule is that the more complex the application, the greater the value of threading.

Typical programs that are inherently MT include:

Independent tasks   A debugger needs to run and monitor a program, keep its GUI active, and display an interactive data inspector, dynamic call grapher, and performance monitor. All in the same address space, all at the same time.

Servers   A server needs to handle numerous overlapping requests simultaneously. NFS®, NIS, DBMSs, stock quotation servers, etc., all receive large numbers of requests that require the server to do some I/O, then process the results and return answers. Completing one request at a time would be very slow.

Repetitive tasks   A simulator needs to simulate the interactions of numerous different elements that operate simultaneously. CAD, structural analysis, weather prediction, etc., all model tiny pieces first, then combine the results to produce an overall picture.

Not Obviously MT Programs

This class comprises those programs that are not inherently MT, but for which threading is reasonable. Here you impose threads upon an algorithm that does not have an obvious decomposition in order to achieve a speedup on an MP machine. Such a program is somewhat harder to write, a bit more difficult to maintain, etc., than its nonthreaded counterpart. But it runs faster. Because of these drawbacks, the (portions of) programs chosen are generally quite simple.

Typical programs in this class include:

Numerical programs   Many numerical programs (e.g., matrix operations) are made up of huge numbers of tiny, identical, and independent operations. They are most easily (well, most commonly) expressed as loops inside of loops. Slicing these loops into appropriate-sized chunks for threads is slightly more complicated, and there would be no reason to do so, save for the order-N speedup that can be obtained on an N-way SMP machine.

Old code   These are the "slightly modified existing systems." This is existing code that makes you think to yourself: "If I just change a few bits here and there, add a few locks, then I can thread it and double my performance."

It's true, it is possible to do this, and there are lots of examples. However, this is a tough situation because you will constantly be finding new interactions that you didn't realize existed before. In such cases (which, due to the nature of the modern software industry, are far too common), you should concentrate on the bottlenecks and look for absolutely minimal submodules that can be rewritten. It's *always* best to take the time to do it right: re-architect and write the program correctly from the beginning.

Automatic Threading

In a subset of cases, it is possible for a compiler to do the threading for you. If you have a program written in such a way that a compiler can analyze its structure, analyze the interdependencies of the data, and determine that parts of your program can run simultaneously without data conflicts, then the compiler can build the threads.

With current technology, the above capabilities are largely limited to Fortran programs that have time-consuming loops in which the individual computations in those loops are obviously independent. The primary reason for this limitation is that Fortran programs tend to have very simple structuring, both for code and data, making the analysis viable. Languages like C, which have constructs such as pointers, make the analysis enormously more difficult. There are MP compilers for C, but far fewer programs can take advantage of such compiling techniques.

With the different Fortran MP compilers,[3] it is possible to take vanilla Fortran 77 or 90 code, make no changes to it whatsoever, and have the compiler turn out threaded code. In some cases it works very well; in others, not. The cost of trying it out is very small, of course.

A number of Ada compilers will map Ada tasks directly on top of threads, allowing existing Ada programs to take advantage of parallel machines with no changes to the code.

Programs Not to Thread

Then there is a large set of programs that it doesn't make any sense to thread. Probably 99 percent of all programs either do not lend themselves easily to threading or run just fine the way they are. Some programs simply require separate processes in which to run. Perhaps they need to execute one task as root, but need to avoid having any other code running as root. Perhaps the program needs to be able to control its global environment closely, changing working directories, etc. Most programs run quite fast enough as they are and don't have any inherent multitasking, such as an icon editor or a calculator application.

In all truth, multithreaded programming is harder than regular programming. There are a host of new problems that must be dealt with, many of which are difficult. Threads are primarily of value when the task at hand is complex.

---

[3]Sun® Fortran MP, Kuck and Associates Fortran compiler, EPC's Fortran compiler, SGI's MP Fortran compiler.

What About Shared Memory?

At this time, you may be asking yourself, "What can threads do that can't be done by processes sharing memory?"

The first answer is "nothing." Anything that you can do with threads, you can also do with processes sharing memory. Indeed, a number of vendors implement a significant portion of their threads library in roughly this fashion. If you are thinking about using shared memory in this way, you should make sure you have (a) plenty of time to kill programming, (b) plenty more time to kill processing, and (c) lots of money to burn buying RAM.

You see: (a) Debugging cross-process programs is tough, and the tools that exist for this are not as good as those for MT. (b) Things take longer. In Solaris, creating a process is about 30 times slower than creating a thread, synchronization variables are about 10 times slower, and context switching about 5 times slower. (c) Processes eat up lots of kernel memory. Building a few thousand threads is no big deal. Building a few thousand processes is.

You can do everything with shared memory. It just won't be as easy or run as fast.

On the other hand... There are a great number of multiprocess programs that work quite well. Moreover there are plenty of instances where separate processes do make more sense. These are normally cases where the frequency of data exchange is limited and the complexity of the interactions is small. One of your jobs will be to figure out what kind of program you're working with.

Threads Standards

There are three different definitions for thread libraries competing for attention today: Win32, OS/2, and POSIX. The first two are proprietary and limited to their individual platforms (Win32 threads run only under NT and Win95, OS/2 threads only on OS/2). The POSIX specification (IEEE 1003.1c, aka *Pthreads*) is intended for all computing platforms, and implementations are available or in development for almost all major UNIX systems (including Linux), along with VMS.

POSIX Threads

The POSIX standard defines the API and behavior that all Pthreads libraries must meet. It is part of the extended portion of POSIX, so it is not a requirement for meeting XPG4, but it is required for X/Open UNIX 98, and all major UNIX vendors have committed to meeting this standard. As of this writing, (July, 1997) almost all UNIX vendors have released a library.

Win32 and OS/2 Threads

Both the NT and OS/2 implementations contain some fairly radical differences from the POSIX standard—to the degree that even porting from one or the other to POSIX will prove moderately challenging. Microsoft has not announced any plans to adopt POSIX. There are freeware POSIX libraries for Win32 (see *Commercial Products* on page 238), and OS/2 also has an optional POSIX library.

DCE Threads

Before POSIX completed work on the standard, it produced a number of drafts that it published for comment. Draft 4 was used as the basis for the threads library in DCE. It is similar to the final spec, but it does contain a number of significant differences. Presumably, no one is writing any new DCE code.

Solaris Threads

Also known as "UI threads," this is the library which SunSoft used in developing Solaris 2 before the POSIX committee completed its work. It will be available on Solaris 2 for the foreseeable future, although we expect most applications writers will opt for Pthreads. The vast majority of the two libraries are virtually identical.

Performance

Even after reading all these wonderful things about threads, there's always someone who insists on asking that ever-so-bothersome question: "Does it work?" For an answer, we turn to some real, live

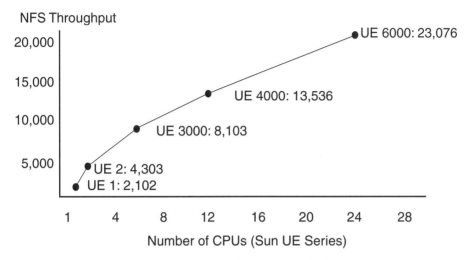

Figure 2–14 *NFS Performance on MP Machines (SPEC '96)*

shipping programs. Some of these are described in greater detail in the MT "Case Studies" (see *Threads Newsgroup* on page 313).

Operating Systems

OSs are large, complex, yet still highly efficient and robust programs. The various OSs have been in daily use by millions of users over the past couple of years and have endured the stress put on them by hundreds of thousands of programmers who are not known for their generosity towards operating system quirks. Mach, Windows NT, Windows 95, Solaris, IRIX, AIX, OS/2, and OSF/1 are all threaded, and many of the other UNIX vendors are also moving toward a threaded kernel.

NFS

Under most UNIX systems, both the NFS client and server are threaded (Figure 2–14). There aren't any standardized benchmarks for the client side, so you'll have to take our word for it that it's faster. On the server side, however, there is the LADDIS benchmark from SPEC.

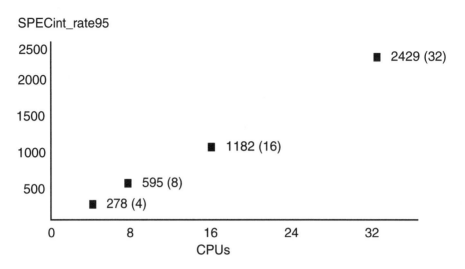

Figure 2–15   *Running SPECrate_fp95 on an SGI Origin/200, 2000 (SPEC '96)*

A great deal of time has been spent optimizing NFS for multiple CPUs, quite successfully.

SPECfp 95

The rule for the SPECfp benchmark is that a compiler is allowed to do pretty much anything it wants to, as long as that same compiler is available to customers and nobody changes the source code at all. The various Fortran 77/90 MP compilers automatically multithread a program with no user intervention, so they are legal. You give the compiler the code, completely unchanged, and it looks to see if there is any possibility of threading it. It is possible to automatically thread 6 of the 14 SPECfp programs. The results are *very* impressive (Table 2.1).

Table 2.1 *SPECfp95 Results for Alpha 4100 5/466 (SPEC '97)*

# CPUs	Tomcatv	Swim	Su2cor	Hydro2d	Mgrid	Turb3d
1	23.8	25.4	10.1	10.0	17.5	19.1
2	33.1	46.2	18.0	15.4	24.5	33.4
4	40.3	83.8	30.3	21.3	34.6	54.9

SPECint_rate95

SPECfp 95 is a reasonable set of benchmarks for single-CPU machines, but it does not give a good picture of the overall performance potential of multiprocessor machines (Figure 2–15). The SPECrate is intended to demonstrate this potential by allowing the vendor to run as many copies of the program as desired (e.g., in one test with 30 CPUs, Sun ran 37 copies of each program). This benchmark does not use the MP compiler.

Summary

Threads allow both concurrent execution in a single address space and parallel execution on multiple processor machines and they also make many complex programs easier to write. Most programs are simple and fast enough that they don't need threads, but for those programs that do need them, threads are wonderful.

3

Foundations

In which we introduce to the underlying structures upon which threads are built, the construction of the thread itself, and the operating system support that allows an efficient implementation.

Implementation vs. Specification

When writing a book of this nature, the authors are often faced with a difficult decision: How much should they restrict themselves to the pure specifications, and how much in the way of implementation should they allow to show through? By talking only about the specifications, the reader is given a pure rendition of what the library should do and is not misled into thinking that because a particular implementation did things one way, they all have to be like that.[1]

Unfortunately, describing only the specification is rather akin to teaching the concepts of mathematics without ever mentioning the existence of numbers.[2] It's clean and pure, but terribly difficult to comprehend fully. So we have chosen to bring in implementation details when we think they will aid in comprehension. The implementation we refer to most is the Solaris one, largely because we know it best.

Please keep in mind that these implementation details are included for your edification, but you should never write programs that depend upon them. They can change at any time, with no notification. Learn from the implementation, write to the specification.

Thread Libraries

There are two fundamentally different ways of implementing threads. The first is to write a user-level library that is substantially self-contained. It will make calls to system routines, and it may depend upon the existence of certain kernel features, but it is fundamentally a user-level library and contains no "magic" hooks into secret kernel routines. All of the defining structures and code for the library will be in user space. The vast majority of the library calls will execute entirely in user space and make no more use of system routines than does any other user-level library.

The second way is to write a library that is inherently a kernel-level implementation. It may define all the same functions as in the first case, but these functions will be completely dependent upon the existence of kernel routines to support them and may well be almost entirely in

---

[1]A specification is a description of what a program is supposed to do. An implementation is an actual program, which hopefully does what the spec says it should. The U.S. constitution is a specification for a country. The United States is an implementation.

[2]Yes, we are members of the "New Math" generation.

kernel space. The user-level portion of the library will be relatively small compared to the amount of kernel-level support it requires. The majority of library calls will require system calls.

Both of these methods can be used to implement exactly the same API, and they overlap in the kinds of kernel support they require. Some implementations of the POSIX standard are of the first kind, while both OS/2 and Win32 threads are of the second type.

In either case, the programmer will use an API that is implemented by a threads library. That library will provide a set of function calls (typically about 50 calls) that is the programmer's sole interface to threads. Everything not provided by those calls must come from the system's other libraries, meaning that 99% of writing a multithreaded program consists of writing regular, old-fashioned code almost the same way as before.

As you read the descriptions of the APIs, you may be struck by the lack of fancy features. This is intentional. These libraries provide a foundation for writing MT programs, but not every detail you might like. They provide you the resources with which to build more elaborate functions. Spin locks, priority-inheriting mutexes, deadlock-recovery features, etc., can be built out of these primitives with relative ease. Thus, if you want very fast, minimal functionality constructs, they are provided. If you want the slower, more complex constructs, you can build them.

We begin by talking about the parts of the system that are not inherently related to threads, but that do define a great deal about how threads must work. We use the specific example of how Solaris deals with the issues involved in building a viable interface between kernel-provided functionality and the user-level threads requirements. Other operating systems and other libraries have chosen different ways of providing this interface, and we do discuss them in general terms. We believe that by understanding one implementation in detail, you will acquire the background needed to fill in the gaps for the other implementations.

The Process Structure

The only thing the kernel knows about is the process structure. And the process structure has changed (slightly) since you last looked at it in traditional multitasking operating systems such as SunOS 4.x (see Figure 3–1).

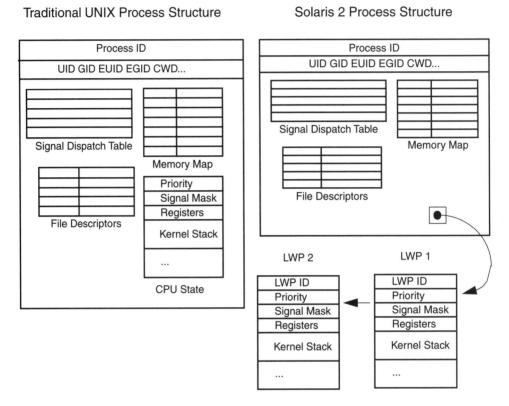

Figure 3–1　*The Process Structure in Traditional UNIX and in Solaris 2*

It used to contain the memory map, the signal dispatch table, signal mask, user ID, group ID, working directory, etc., along with runtime statistics, CPU state (registers, etc.), and a kernel stack (for executing system calls). In Solaris 2, the last couple bits have been abstracted out and placed into a new structure called a *lightweight process* (LWP).[3] So, a process contains all of the above, except for the runtime statistics, CPU state, and kernel stack, which are now part of the LWP structure. A process thus contains some number of LWPs (one for a "traditional"

---

[3]The other operating systems that support user-level threads have different ways of dealing with the same issue. Some of them copy the entire process structure for each thread, some of them don't do anything. The concept of a separate, schedulable entity, such as the LWP, proves to be an excellent pedagogical concept, and the other designs can be easily described in terms of LWPs. LWP is, of course, a Solaris term.

process, more for a multithreaded process). Just as the threads all share the process variables and state, the LWPs do the same.

The process structure shown in Figure 3–1 is in kernel space—below the solid line in the figures. It is not directly accessible by any user code. User code can only access it via a system call. That restriction allows the kernel to check the legality of the call and prevent user code from doing things it shouldn't, either by intention or mistake. Because a system call is required to access the process structure information, it is a more costly operation than a function call.

Lightweight Processes

A lightweight process[4] can be thought of as a virtual CPU that is available for executing code. Each LWP is separately scheduled by the kernel. It can perform independent system calls and incur independent page faults, and multiple LWPs in the same process can run in parallel on multiple processors.

LWPs are scheduled onto the available CPU resources according to their scheduling class and priority, as illustrated later in Figure 3–4 on page 41. Because scheduling is done on a per-LWP basis, each LWP collects its own kernel statistics—user time, system time, page faults, etc. This also implies that a process with two LWPs will generally get twice as much CPU time as a process with only one LWP. (This is a wild generalization, but you get the idea—the kernel is scheduling *LWPs*, not processes.)

An LWP also has some capabilities that are not exported directly to threads, such as kernel scheduling classes. A programmer can take advantage of these capabilities while still retaining use of all the thread interfaces and capabilities by specifying that the thread is to remain permanently bound to an LWP (known as *System Contention Scope Scheduling*, and discussed further in *Realtime LWPs* on page 75).

LWPs are an implementation technique for providing kernel-level concurrency and parallelism to support the threads interface. There is no reason for you to ever use the LWP interface directly. Indeed, you should specifically avoid it. It gains you nothing but costs you your portability.

---

[4]SunOS 4.x had a library known as the LWP library. There is no relationship between Solaris 2 LWPs and SunOS 4.x LWPs.

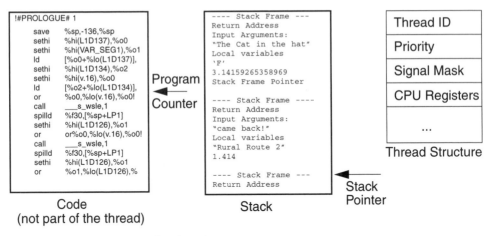

Figure 3–2   *The Contents of a Thread*

Threads and LWPs

In a typical, traditional, multitasking operating system, a process comprises memory, the CPU register state, and some system state (file descriptors, user ID, working directory, etc., all stored in the *process structure*). When it's time to context switch two processes, the kernel saves the registers in the process structure, changes some virtual memory pointers, loads the CPU registers with data from the other process structure, and continues.

When context-switching two threads, the registers are saved as before, but the memory map and the "current process" pointer remain the same. The idea is that you have a single program, in one memory space, with many virtual CPUs running different parts of the program concurrently.

What actually makes up a thread are (see Figure 3–2): its own stack and stack pointer; a program counter; some thread information, such as scheduling priority, and signal mask, stored in the thread structure; and the CPU registers (the stack pointer and program counter are actually just registers).

Everything else comes from either the process or (in a few cases) the LWP. The stack is just memory drawn from the program's heap. A thread *could* look into and even alter the contents of another thread's

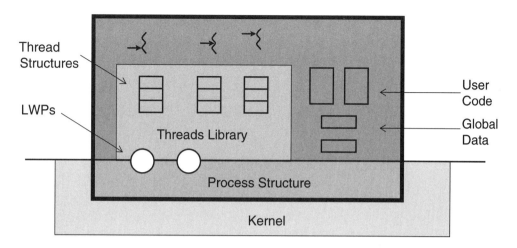

Figure 3–3   *How the Threads Library Fits into a Process*

stack if it so desired. (Although you, being a good programmer, would never do this, your bugs might.)

Putting all this together, we end up with a picture such as Figure 3–3. The threads, their stacks, the code they run, and the global data that they share, are all in user space, directly under user control. The thread structures are also in user space, but completely under control of the threads library. There is no legal[5] way for a user program to access those structures directly. The library itself, like every other system library, is just regular user code that you could have written yourself.

The LWPs are part of the process structure, but we show them crossing the line because this is how we think of their use. They are the main vehicle for processing from the threads library's point of view, so we show them in illustrations crossing that boundary, although they are, strictly speaking, in kernel space. The actual process structure is completely in kernel space.

As you can deduce, this definition of threads residing in a single address space means that the entire address space is seen identically by all threads. A change in shared data by one thread can be seen by all the other threads in the process. If one thread is writing a data structure

---

[5]Because this is in user space, there is no way to prevent you from accessing those structures if you really want to, unlike the process structure, where you cannot do so. But once again, don't! If the API doesn't give you what you think you need, you're probably doing something wrong. (*Don't do that!*)

while another thread is reading it, there will be problems (see *Race Conditions* on page 125).

As threads share the same process structure, they also share most of the operating system state. Each thread sees the same open files, the same user ID, the same working directory; each uses the same file descriptors, *including the file position pointer*. If one thread opens a file, another thread can read it. If one thread does an `lseek()` while another thread is doing a series of reads on the same file descriptor, the results may be, uh…, surprising.

The other important aspect of the threads library being a user-level library is that it doesn't change UNIX at all. *All UNIX semantics are retained*, and old, nonthreaded programs continue to run exactly the same way they always did. The same compilers you're using still work. All the same tools still work the same way.[6]

Solaris Multithreaded Model

In this model (see Figure 3–4), threads are the portable application-level interface. Programmers write applications using the threads library. The library schedules the threads onto LWPs. The LWPs in turn are implemented by kernel threads[7] in the kernel. These kernel threads are then scheduled onto the available CPUs by the standard kernel scheduling routine, completely invisible to the user. At no time will the programmer ever need to go below the public threads interface. Indeed, doing so will seriously compromise the portability and upward compatibility of the program.

System Calls

A system call is the way multitasking operating systems allow user processes to get information or request services from the kernel. Such things as "Write this file to the disk" and "How many users are on the

---

[6]You may not always like the *results*, however. The data will be the same as before, but with MT programs you often discover that what you *really* want is something different. (See Chapter 15, *Tools*.)

[7]All of the kernels are implemented using a threads library, often similar to Pthreads (Solaris kernel threads are very similar, DEC uses OFS's Mach threads which are quite different). These *kernel threads* are used to implement LWPs. The kernel also uses them for its own internal tasks, such as the page daemon. The term "kernel thread" is not used uniformly, and many people use it to refer to LWPs (or logical equivalent). We will not deal with kernel threads at all.

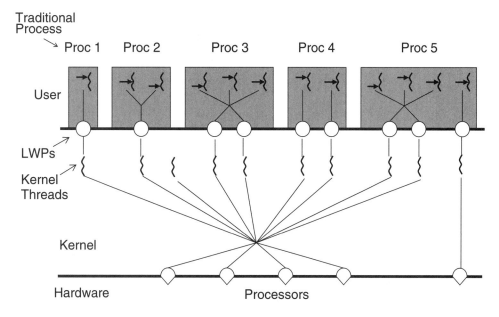

Figure 3–4 *The Solaris Multithreaded Architecture*

system?" are done with system calls. We divide system calls into two categories, blocking and nonblocking calls (aka *synchronous* and *asynchronous I/O*). In a blocking call, such as "Read this file from the disk," the program makes the call, the operating system executes it and returns the answer, and the program proceeds. If a blocking system call takes a long time, then the program just waits for it. (Usually another process will be scheduled while this one is waiting.)

In a nonblocking system call such as "Write this file to the disk without waiting," the program makes the call, the operating system sets up the parameters for the write, then returns, and the program continues. Exactly when the disk write actually occurs is not particularly important, and the program is able to continue working. A nonblocking system call may send the process a signal to tell it that the write is completed. Asynchronous I/O is important for many nonthreaded applications, as it allows the application to continue to work, even while there is I/O pending.

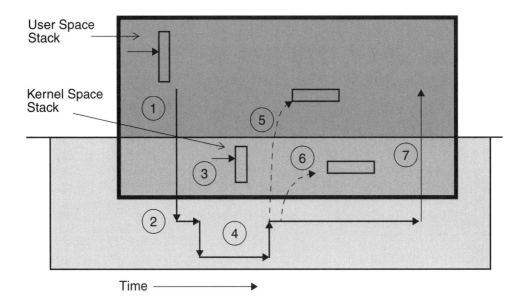

Figure 3–5 *The Operation of a System Call*

When a process makes a system call (see Figure 3–5), the following events occur:

1. The process traps to the kernel.
2. The trap handler runs in kernel mode and saves all of the registers.
3. The handler sets the stack pointer to the process structure's kernel stack.
4. The kernel runs the system call.
5. The kernel places any requested data into the user-space structure that the programmer provided.
6. The kernel changes any process structure values affected.
7. The process returns to user mode, replacing the registers and stack pointer, and returns the appropriate value from the system call.

Of course, system calls don't always succeed. They can out-and-out fail (e.g., if you supply an incorrect argument), in which case they return a failure value and set `errno`. Or they can be interrupted by a signal (see *Signals* on page 43), in which case the call is forced out of the kernel, the signal handler is run, and the system call returns `EINTR`. Presumably the program will see this value and repeat the system call. (As a diligent programmer, you always check for these things, right?[8])

What happens in a process with multiple LWPs? Almost exactly the same thing. The LWP enters the kernel, there's a kernel stack for each LWP, all the usual things happen, and the system call returns. And if several LWPs make system calls? They all execute independently and everything works as expected. With the usual caveats.

If several calls affect the same data, things could turn ugly. For example, if two threads issue calls to change the working directory, one of them is going to get a surprise. Or if two threads do independent calls to `read()`, using the same file descriptor, the file pointer will not be coordinated by either one of them, resulting in one thread reading from a different place than it expected. We'll deal with these issues later.

The really nice thing about different threads being able to execute independent system calls is when the calls are blocking system calls. Ten different threads can issue ten synchronous reads, all of which block, and yet all the other threads in the process can continue to compute. Cool.

Signals

Signals are the mechanism that UNIX uses in order to get asynchronous behavior in a program.[9] In non-threaded programs it works this way: Your program is running along normally, minding its own business. Then something (another process or the kernel) sends a signal to your process. The kernel then stops your process in its tracks and forces it to run some other function (it is probably one you have written). That function runs, doing whatever it wants; then it can either return (and your program will then resume right where it left off), or it can do a `siglongjmp()` (in which case your program resumes at the `sigsetjmp()` location), or it can just call `exit()` (causing the entire process to exit).

---

[8]Nor do we. But we know we should.

[9]Neither NT nor OS/2 implements anything like signals, making interruptible behavior difficult to achieve.

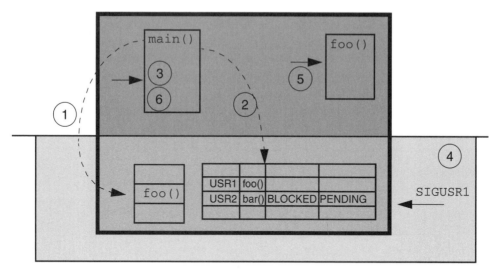

Figure 3–6   *The Operation of a Signal*

So, a typical program will start up in main(), as in Figure 3–6. When a process makes a system call, the following events occur:

1. The program will call sigaction() to declare some function to be the *handler* for a given signal (say, function foo() will handle SIGUSR1). The kernel will put a pointer to that handler into the process structure's signal dispatch table.

2. Next, your program will call sigprocmask() to tell the kernel which signals it is willing to accept (here, SIGUSR1, yes; SIGUSR2, no).

3. Finally your program takes off and starts doing what you wrote it to do.

4. Now, when some other process sends your process SIGUSR1, your program will stop what it's doing....

5. and run the handler code you wrote. You have no idea what your program might be doing when the signal arrives. That's the idea with signals—they can be completely asynchronous.

6. When the signal handler is done, it typically just does a return, and your program continues where it left off, as if nothing had happened.

In a threaded program, we will discover that threads allow us to accomplish the same tasks in a much simpler fashion.

Summary

Threads libraries can be implemented as self-contained user-level libraries or as kernel-based routines. The same program can be written in either, the difference being often quite minor. The main distinction of threads vs. processes is that threads share all process resources and data.

4

Lifecycle

In which the reader is treated to a comprehensive explanation of the intricacies in the life of a thread—birth, life, and death. Even death by vile cancellation. A small program which illustrates all of these stages concludes the chapter.

Thread Lifecycle

The fundamental paradigm of threads is the same in all of the libraries. In each of them, the program starts up in the same fashion as single threaded programs always have—loading the program, linking in the dynamic libraries, running any initialization sections and finally starting a single thread running `main()` (the main thread). For an MT program, all the same things occur and one of the libraries linked in will be the threads library. The main function will then be free to create additional threads as the programmer sees fit.

In the simplest case, you can call the create function with a function to run and an argument for the function to run on. Everything else will then take default values. Should you desire to pass your start routine more than a single argument, you must create a structure and pass the multiple arguments in that. As you can see from Code Examples 4–1 through 4–3, all of the libraries have very similar creation functions and operate in very similar fashions.

Conversely, a thread is exited by calling the appropriate thread exit function or simply returning from the initial function. Beyond the actual call to the create function, there is no parent/child relationship—any thread can create as many threads as it pleases and after creation there will be no relationship between the creator and createe.

```
pthread_create(&tid, NULL, start_fn, arg);
pthread_exit(status);
```

Code Example 4–1: *A Simple Call to Create a POSIX Thread*

```
DosCreateThread(NULL, start_fn, arg, NULL, NULL);
DosExit(EXIT_THREAD, uExitCode);
_beginthread(start_fn, NULL, StackSize, arg);
_endthread();
```

Code Example 4–2: *A Simple Call to Create an OS/2 Thread*

```
CreateThread(NULL, NULL, start_fn, arg, NULL, &tid)
ExitThread(status);
_beginthreadx(NULL, 0, start_fn, arg, NULL, &tid);
_endthreadx(status);
_beginthread(start_fn, 0, arg);
_endthread();
```

Code Example 4–3: *A Simple Call to Create a Win32 Thread*

Each thread has a thread ID (TID), which may be used to control certain aspects (scheduling classes, cancellation, signals, etc.) of that thread. (Win32 defines both a TID and a *handle*, both of which uniquely identify a thread. The TID is defined inside the process, the handle across all processes. Some functions use the TID, others the handle.) POSIX TIDs are of type `pthread_t`, which is an opaque datatype and should not be confused with any other datatype (see *POSIX Thread IDs* on page 177).

Both OS/2 and Win32 have several different functions to create and exit threads. These different functions allow them some extra latitude in how much initialization is done. Unfortunately, the different functions have non-overlapping sets of functionality, making it somewhat challenging to choose the correct one. Threads in both OS/2 and Win32 are kernel objects and have access to some kernel-level resources that are not shared by other threads in the process. For example, only the thread that creates a window can receive messages from it. (This seems like an unnecessary burden on the programmer.) POSIX has no such restrictions.

For Win32, the thread handle is a system-level reference to the thread structure, and it must be closed before that structure can be freed.

Returning Status and Memory

Sometimes you specifically want to wait for a thread to exit (see Figure 4–1). Perhaps you've created 20 threads to do 20 pieces of a task and you can't continue until they are all finished. One method is to call the wait (in POSIX, *join*) function on each of the desired thread IDs.

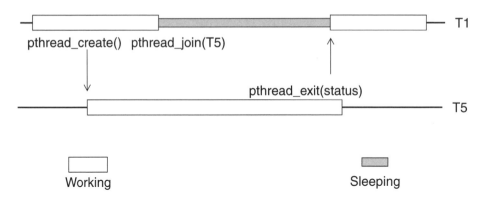

Figure 4–1   *Using* `pthread_join()` *and* `pthread_exit()`

The caller will block until each of the specified threads has exited. The other way is to use normal synchronization functions, (see *Using Semaphores to Count Exiting Threads* on page 93).

In addition to waiting for the threads to exit, the caller can receive a status from the exiting threads (Win32 and POSIX only). To ensure no deadlocks occur, it makes no difference if the waiting thread calls the join function first or if the exiting thread calls the exit function first. Calling `return(status)` from the start routine implicitly calls the exit function with that value.

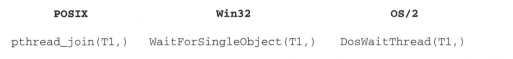

POSIX	Win32	OS/2
`pthread_join(T1,)`	`WaitForSingleObject(T1,)`	`DosWaitThread(T1,)`

Code Example 4–4:   *Waiting for Threads to Exit*

Not all Pthreads can be joined. At creation time, you can specify that you intend *not* to join a thread, creating a so-called *detached thread*. You can specify that you *do* intend to do a join, creating a *nondetached thread*. Any thread can call `pthread_join()` on any other non-detached thread, but the exiting thread can be joined only once. (In UI threads it was possible to request a join on "any thread" by passing NULL instead of a thread ID. This was a bad idea and not continued in POSIX.) The main thread is always a nondetached thread, so it can be joined.

Win32 and OS/2 do not have this detached thread concept—all threads may be waited for. In Win32, any thread (except those created with `_beginthread()`) can also return status. In OS/2, no thread can return status.

Don't Wait for Threads, Don't Return Status

When should you wait for a thread? Our *opinion* is never. Consider: Why do you care when a thread exits? Because you are waiting for that thread to complete some task, the results of which some other thread needs. By doing a join on that thread, you are implicitly assuming that the task will be complete when the thread exits. While this may indeed be true, it would be conceptually cleaner if you simply waited for the task itself, using one of the synchronization variables discussed in Chapter 6, *Synchronization*. In many of our examples we simply count the number of threads that exit.

As for returning status, the same argument applies. It isn't the thread that has status to return, it's the task that the thread was executing that has status, and that status may be handled without calling join.

The one case in which you do wish to know that the thread has exited occurs when you have allocated the thread's stack yourself and need to free that space. Here, joining the thread is essential. The one case in which you need an actual status from the thread occurs when the thread might be cancelled (killed by another thread—see *Cancellation* on page 137). A cancelled thread will return the status of `PTHREAD_CANCELED`.

In all honesty, there are plenty of programs that don't take our advice and work just fine. You don't have to take our advice either, but you should consider it before making your decision.

That's Not a Bug, That's a Feature!

Nondetached threads are not the most common case, but they are the default. You have to be careful with this, because it bites. If you try to join on a detached thread, `pthread_join()` will probably return an error (although this is actually considered a programming error and it may crash!). If you forget to join on a nondetached thread, however, it will simply remain a zombie, not free its storage, and you will have a big memory leak.

You see, a detached thread will clean up after itself upon exit, returning its thread structure, TSD array, and stack to the heap for reuse. A nondetached thread will clean up after itself only *after* it has been joined.[1] And as you create and exit more threads, your application will use up more and more of your address space, and finally die a slow and horrible death, for which you will bear sole responsibility.

It is possible to change the detach status of a thread dynamically (`pthread_detach()`), should you change your mind and decide not to join a thread, although this seems like a bad idea and likely to lead to massive confusion.

Exiting the Process

The semantics of `exit()` are retained in MT programs for POSIX, Win32, and OS/2. When any thread in a process calls `exit()`, the process exits, returning its memory, system resources, process structure, all LWPs, etc. If `main()` "falls off the bottom" of the initial thread, the main thread makes an implicit call to `exit()`, also killing the process.

When any other thread falls off the bottom of its initial function, it implicitly calls `pthread_exit()`, exiting only that one thread. In the special case in which the main thread calls the thread exit function directly, that thread exits but does not call `exit()`, and the process continues. This situation is true for POSIX and Win32, but OS/2 requires the main thread to stay alive.

Finally, should all user threads exit (the library may create threads for its own use and they will not be counted), the thread library will detect this and call `exit()` itself. This situation is not typical, however, as you will generally sense when it's time to exit your process, and you should call `exit()` explicitly.

---

[1] Sure, it could clean up some of its structures at `pthread_exit()` time, but that would imply that we expect programmers to make this mistake. By doing it this way, it's actually simpler, because big memory leaks are much easier to find than small ones.

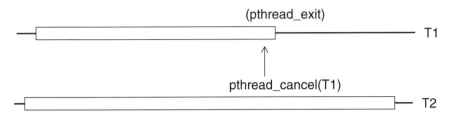

Figure 4–2   *Cancellation*

Suspending a Thread

UI, Win32, and OS/2 all have a function to force a thread to suspend its execution for an arbitrary length of time and a second function to cause the thread to resume (e.g., in UI, `thr_suspend()` and `thr_continue()`). These functions were included for the purpose of allowing such things as garbage collectors and debuggers to gain full control of a process. As such, they are useful, however for almost any other purpose they are the *wrong thing*. Because a suspended thread may hold locks that a controller thread needs, it is almost impossible to use them effectively. POSIX does not include suspension in its API. Instead it allows the vendors to write private versions of these functions in the vendor's debugging interface (see *Threads Debugger Interface* on page 204).

Cancellation

It is possible for one thread to tell another thread to exit. This is known as cancellation in POSIX and simply as "killing a thread" in OS/2 and Win32. (UI threads do not have anything like this.) In theory it's quite simple. T1 (Figure 4–2) tells T2 to exit, and it does. There is no relationship between the threads. Maybe T2 created T1, maybe T3 created both of them, maybe something else.

POSIX	**OS/2**	**Win32**
`pthread_cancel(T1);`	`DosKillThread(T1);`	`TerminateThread(T1);`

Code Example 4–5:   *Cancellation in the Three Libraries*

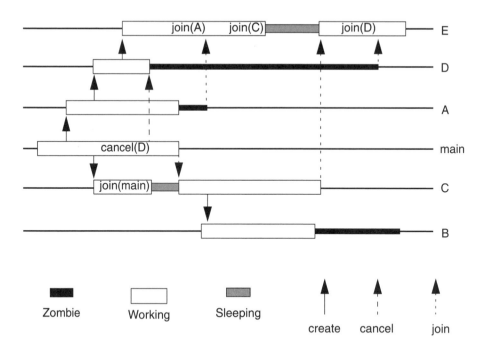

Figure 4–3   *POSIX Thread Create and Join*

How to make cancellation work correctly, in bounded time, and without destroying any data is a different story. That part is highly complex and handled in Chapter 9, *Cancellation*.

An Example: Create and Join

In Figure 4–3 we make a series of calls to `pthread_create()`, `pthread_join()`, `pthread_cancel()`, and `pthread_exit()`. The basic code is very simple and should require little explanation. A series of well-placed calls to `sleep()` arranges for the threads to execute in exactly the order we desire. Removing those calls will cause the speed and order of execution to change, but will not affect the correctness of the program.

Things to note about this program include:

- One of the include files is `pthread.h`. Later we'll see other include files.

- The use of `pthread_self()` to return the thread ID, and `thread_name()` to produce a printable string for the TID.[2]

- All of the threads are time-shared. This is what the constant `PTHREAD_SCOPE_SYSTEM` does for us. We'll explain in detail later.

- All of the threads are joinable (unusual for our programs). This capability is actually the default, but we make it explicit with the constant `PTHREAD_CREATE_JOINABLE`.

- We return status values from the different threads (also unusual for us). Normally we'll use `pthread_exit()` all of the time, but we use `return()` in `sub_a()` and `sub_d()` just to prove it works.

- We test for error return values from a number of functions (e.g., `pthread_create()`) by using a wrapper function we wrote with a similar name (e.g., `PTHREAD_CREATE()` —see *Return Values and Error Reporting* on page 181).

All code examples in this book are available from the web (see *Code Examples* on page 314).

```
/*
  Simple program that just illustrates thread creation,
    thread exiting,
  waiting for threads, and returning status from threads.
*/

/*
cc -o multi_thr multi_thr.c -L. -R. -g -lpthread -lthread
    -lthread_extensions -lposix4
*/

#define _POSIX_C_SOURCE 199506L

#include <stdio.h>
#include <stdlib.h>
#include <pthread.h>
#include <time.h>
#include "thread_extensions.h"
/* Function prototypes for thread routines */
```

Code Example 4–6:   *POSIX Thread Create and Join (`multi_thr.c`)*

---

[2]The functions prefixed with "`thread`" are from our library, `thread_extensions.so`.

```
void *sub_a(void *);
void *sub_b(void *);
void *sub_c(void *);
void *sub_d(void *);
void *sub_e(void *);

pthread_t thr_a, thr_b, thr_c, thr_d, thr_e, thr_main;
pthread_attr_t attr;
int zero;


int time1()
{return(time(NULL)-zero);}


void *sub_a(void *arg)
{int err, i;
 pthread_t tid = pthread_self();

 printf("[%2d] A: \t In thread A [%s]\n", time1(),
                                    thread_name(tid));
 sleep(1);
 PTHREAD_CREATE(&thr_d, &attr, sub_d, NULL);
 printf("[%2d] A: \t Created thread D [%s]\n", time1(),
                                    thread_name(thr_d));

 sleep(3);
 printf("[%2d] A: \t Thread exiting...\n", time1());
 return((void *)77);        /* Same as pthread_exit((void *)77) */
}


void *sub_b(void *arg)
{pthread_t tid = pthread_self();
 printf("[%2d] B: \t In thread B [%s]\n", time1(),
                                    thread_name(tid));

 sleep(4);

 printf("[%2d] B: \t Thread exiting...\n", time1());
 pthread_exit(NULL);
}


void *sub_c(void *arg)
{void *status;
```

Code Example 4–6:   *(cont.) POSIX Thread Create and Join*

```
int err, i;
pthread_t tid = pthread_self();
char *name = thread_name(tid);

printf("[%2d] C: \t In thread C [%s]\n", time1(), name);
sleep(2);

printf("[%2d] C: \t Joining main thread...\n", time1());
if (err=pthread_join(main_thr, &status))
  printf("pthread_join Error. %s", strerror(err)), exit(1);
printf("[%2d] C: \t Main thread [%s] returning status: %d\n",
  time1(), thread_name(main_thr), (int) status);

sleep(1);

PTHREAD_CREATE(&thr_b, &attr, sub_b, NULL);
printf("[%2d] C: \t Created thread B [%s]\n", time1(),
                                 thread_name(thr_b));

sleep(4);
printf("[%2d] C: \t Thread exiting...\n", time1());
pthread_exit((void *)88);
}

void *cleanup(void *arg)
{pthread_t tid = pthread_self();
 char *name = thread_name(tid);

  printf("[%2d] D: \t %s cancelled! \n", time1(), name);
}




void * sub_d(void *arg)
{int err, i;
 pthread_t thr_e;
 void *status;
 pthread_t tid = pthread_self();

 printf("[%2d] D: \t In thread D [%s]\n", time1(),
                                 thread_name(tid));

 pthread_cleanup_push(cleanup, NULL);
 pthread_setcanceltype(PTHREAD_CANCEL_ASYNCHRONOUS, NULL);
 pthread_setcancelstate(PTHREAD_CANCEL_ENABLE, NULL);
```

Code Example 4–6: *(cont.) POSIX Thread Create and Join*

```
  sleep(1);
  PTHREAD_CREATE(&thr_e, &attr, sub_e, NULL);
  printf("[%2d] D: \t Created thread E [%s]\n", time1(),
                                   thread_name(thr_e));

  sleep(5);

    /* D should get cancelled before this runs. */
  printf("[%2d] D: \t Thread exiting...\n", time1());
  pthread_cleanup_pop(0);
  return((void *)55);
}

void * sub_e(void *arg)
{int err, i;
 void *status;
 pthread_t tid = pthread_self();

 printf("[%2d] E: \t In thread E [%s]\n", time1(),
                                   thread_name(tid));
 sleep(3);
 printf("[%2d] E: \t Joining thread A...\n", time1());
 if (err=pthread_join(thr_a, &status))
   printf("pthread_join Error. %s", strerror(err)), exit(1);
 printf("[%2d] E: \t Thread A [%s] returning status: %d\n",
    time1(), thread_name(thr_a), (int) status);

 sleep(2);

 printf("[%2d] E: \t Joining thread C...\n", time1());
 if (err=pthread_join(thr_c, &status))
   printf("pthread_join Error. %s", strerror(err)), exit(1);
 printf("[%2d] E: \t Thread C [%s] returning status: %d\n",
    time1(), thread_name(thr_c), (int) status);

 sleep(2);
 printf("[%2d] E: \t Joining thread D...\n", time1());
 if (err=pthread_join(thr_d, &status))
   printf("pthread_join Error. %s", strerror(err)), exit(1);
 if ((void*) status == (void*) PTHREAD_CANCELED)
   printf("[%2d]E:Thread D [%s] returning status:PTHREAD_CANCELED",
           time1(), thread_name(thr_c));
 else
   printf("[%2d] E: \t Thread D [%s] returning status: %d\n",
     time1(), thread_name(thr_c), (int) status);
```

Code Example 4–6:   *(cont.) POSIX Thread Create and Join*

```
  sleep(1);
  printf("[%2d] E: \t Thread exiting...\n", time1());
  pthread_exit((void *)44);
}

main()
{
 int err;

 zero = time(NULL);
 main_thr = pthread_self();
 printf("Time Thread \t Event\n");
 printf("==== ====== \t =====\n");
 printf("[%2d] Main: \t Started [%s]\n", time1(),
                                      thread_name(main_thr));

 PTHREAD_ATTR_INIT(&attr);
 pthread_attr_setscope(&attr, PTHREAD_SCOPE_SYSTEM);
 pthread_attr_setdetachstate(&attr, PTHREAD_CREATE_JOINABLE);

 sleep(1);
 PTHREAD_CREATE(&thr_a, &attr, sub_a, NULL);
 printf("[%2d] Main: \t Created thread A [%s]\n", time1(),
                                      thread_name(thr_a));

 sleep(1);
 PTHREAD_CREATE(&thr_c, &attr, sub_c, NULL);
 printf("[%2d] Main: \t Created thread C [%s]\n", time1(),
                    thread_name(thr_c));

 sleep(2);
 printf("[%2d] Main: \t Cancelling thread D [%s]\n", time1(),
                    thread_name(thr_c));
 pthread_cancel(thr_d);

 sleep(1);
 printf("[%2d] Main: \t Thread exiting...\n", time1());
 pthread_exit((void *) NULL);
}
```

Code Example 4–6: *(cont.) POSIX Thread Create and Join*

Note that there are several odd casts (e.g., (void *) PTHREAD_CANCELED) that shouldn't be required, but are included due to minor bugs between Solaris, IRIX, HP-UX, and Digital UNIX.

Summary

The basic paradigm of thread creation is to build a new entity that will run a given function on a given argument. Threads can wait for each other, kill each other, or simply exit themselves. We showed a small program that illustrated each of these.

5

Scheduling

In which we explain the myriad details of the different scheduling models and the various alternative choices that could be made, describe context switching in detail, and delve into gruesome detail of the various POSIX options and parameters. There is a light at the end of the tunnel, however.

Different Models of Kernel Scheduling

There are three primary techniques for scheduling threads onto kernel resources (and indirectly, onto CPUs). Two of them involve the use of LWPs (or something similar). These are the techniques from which the designers of the various operating systems had to choose. They wanted a model that would adequately support the complexity of the operating system and still meet the various demands of dedicated programmers. All three models are perfectly reasonable and give the programmer different sets of trade-offs, simultaneously building programs that do exactly the same things with different levels of efficiency.

All three of these models are in use by different vendors.

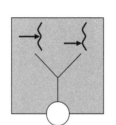

Many Threads on One LWP

The first technique is known as the "Many-to-One" model. It is also known as "co-routining."[1] Numerous threads are created in user space, and they all take turns running on the one LWP. Programming on such a model will give you a superior programming paradigm, but running your program on an MP machine will not give you any speedup, and when you make a blocking system call, the whole process will block. However, the thread creation, scheduling, and synchronization are all done 100 percent in user space, so they're done fast and cheap and use no kernel resources. The DCE threads library followed this model on HP-UX 10.20.

There is a clever hack[2] used for blocking system calls in some threads libraries (e.g., DCE threads) that is worth mentioning. The library puts a "jacket" routine around each blocking system call. This jacket routine replaces the blocking system call with a nonblocking one. Thus, when a thread makes a blocking system call, the library can put that thread to sleep and allow another one to run. When the signal comes back from the kernel, saying that the system call is complete, the library figures out which thread made the call and wakes up that sleeping thread, and everything proceeds as if the thread had blocked in the first place. It's hassle-free async I/O!

---

[1] The exact use of this term varies from book to book, but in broad terms, this is accurate.

[2] "Speak for yourself! I had to code and debug the monster and I still have to explain it to users."—Dave Butenhof, reviewing this section.

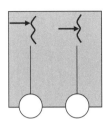

One Thread per LWP

The "One-to-One" model allocates one LWP[3] for each thread. This model allows many threads to run simultaneously on different CPUs. It also allows one or more threads to issue blocking system calls as the other threads continue to run—even on a uniprocessor.

This model has the drawback that thread creation involves LWP creation; hence it requires a system call, as does scheduling and synchronization. In addition, each LWP takes up additional kernel resources, so you are limited in the total number of threads you can create. Win32 and OS/2 use this model. Some POSIX implementations (DCE, IBM's draft 7, Peterson's LinuxThreads) also use it.

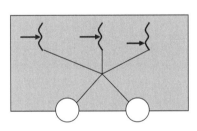

Many Threads on Many LWPs (Strict)

The third model is the strict "Many-to-Many" model. Any number of threads are multiplexed onto some (smaller or equal) number of LWPs. Thread creation is done completely in user space, as are scheduling and synchronization (well, almost). The number of LWPs may be tuned for the particular application and machine. Numerous threads can run in parallel on different CPUs, and a blocking system call need not block the whole process. As in the Many-to-One model, the only limit on the number of threads is the size of virtual memory.[4] No one actually uses this strict version.

---

[3]Remember, when you read about how a vendor implements this model, the vendor may not distinguish between the thread and the (possibly conceptual) LWP. The vendor may simply refer to the thread and expect you to understand that it's a single entity containing everything.

[4]On a 32-bit machine, this is roughly 2 GB (total virtual memory) / 8 KB (minimum stack size) = 256,000 threads.

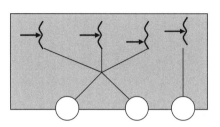

The Two-Level Model

The "Two-Level Model" (known commonly as the "Many-to-Many" model) is a strict Many-to-Many model with the ability to specifically request a One-to-One binding for individual threads.

This model is probably the best of the choices. Several operating systems now use this model (Digital UNIX, Solaris, IRIX, HP-UX). Win32 has a "fibers" library, which sits on top of its threads and gives a rough approximation to the two-level model. However, fibers have a completely different API and require explicit context-switching, so it's best not to consider them to be threads. The two-level model creates a bit more work for the library writers than the other models, but gives the programmer the optimal model with which to work.

Thread Scheduling

As we have just seen, there are two basic ways of scheduling threads: process *local* scheduling (also known as *Process Contention Scope*, or *Unbound Threads*—the Many-to-Many model) and system *global* scheduling (also known as *System Contention Scope*, or *Bound Threads*—the One-to-One model). These scheduling classes are known as the *scheduling contention scope*, and are defined only in POSIX. Process contention scope scheduling means that all of the scheduling mechanism for the thread is local to the process—the threads library has full control over which thread will be scheduled on an LWP. This also implies the use of either the Many-to-One or Many-to-Many model.

System contention scope scheduling means that the scheduling is done by the kernel. POSIX allows both (it doesn't require both), whereas both Win32 and OS/2 specify only global scheduling.

Globally scheduled threads also have a *policy and a priority* associated with them, which further refines the scheduling details at the kernel level. These policies are part of the optional portion of the POSIX specification, and currently none of the vendors implements every possible option.

The whole subject of scheduling is fraught with problems. Both the scheduling of threads and the scheduling of processes themselves have problems in all operating systems that have never been resolved to

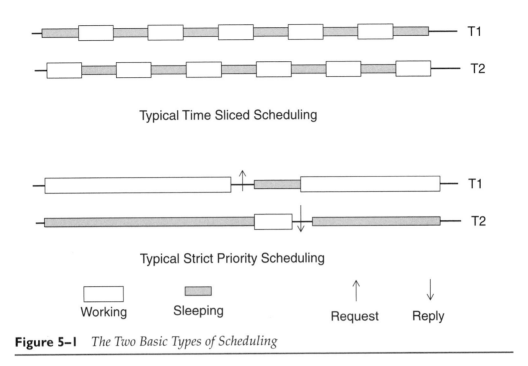

Typical Time Sliced Scheduling

Typical Strict Priority Scheduling

Working   Sleeping   Request   Reply

Figure 5–1   *The Two Basic Types of Scheduling*

everyone's satisfaction. In brief, there are two basic situations in which we find ourselves (see Figure 5–1).

The first case (the "independent" case) occurs when two processes (or threads) are running almost completely independently—neither ever has anything it wants from the other, and both would happily chew up every CPU cycle they could get. For example, consider two developers working on different projects on the same machine. Time-slicing is necessary for both of them to get a fair share of the machine.

The other situation (the "dependent" case) occurs when the two processes depend directly upon each other. One process needs another to perform some task before it can continue—a text editor cannot do anything until the file system has delivered files to it to work on, and the file system has nothing to do until the text editor requests some services from it. In such a case, time slicing is of no use at all. In Figure 5–1, we show two independent threads being time sliced, and two dependent threads that require some resource. In the second case, T1 is allowed to run as long as it wants to. It could run forever, if only it didn't need to exchange that resource with T2.

A real machine is typically faced with both situations all the time, along with the judgments of users and system administrators as to the relative importance of the various processes.

We will not attempt to solve these problems here. Suffice it to say that the use of these techniques results in less than perfect scheduling algorithms, but we have done fairly well with them over the past 30–40 years nonetheless.

We will now go into some of the gory details of how scheduling is done. The major point we make is that most threaded programs are of the "dependent" case above, and scheduling is accomplished mainly by dependence upon the program's need for synchronization.

Process Contention Scope

PCS scheduling is done by the threads library. The library chooses which unbound thread will be put on which LWP. The scheduling of the LWP is (of course) still global and independent of the local scheduling. While this does mean that unbound threads are subject to a funny, two-tiered scheduling architecture, in practice, you can ignore the scheduling of the LWP and deal solely with the local scheduling algorithm.

There are four ways to cause an active thread (say, T1) to context switch. Three of them require that the programmer has written code. These methods are largely identical across all of the libraries.

1. **Synchronization**. By far the most common means of being context switched (a wild generalization) is for T1 to request a mutex lock and not get it. If the lock is already being held by T2, then the T1 will be placed on the sleep queue, awaiting the lock, thus allowing a different thread to run.

2. **Pre-emption**. A running thread (T6) does something that causes a higher priority thread (T2) to become runnable. In that case, the lowest priority active thread (T1) will be pre-empted, and T2 will take its place on the LWP. The ways of causing this to happen include releasing a lock, changing the priority level of T2 upwards or of T1 downwards.

3. **Yielding**. If the programmer puts an explicit call to `sched_yield()` in the code that T1 is running, then the

scheduler will look to see if there is another runnable thread (T2) of the *same* priority (there can't be a higher priority runnable thread). If there is one, then that one will be scheduled. If there isn't one, then T1 will continue to run.

4. **Time-Slicing.** If the vendor's PCS allows time slicing (like Digital UNIX, unlike Solaris), then T1 might simply have its time slice run out and T2 (at the same priority level) would then receive a time slice.

A bit of reflection will show the reader that two of the methods can be executed entirely in user space, with the thread-level context switch requiring about 10 microseconds on a 167 MHz UltraSPARC. Pre-emption, however, is a bit more involved and requires a system call to execute (see *Pre-emption* on page 74).

In actual practice, you, the programmer, will spend very little time thinking about issues of scheduling. When a thread needs a common resource, it uses a lock. If it doesn't get the lock, it blocks, and another thread runs. Sooner or later the owner will release the lock, and the first thread will become runnable again.

The scheduler for PCS threads has a simple algorithm for deciding which thread to run. Each thread has a priority number associated with it. The runnable threads with the highest priorities get to run. These priorities are *not* adjusted by the threads library. The only way they change is if the programmer writes an explicit call to `pthread_setschedparam()`. This priority is an integer in C. We don't give you any advice on how to choose the value, as we find that we don't use it much ourselves. You probably won't, either.

The natural consequence of the above discussion on scheduling is the existence of four scheduling states for threads. (The astute reader may have already figured this all out and skip this section.)

A thread may be in one of the following states:

Active: It is on an LWP.[5]

Runnable: It is ready to run, but there just aren't enough LWPs for it to get one. It will remain here until an active thread loses its LWP or until a new LWP is created.

---

[5]Whether or not the LWP is on a CPU is irrelevant.

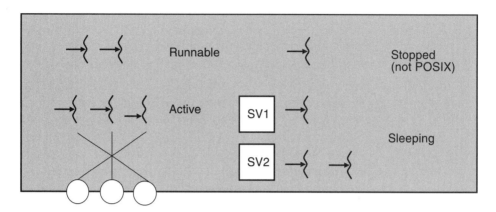

Figure 5–2   *Some Process Contention Scope Threads in Various States*

Sleeping: It is waiting for a synchronization variable.

Stopped (not in POSIX):   A call to the suspension function has been made. It will remain in this state until another thread calls the continue function on it.

Zombie: It is a dead thread and is waiting for its resources to be collected. (This is not a recognizable state to the user, though it might appear in the debugger.)

Figure 5–2 shows a process with eight PCS threads and three LWPs. Five of the threads want to run, but only three can do so. They will continue to run as long as they want or until one of them makes a threads library call that changes conditions, as noted above. The two runnable threads are of equal or lower priority than the three active ones, of course. Should one of the sleeping or stopped threads be made runnable, then whether they actually become active will be a question of priority levels. If the newly runnable thread is of higher priority than one of the active threads, then it will displace the lowest priority active thread. If it is of lower priority than all of them, then it won't. If it is of *equal* priority, then we make no guarantees. You should not write a program assuming anything about this condition.

The LWPs that are to be used by the unbound threads are set up in a pool and are identical in all respects. This setup allows any thread to execute on any of the LWPs in this pool. You should not change any attributes of these LWPs (e.g., scheduling class, "nice" level), as you don't

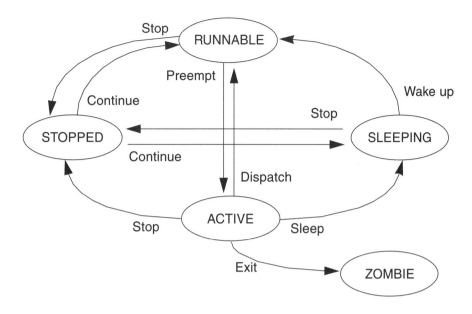

Figure 5–3 *Simplified View of Thread State Transitions*

know which thread will be running on them at any given time. Should you want a special LWP, you'll want a bound thread to run on it.

When a PCS thread exits, or goes to sleep (Figure 5–3), and there are no more runnable threads, the LWP that was running the thread goes to sleep in the kernel. When another thread becomes runnable, the idling LWP wakes up and runs it. Should an LWP remain idle for an extended length of time (five minutes for Solaris 2.5), the threads library may kill it. You will never notice this. Should your application become more active later, more LWPs will be created for you.

When a System Continuation Scope (SCS) thread blocks on a synchronization variable, its LWP must also stop running. The LWP does so by making a system call that puts it to sleep. When the synchronization variable is released, the thread must be awakened. This is done by making a system call to wake up the LWP. The LWP then wakes up, and the thread resumes running. Much the same thing happens when a locally scheduled thread blocks on a cross-process synchronization variable. In both cases the LWP goes to sleep in the kernel until the synchronization variable is released. This description is pretty much the same for Win32, and OS/2. Only the names are different.

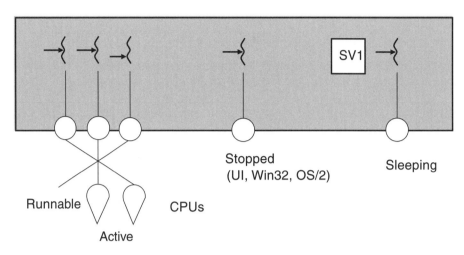

Figure 5–4   *Some System Contention Scope Threads in Various States*

System Contention Scope

An SCS thread is nothing more than a typical thread that is permanently bound to a specific LWP. The LWP runs only that thread and that thread runs only on that LWP. This means that this thread is never merely runnable. It is either sleeping on a synchronization variable, suspended, or active (Figure 5–4). It is never prevented from getting time (that is, "virtual time"—time on an LWP) when it wants it.

Both OS/2 and Win32 have only SCS scheduling, and it is completely handled by the normal kernel scheduler. There are a number of different scheduling classes for the different operating systems (batch, timesharing, interactive, realtime, etc.), which we will touch on later. Suffice it to say that with a SCS thread, you can set the kernel-level scheduling class and priority using the process-level API.

So, when do you want to use SCS threads? The answer is unclear. For some time the common wisdom was, "Only use globally scheduled threads when an event outside the process requires immediate processing by that particular thread or when you want time slicing. If you use globally scheduled threads everywhere, your program will use a lot more kernel resources than it presumably needs." Since that was first said, we have had some reservations. After spending more time with actual programs, we're more inclined to say the opposite! Use PCS threads only when you are going to have very large numbers of threads and use SCS threads normally.

This change of mind is not as egregious as it may sound. The logic is that if your program is computationally intensive, then you're probably expecting all threads to be either computing or waiting for I/O 95% of the time. So you're unlikely to be doing much local context switching anyway. On top of this, a number of empirical studies indicate that SCS threads end up being faster (we don't know why!). Finally, if you have a kernel-level LWP tracing tool, it's very nice to know which thread will be on which LWP.

The primary conclusion in both cases is that you should see no particular differences between locally and globally scheduled threads as long as there are sufficient LWPs.

Context Switching

Context switching is a rather complicated concept and has many details of significance, so it is difficult to explain in just a few paragraphs. Nonetheless, we shall try. If you don't feel that you have a firm grasp of how it works, you should go bug a friend to explain all of the subtle nuances. Threads or no threads, you should understand this concept thoroughly.

A context switch is the act of taking an active thread off its LWP and replacing it with another one that is waiting to run. This concept extends to LWPs and traditional processes on CPUs, also. We will describe context switching in traditional, process/CPU terms.

The state of a computation is embodied in the computer's registers—the program counter, the stack pointer, general registers, along with the MMU's (Memory Management Unit) page tables. These, plus the memory contents, disk files, and other peripherals, tell you everything about the computer. When it's time to context switch two traditional processes, all the register state must be changed to reflect the new process that we wish to run. It works approximately like this:

- All the current registers are stored into the process structure for P1.
- All the stored register values from the process structure for P2 are loaded into the CPU's registers.
- The CPU returns to user mode, and voila! P1 is context switched out and P2 is context switched in and running.

All the other data in the process structure (working directory, open files, etc.) remains in the process structure where it belongs. If a process wishes to use that data, it will reference it from the process structure. When two LWPs in the same process context switch, all of the above happens in much the same fashion.

Notice also that a context switch must be done by the CPU itself. One CPU cannot do the context switch for another. CPU1 can send an interrupt to CPU2 to let it know that it should context switch, but CPU1 cannot actually change the registers in CPU2. CPU2 has to want to context switch.

Finally, context switching for PCS threads involves much the same procedure. A thread (T1) decides that it has to context switch (perhaps it is going to sleep on a synchronization variable). It enters the scheduler. The CPU stores its register state into the thread structure for T1, then it loads the registers from another thread (T2) into the CPU and returns from the scheduler as T2. No system calls need be involved. It is possible that it happens completely in user space and is very fast.

It may be a bit unclear what the role of the LWP is when threads context switch. The role is invisible. The threads save and restore CPU registers with no regard to the LWP at all. The threads scheduler does not do anything to the LWP structure. Should the operating system decide to context switch the LWP, it will do so completely independently of what the LWP happens to be doing at that time. Should two threads be in the middle of context switching when the kernel decides to context switch the LWP, it still makes no difference. The threads' context switch will just take a little longer.

Consider the situation in Figure 5–5. Three threads are runnable on two LWPs at time 0. Thread T1 holds a mutex, M. Clearly, T1 and T2 will be the active threads, as they have the highest priorities. We'll imagine that T1 is on LWP1, and T2 on LWP2, while T3 is on the runnable queue.

Approaching time 1, T2 attempted to lock M and failed. So, as part of the code for `pthread_mutex_lock()`, T2 put itself onto the sleep queue for M, then called the scheduler. The scheduler code ran (still as T2) and decided to run T3. Next, the scheduler stored away the CPU registers into T2's thread structure and loaded the registers from T3's. (At this particular instant, it's not defined which thread is running on LWP2, and it's not important, either.) At time 1, the scheduler code finishes its work and returns with T3 running on LWP2.

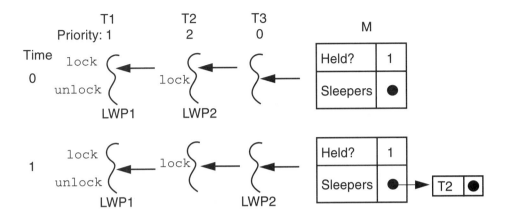

Figure 5–5 *How a Context Switch Works*

At time 2, T1 releases the mutex. As part of the code for `pthread_mutex_unlock()`, it takes the first thread off of M's sleep queue (T2) and makes it runnable and releases the mutex. Finally, it calls the scheduler.

The scheduler notices that there's a runnable thread (T2) that has a higher priority than one of the active threads (T3). The scheduler then sends a signal in order to pre-empt the thread on LWP2. Now the scheduler has done its work. It returns, and T1 continues to run. This is the state of the world at time 2 (with a signal pending).

For some short period of time, T3 continues to run. When the signal arrives from the kernel, T3 is interrupted and forced to run the signal handler. That, in turn, calls the scheduler, which context switches T3 out and T2 in. And that's it! At time 3, T1 and T2 are both active, T3 is runnable, and T2 holds the mutex.

There are a couple things to notice here. There's no guarantee that T2 will get the mutex. It's possible that T1 could have reclaimed it; it's even possible that T3 could have snatched it away just before the signal arrived. If either of these events occurred, the net result is that a bit of time would have been wasted, but they would both work perfectly. This scenario works as described, irrespective of the number of CPUs. If this runs on a multiprocessor, it will work exactly the same way as it does on a uniprocessor, only faster.

In this example, we have described two context switches. The first one was voluntary—T2 wanted to go to sleep. The second was involuntary (pre-emptive)—T3 was perfectly happy and only context switched because it was forced to.

Pre-emption

Preemption is the process of rudely kicking a thread off its LWP (or an LWP off its CPU) so that some other thread can run instead. (This is what happened at time 3.) For SCS threads, preemption is handled in the kernel by the kernel scheduler. For PCS threads, it is done by the thread library. Pre-emption is accomplished by sending the LWP in question a signal specifically invented for that purpose.[6] The LWP then runs the handler, which in turn realizes that it must context switch its current thread and does so. (You will notice that one LWP is able to direct a signal to another specific LWP in the case in which they are both in the same process. You should never do this yourself. You may send signals to threads, but never to LWPs.)

Pre-emption requires a system call, so the kernel has to send the signal, which takes time. Finally the LWP, to which the signal is directed, must receive it and run the signal handler. Context switching by preemption is involuntary and is more expensive than context switching by "voluntary" means. (You will never have to think about this while programming.)

The above discussion of context switching and pre-emption is accurate for all the various libraries. It is accurate for threads on LWPs, and for LWPs (or traditional processes) on CPUs, substituting the word "interrupt" for "signal."

How Many LWPs?

The UI threads library has a call, `thr_setconcurrency()`, which tells the library how many LWPs you'd like to have available for PCS threads. (The X/Open extension to Pthreads includes `pthread_setconcurrency()`.) If you set the number to ten, and you have nine threads, then when you create a tenth thread, you'll get a tenth LWP. When you create an eleventh thread, you won't get another LWP. Now the caveat. This is a *hint* to the library as to what you'd like. You may not get what you ask for! You might even get more. Your program must run correctly without all the LWPs you want, though it

---

[6]In Solaris, it's SIGLWP. This is a kernel-defined signal that requires a system call to implement. Digital UNIX uses a slightly different mechanism, but the results are the same.

may run faster if it gets them. In practice, this becomes an issue only when your program needs a lot of LWPs.

You've got the power, but how do you use it wisely? The answer is totally application dependent, but we do have some generalities. (N.B.: *Generalities*. If you need a highly tuned application, you've got to do the analysis and experimentation yourself.) We assume a dedicated machine.

- If your program is completely CPU-bound, then one LWP per CPU will give you maximum processing power. Presumably you'll have the same number of threads.
- If your program is highly CPU-bound *and* you do some I/O, then one LWP per CPU and enough to cover all simultaneous blocking system calls[7] is called for.
- If your program is only I/O bound, then you'll want as many LWPs as simultaneous blocking system calls.

Realtime LWPs

Just because a thread is bound to an LWP does not imply that the LWP is going to be scheduled on a CPU immediately. Depending upon the nature of your application requirements, you may need to alter the kernel-level scheduling priority of that LWP. If you need merely to ensure that it gets a CPU within a second, then relying upon the normal time-slicing scheduler is probably sufficient. If response is required on the order of 100 ms, then simply raising the timesharing class priority of the LWP is probably sufficient.

It's when you require response in the 2–100 ms range that things get interesting. You will need to put the LWP into the realtime scheduling class. You do all of the typical realtime tricks—no blocking system calls, probably no I/O,[8] no paging (you'll need to lock down all the memory that your thread will use: functions, stack, data.), etc. ("Etc." means that there is plenty more involved that we haven't thought about, but that you'd better. Realtime processing is a tricky thing; be very careful!) Both Win32 and OS/2 also have realtime scheduling classes.

---

[7] Blocking system calls include all calls to the usual system calls such as `read()`, but also any thread that blocks on a cross-process synchronization variable should be counted. Bound threads are independent of this, as they each have their own LWP.

[8] For I/O, you'd typically set up the buffers in the realtime thread but then allow a normal thread to execute the I/O call on those buffers.

POSIX defines three scheduling classes for realtime threads, SCHED_RR, SCHED_FIFO, and SCHED_OTHER. They are all optional and are not implemented in all of the current operating systems (e.g., Digital UNIX and IRIX do all three, Solaris does only SCHED_OTHER). In actual practice, the two optional classes are quite reasonably replaced with the existing realtime scheduling algorithms. They are only interesting when you have several threads with the same realtime priority level that are competing for the CPU. This is unusual.

SCHED_FIFO

Assume a realtime situation such as in Figure 5–6, where T1 is of highest priority. It gets a CPU whenever it is runnable (like now). T2 is currently blocked, and T3 and T4 are of lower priority and get a CPU only when the others don't want it. T3 was the first one to go onto the queue, so it will always get a CPU before T4 does.

If T1 blocks, then T4 will get a CPU. As soon as T1 unblocks, T4 will lose that CPU. Should T2 unblock, then T3 will lose its CPU, but regain it as soon as T2 blocks again. There is no time slicing, and threads never change their priorities (unless the programmer makes a call to pthread_setschedparam()).

SCHED_RR

This operation is much the same as SCHED_FIFO, save that there is time slicing and threads rotate in their queues. So, in Figure 5–6, after one time slice, T3 will lose the CPU and T4 will get to run. At the end of T4's time slice, T3 will get to run again. T1, being of higher priority, will continue to run as long as it wants.

Should T1 block or T2 unblock, the behavior will be identical to SCHED_FIFO.

SCHED_OTHER

POSIX puts no limits on the behavior of this option. In Solaris, this is identical to that of SCHED_FIFO, save that no guarantee is made about which of T3 or T4 will run. In Figure 5–6, should T2 unblock, then T3 will lose its CPU. When T2 blocks again, there is no guarantee which of T3 or T4 will run, but the chosen thread will be able to run as long as it wants. Other systems do different mappings.

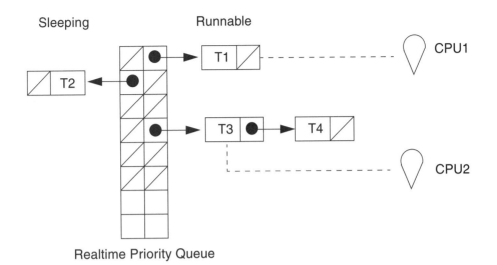

Figure 5–6 *Realtime Scheduling Operation*

Specifying Scope, Policy, Priority, and Inheritance

There are four aspects of scheduling attributes (see *Attribute Objects* on page 170) which you can set when creating a new thread. You can set the scheduling:

Scope pthread_attr_setscope() allows you to select either PTHREAD_SCOPE_PROCESS (local scheduling, unbound threads) or PTHREAD_SCOPE_SYSTEM (global scheduling, bound threads).

Policy pthread_attr_setschedpolicy() allows you to select SCHED_RR, SCHED_FIFO, or SCHED_OTHER, or other implementation-defined policies.

Priority pthread_attr_setschedparam() allows you to set the priority level of a thread by setting the sched_param struct element param.sched_priority. You can also change the parameters of a running thread via pthread_setschedparam(). POSIX gives no advice on how to use the priority levels provided. All you know is that for any given policy, the priority level must be between

`sched_get_priority_max`(*policy*) and
`sched_get_priority_min`(*policy*).

Inheritance   `pthread_setinheritsched()` allows you to specify whether the scheduling policy and parameters will be inherited from the creating thread (PTHREAD_INHERIT_SCHED), or will be set directly by the other functions (PTHREAD_EXPLICIT_SCHED).

Unless you are doing realtime work, only scope is of interest, and that will almost always be set to PTHREAD_SCOPE_SYSTEM. POSIX does not specify default values for these attributes, so you should really set all four.

Avoid Realtime

You might require a realtime thread when you have the undivided attention of a user and are doing constant updating (e.g., mouse tracking, video or audio playback), or when you are doing machine feedback and control (e.g. autonomous vehicle navigation, robotics). Other instances include when you are doing realtime data collection with analysis.

You might think you need realtime thread, but don't, when you update displays with the *divided* attention of a human (if you're 100 ms late in seeing the latest from the stock ticker, no big deal). *Avoid using the realtime class if you possibly can.*

Allocation Domains

POSIX recognizes the desire of some programmers for closer control over the scheduling of LWPs onto CPUs. Unfortunately, there is little convergence on the methods of doing so by the vendors, so there is little that POSIX can say about it. Basically POSIX defines allocation domains, which are sets of CPUs. The programmer then specifies that certain LWPs are allowed to execute on the CPUs in the chosen domains. All of these functions are implementation-specific.

Do allocation domains really gain you anything? In certain realtime applications, yes. Otherwise, probably not. Our *opinion* is that you are more likely to bog your program down with excessive complexity than to improve it if you use them in most programs.

Binding LWPs to Processors

It's often possible to ensure that a given LWP will always run on a selected processor. It's also possible to ensure that a given LWP will run to the exclusion of all other LWPs in all processes by putting it into the realtime class. Doing both effectively binds the processor to the LWP so long as the LWP wants to run.

The question of when these things are useful has a somewhat tricky answer, and it changes with new operating system releases. If schedulers worked perfectly and had ESP, you would never bind an LWP to a CPU. In practice, it's *sometimes* otherwise.

Happiness Is a Warm Cache

The main issue is that of cache memory latency. The current batch of PCs and workstations have external caches of significant size (typically 1–4 megabytes). To replace the contents of such a cache completely can take a very long time (upwards of 100 ms, depending upon individual architecture). If an LWP is running on CPU 0 and it is context switched off for a short time, then the vast majority of that cache will still be valid. So, it would be much better for that LWP to go back onto CPU 0.

The normal schedulers in the various OSs endeavor to do precisely that via *processor affinity*. Solaris, for example, will delay running an LWP on CPU 1, should that LWP have previously been on CPU 0. If CPU 0 becomes available relatively quickly (currently, 30 ms—three clock ticks), then that LWP will be put back on CPU 0. If CPU 0 does not become available within that time frame, then the LWP will be scheduled on whatever CPU is available.

We know of some instances where it has proven valuable to do processor binding of LWPs. If you are considering this, test first. *You should not even consider processor binding unless you already know that there's a clear problem of this nature.* And you must be aware that everything may be different on a different architecture or different OS release. The details of these issues are well beyond the scope of this book, and we wish to caution you that it is rare for anyone to have to address these issues.

When Should You Care About Scheduling?

There are times when you will want to deal with scheduling directly, but those times are few and far between for any of the libraries. If you find yourself thinking about this a lot, you're probably doing something wrong. Some examples:

It is possible to design a server program where each thread runs forever, picking up requests off the net, processing them, and returning for more. It is possible for an unbound thread to get starved out in this situation. In this case you should add LWPs for the purpose of effecting a time-slicing scheme.

A program that used a set of threads to produce data and another single thread to push that data out to some device in real time needs to ensure that the output thread runs when it needs to. Here a higher priority would be in order. In the Delphax/Uniq case study (see *Vendor's Threads Pages* on page 314), where they built a high-speed printer driver, they found it worthwhile to make a bound thread and put the LWP into the realtime class.

In spite of all the attention we just paid to explaining it, you will not write much (if any!) code to deal with. If the library writers did their job well, everything will "just work," without any effort on your part at all. In most MT programs, the different threads all depend upon one another, and it doesn't really matter which one runs first. Sooner or later, the running threads will need something from the other threads, and they will be forced to sleep until those other threads have produced that something.

Summary

Several scheduling models exist, most of which are overkill. For all but truly exceptional programs, the normal vendor scheduler does a fine job and that, along with proper synchronization, means we don't have to worry about scheduling at all. Realtime folks are on their own.

6

Synchronization

In which the reader is led on a hunt for the intimidating synchronization variable and discovers that it is not actually as frightening as had been thought. Programs illustrating the basic use of the POSIX primitives are shown.

Synchronization Issues

In order to write any kind of concurrent program, you must be able to synchronize the different threads reliably. Failure to do so will result in all sorts of ugly, messy bugs. Without synchronization, two threads will start to change some data at the same time, one will overwrite the other. To avoid this disaster, threads must reliably coordinate their actions.

```
              Thread 1                              Thread 2
bal = GetBalance(account);              bal = GetBalance(account);
bal += bal * InterestRate;              bal += deposit;
                                        PutBalance(account, bal);
PutBalance(account, bal);
```

Code Example 6–1:   *Why Synchronization Is Necessary*

Atomic Actions and Atomic Instructions

Implementation of synchronization requires the existence of an atomic *test and set* instruction in hardware. This is true for uniprocessor, as well as multiprocessor, machines. Because threads can be pre-empted at any time, between any two instructions, you must have such an instruction. Sure, there might be only a 10-nanosecond window for disaster to strike, but you still want to avoid it.

A test and set instruction tests (or just loads into a register) a word from memory and sets it to some value (typically 1), all in one instruction with no possibility of anything happening in between the two halves (e.g., an interrupt or a write by a different CPU). If the value of the target word *is* 0, then it gets set to 1 and you are considered to have ownership of the lock. If already is 1, then it gets set to 1 (i.e., no change) and you don't have ownership. All synchronization is based upon the existence of this instruction.

```
try_again:     ldstub address -> register
               compare register, 0
               branch_equal got_it
               call go_to_sleep
               jump try_again
got_it:        return
```

Code Example 6–2:   *Assembly Code for the Basic Mutual Exclusion Lock*

In SPARC machines, the test and set instruction is `ldstub` ("load and store unsigned byte"), which loads a byte into a register while setting that byte to all ones. Code Example 6–2 shows how it can be used to create a basic lock. The important thing to understand here is that no matter how many different threads on how many different CPUs call `ldstub` at the same time, only one of them will get ownership. Exactly how the `go_to_sleep` function works is unimportant. Indeed, even if it did nothing at all, and just jumped right back to `try_again`, the locking code would still work (see *Spin Locks* on page 114). Notice that there is no guarantee that a thread that goes to sleep will get the lock when it wakes up.

Other types of atomic instructions are used on other machines, most of which are logically equivalent. The one type of instruction substantially different is the *compare and swap* style instruction, which compares one word of main memory with a register and swaps the contents of that word with a second register when equal. This type of instruction allows some other types of atomic actions which are qualitatively distinct (see *LoadLocked/StoreConditional and Compare and Swap* on page 291), giving significantly superior performance for specific situations.

Critical Sections

A critical section is a section of code that must be allowed to complete atomically with no interruption that affects its completion. We create critical sections by locking a lock (as in Code Example 6–2), manipulating the data, then releasing the lock afterwards. Such things as incrementing a counter or updating a record in a database need to be critical sections. Other things may go on at the same time, and the thread that is executing in the critical section may even lose its processor, but no other thread may enter the critical section. Should another thread want to execute that same critical section, it will be forced to wait until the first thread finishes.

Critical sections are typically made as short as possible and often carefully optimized because they can significantly affect the concurrency of the program. As with all of the code in this book, we rely upon the programmer to obey the rules for using critical sections. There is no external enforcement that prevents a sloppy programmer from manipulating data without holding the proper lock.

Lock Your Shared Data!

All shared data must be protected by locks. Failure to do so will result in truly ugly bugs. Keep in mind that all means *all*. Data structures are passed to other threads and global variables are the obvious examples.[1] All data structures that can be accessed by multiple threads are included. *Static variables* are included.

Statics are just global variables that can be seen by only one function or functions in one file. It was somewhat convenient to use these in the single-threaded programs of yore, but in MT programs they are disasters waiting to strike. You should reconsider your use of statics very carefully. If you do use 'em, lock 'em first!

Synchronization Variables

A set of functions manipulate special structures in user memory. POSIX implements three *synchronization variables* and the function `pthread_join()` to provide this functionality. Win32 and OS/2 both provide synchronization variables of a slightly different nature. In all the libraries, these provide the only reliable means to coordinate the interactions of your threads. There are other tricky things you can do to coordinate your threads, but they won't work reliably because the hardware is designed assuming that you will be using synchronization variables.

There are two basic things you want to do. Thing one is that you want to protect shared data. This is what locks do. Thing two is that you want to prevent threads from running when there's nothing for them to do. You don't want them spinning, wasting time. This is what semaphores, condition variables, join, barriers, etc. are for.

Mutexes

The mutual exclusion lock is the simplest and most primitive synchronization variable. It provides a single, absolute owner for the section of code (thus a critical section) that it brackets between the calls to `pthread_mutex_lock()` and `pthread_mutex_unlock()`. The first thread that locks the mutex gets ownership, and any subsequent attempts to lock it will fail, causing the calling thread to go to sleep. When the owner unlocks it, one of the sleepers will be awakened, made runnable, and given the *chance* to obtain ownership. *It is possible that some other thread will call* `pthread_mutex_lock()` *and get ownership before the newly awakened thread does.* This is perfectly

---

[1] It is, of course, possible to have global variables that are not shared, but this would be rather unusual. Be very careful if you think you have one. If you're wrong, you're going to be unhappy when something breaks.

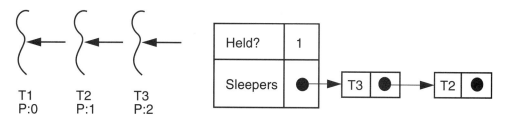

Figure 6–1 *A Mutex with Several Threads Sleeping on It*

correct behavior and must not affect the correctness of your program.[2] It's unusual to write code that would be affected by this behavior (see *FIFO Mutexes* on page 109).

In Figure 6–1, three threads all need a mutex. They have different priorities ("P:"), which determine the order in which they go onto the sleep queue. The threads have requested the lock in the order: T1, T2, T3. As the first to try, T1 owns the lock, and T3 will be awakened as soon as T1 releases it, even though T2 requested the lock before T3. Note that the mutex *doesn't* know who owns it.[3]

POSIX	**Win32**

```
pthread_mutex_lock(m)
...
pthread_mutex_unlock(m)
```

```
WaitForSingleObject(m)
...
ReleaseMutex(m)
```

OS/2

```
DosRequestMutexSem(m)
...
DosReleaseMutexSem(m)
```

Code Example 6–3: *Using Mutexes in the Different Libraries*

---

[2]In the absurd case of two threads trying to increment a counter, it is possible that only one of them will ever run, even though the program was written "correctly." The probability of T1 failing to get the mutex 1000 times in a row is always tiny and is only of interest to the rarest of non-realtime programs. As for those realtime folks... They have a lot of issues not covered in this book. We don't know RT and we're not going to guess.

[3]POSIX doesn't prevent a mutex from recording its owner, it just doesn't require it. Some implementations can be much faster if ownership is not recorded.

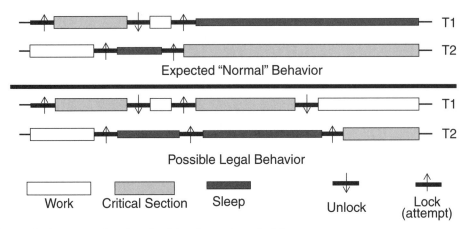

Figure 6–2   *Execution Graph of the Operation of a Mutex*

Because mutexes protect sections of code, it is not legal for one thread to lock a mutex and for another thread to unlock it. Depending upon the library implementation, this might not result in a runtime error, but it is illegal. The locking may occur in one function, while the unlocking occurs in another; locks may overlap in their use (lock 2, unlock 1, lock 3, unlock 2, etc.), but under no circumstances should you ever release a lock from the wrong thread. If you think you need this kind of behavior, you should (a) think really hard about what you're doing, and (b) look at semaphores. (Look at the use of `death_lock` in *A Cancellation Example* on page 142.)

In the execution graph for mutexes shown in Figure 6–2, we see the timing behavior of locks. The graph is shown for two threads on two CPUs, but for a uniprocessor the behavior will be identical, save that there will be gaps in each time line as the CPU context switches. Those gaps will affect neither the correctness of the code nor the probability of encountering race conditions in correctly locked code (see *Race Conditions* on page 125).

Code Example 6–4 and Figure 6–3 show the proper way to use mutexes while putting items onto a list (as T1 is doing) and taking them off (T2). Should two threads call `remove()` at the same time, one of them will get mutex ownership while the other will have to go to sleep. When the mutex is released, the sleeper will be awakened, but it is possible that either T1 or a third thread could slip in at just the right instant and get the lock. In this case the new thread, instead of the sleeper, would

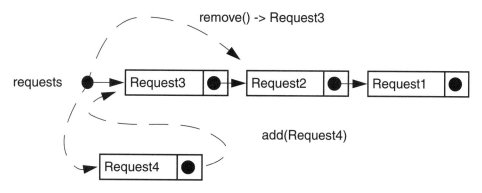

Figure 6–3 *Protecting a Shared List with a Mutex*

remove `Request2` from the list. Presumably all the threads will be executing the same code, so it won't make any difference which thread actually gets to process the request.

| **Thread 1** | **Thread 2** |

```
add(request_t *request)
{   pthread_mutex_lock(&lock);
    request->next = requests;
    requests = request;
    pthread_mutex_unlock(&lock);
}
```

```
request_t *remove()
{   pthread_mutex_lock(&lock);
    ...sleeping...

    request = requests;
    requests = requests->next;
    pthread_mutex_unlock(&lock)
    return(request);
}
```

Code Example 6–4: *Protecting a Shared List with a Mutex*

In Code Example 6–4, you will notice that we're placing new requests onto the front of the queue, and also taking old requests off of the front. You probably wouldn't do this with your own programs, but for pedagogical purposes, it suits us quite well. For example, if the consumers start falling behind the producers, you will be able to see that some requests end up at the back of the list and are never processed.

For the (rare) situation when you do not want to go to sleep, a trylock function is included in each API. In POSIX, `pthread_mutex_trylock()` returns 0 if you get the lock, and `EBUSY` if you don't. (OS/2 and Win32 functions have timeouts for the same purpose.) If you get `EBUSY`, you'll have to figure out something else to do, as entering the critical section anyway would be highly antisocial. This function is used very rarely, so if you think you want it, look very carefully at what you're doing![4] (See *Making malloc() More Concurrent* on page 210.)

It is important to realize that although locks are used to protect data, what they *really* do is protect that section of code that they bracket. There's nothing that forces another programmer (who writes another function that uses the same data) to lock his code. Nothing but good programming practice.

Win32 provides a similar mutex, along with a *critical section*,[5] which is quite similar. OS/2 calls mutexes *mutex semaphores*, but defines much the same behavior (there are a bunch of added bells and whistles). Both Win32 and OS/2 mutexes are recursive—meaning that the same thread can lock the mutex multiple times.

Semaphores

In the 19th century, when trains were still advanced technology and railroad tracks were exotic and expensive, it was common to run single sets of tracks and restrict the trains to travel in only one direction at a time. *Semaphores* were invented to let the trains know if other trains were on the rails at the same time. A semaphore was a vertical pole with a metal flag adjusted to hang at either 45 or 90 degrees to indicate the existence of other trains.

In the 1960s, E. W. Dijkstra, a professor in the Department of Mathematics at the Technological University, Eindhoven, Netherlands, extended this concept to computer science. A *counting semaphore*[6] (aka *PV semaphore*) is a variable that can increment arbitrarily high, but decrement only to zero. A `sem_post()` operation (aka "V"—*verhogen*

---

[4]We apologize if these warnings seem a bit much. We realize that *you* understand the issues involved. We just want to make it clear for that other programmer.

[5]We find it is somewhat confusing to use a generic term like critical section, which refers to a concept, for the name of a specific synchronization variable.

[6]The word semaphore has come to take on other meanings in computer science. System V semaphores, for example, are much more elaborate objects than counting semaphores.

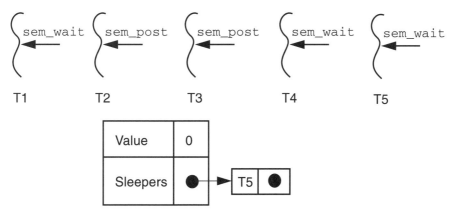

Figure 6–4 *How a Semaphore Operates*

in Dutch) increments the semaphore, while a `sem_wait()` (aka "P"—*Proberen te verlagen*) attempts to decrement it. If the semaphore is greater than zero, the operation succeeds; if not, then the calling thread must go to sleep until a different thread increments it.

A semaphore is useful for working with "train-like" objects, that is, what you care about is whether there are either zero objects or more than zero. Buffers and lists that fill and empty are good examples. Semaphores are also useful when you want a thread to wait for something. You can accomplish this by having the thread call `sem_wait()` on a semaphore with value zero, then have another thread increment the semaphore when you're ready for the thread to continue.

In Figure 6–4, the semaphore started with a value of zero. The threads have executed their respective operations in the order: T1, T2, T3, T4, T5. After T1 executed its `sem_wait()`, it had to wait (as the value was zero). When T2 did the `sem_post()`, T1 was awakened, and decremented the value back to zero. T3 did a `sem_post()`, incrementing the value to one. When T4 did its `sem_wait()` it could continue without waiting at all. Finally, T5 called `sem_wait()`, and is still waiting.

Although there is a function `sem_getvalue()` which will return the current value of a semaphore, it is virtually impossible to use correctly because what it returns is what the value of the semaphore *was*. By the time you use the value it returned, it may well have changed. If you find

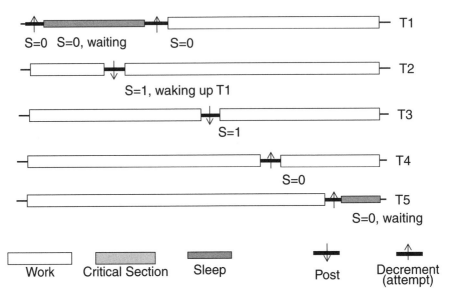

Figure 6–5 *Execution Graph of the Operation of a Semaphore*

yourself using `sem_getvalue()`, look twice; there's probably a better way to do what you want.

```
        POSIX                                Win32
sem_wait(&s);                    WaitForSingleObject(s,...);
sem_post(&s);                    ReleaseSemaphore(s,...);
```

Code Example 6–5: *Basic Use of Counting Semaphores (OS/2 has none)*

Win32 implements counting semaphores with similar definitions. OS/2 does not implement them at all, though building them would not be difficult.

In the execution graph below (Figure 6–5) we see the operation of Code Example 6–5. Notice that when T1's decrement attempt fails, it simply goes to sleep and tries it again later. Another thread could jump in and decrement the value just as thread T1 was waking up, in which case T1 would have to go back to sleep. As with mutexes, this is usually not a problem.

POSIX semaphores are unique among synchronization variables in one particular fashion: They are *async safe*, meaning that it is legal to call `sem_post()` from a signal handler (see *Async Safety* on page 161). No other synchronization variable is async safe. So, if you want to write a signal handler that causes some other thread to wake up, this is the way to do it.

If you look at the definition of semaphores, you will also notice that they may return from a wait with a legal, non-zero value, `-1`, with `errno` set to `EINTR`. This means that the semaphore was interrupted by a signal and *it did not successfully decrement*. Your program must not continue from this point as if it did.

Correct usage of a semaphore therefore requires that it be executed in a loop. If you block out all signals, then, and only then, can you use semaphores without a loop. Of course you would need to be completely certain that no one who maintains your code ever allows signals. In all of our code, we simply use a help function:

```
void SEM_WAIT(sem_t *sem)
{   while (sem_wait(sem) != 0) {}}
```

Code Example 6–6: *Semaphore Ignoring* `EINTR`
                     (`thread_extensions.c`)

The logic for this `EINTR` behavior is that you might want your thread to do something different, should it be interrupted by a signal. Admittedly we have never run into such a situation; nonetheless, there it is.

A typical use of semaphores is in Code Example 6–7. This is a producer/consumer example in which one thread is continually receiving requests from the net, which it adds to a list, while the other thread is busy removing items from that list and processing them. It is particularly interesting to notice that the number of items on the list is contained in the semaphore, but the program never actually gets to look at that number. Should the producer place twenty items on the list all at once, the consumer function will be able to call `sem_wait()` twenty times without blocking. The twenty-first time, the semaphore will be zero, and the consumer will have to wait. Because the critical sections are so small, the chance of any thread ever blocking on the mutex is very small.

In Code Example 6–7, the main things to notice are that `get_request()` allocates the memory for the request structure that will be appended to the list, while `process_request()` is responsible for freeing it. This code may be safely run by any number of threads running the producer, and any number running the consumer. In no case will a consumer ever attempt to remove a request from an empty list. The semaphore actually encodes the minimum length of the list. During the brief moments between the time a producer places a request onto the list and the semaphore is incremented, the semaphore value is one less than the actual length of the list. For now, this is fine.

The list is unbounded and may continue to grow longer until memory is exhausted. This is a problem with our example code that must be solved. You should be able to come up with a solution yourself now. We'll get to it a bit later.

```
request_t *get_request()
{request_t *request;
    request = (request_t *) malloc(sizeof(request_t));
    request->data = read_from_net();
    return(request)
}

void process_request(request_t *request)
{   process(request->data);
    free(request);
}

producer()
{request_t *request;
 while(1)
    {request = get_request();
     add(request);
     sem_post(&requests_length);
    }
}

consumer()
{request_t *request;
 while(1)
    {SEM_WAIT(&requests_length);
     request = remove();
     process_request(request);
    }
}
```

Code Example 6–7:   *The Classic Producer/Consumer Example*
(one_queue_problem.c)

Using Semaphores to Count Exiting Threads

Sometimes we do want to know when a set of threads have completed their work. One way of doing this is to use a semaphore as a sort of barrier (distinct from the *Barriers* on page 116). Each exiting thread will increment the semaphore, and the thread waiting for them will call sem_wait() once for each thread in question. This gives a convenient replacement for pthread_join(). This code is used in *A Stoppable Producer/Consumer Example* on page 101.

```
    /* Block *one* thread, waiting for the others. */
void thread_single_barrier(sem_t *barrier, int count)
{
  while (count > 0)
    {SEM_WAIT(barrier);
     count--;
    }
}
```

Code Example 6–8: *A Simple Barrier to Block One Thread*

A Different View of Semaphores

Now let's look at a different picture of how a semaphore works. Figure 6–6 depicts the actual operation of sem_wait() and sem_post() on Solaris 2.5. As the value of the semaphore is a shared data item, it must be protected by a mutex (or logical equivalent). This mutex is part of the semaphore structure and is hidden from the programmer. The first thing sem_wait() does is lock that mutex. Then it checks the value. If it is greater than zero, the value is decremented, the hidden mutex is released, and sem_wait() returns.

If the value of the semaphore is zero, then the mutex will be released, and the thread will then go to sleep. Upon waking up, the thread then must repeat the operation, reacquiring the mutex and testing the value.

The operation of sem_post() is quite simple. It locks the mutex, increments the value, releases the mutex and wakes up one sleeper (if there is one). The results are exactly what you expect. Even though you

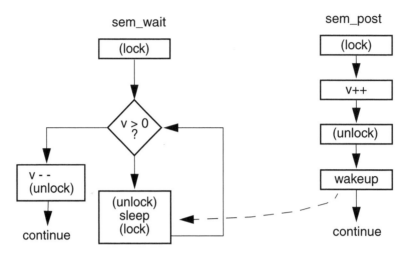

Figure 6–6   *A Flow Chart for Semaphores*

have no idea what the scheduling order might be, it is impossible to accidently decrement the value below zero, and no thread can ever get "stuck" on the sleep queue when the value is greater than zero. There are timing gaps where things *look* momentarily inconsistent, and it is possible for a thread to be awakened by mistake, but the end results are always correct.

A semaphore is perfect for situations where you want to count things and have threads sleep when some limit is hit. If you wish to count *up* to some number, say for a list limited to ten items, you simply view the semaphore as counting the number of "spaces" in the list, initialize it to ten and count down (see *Controlling the Queue Length* on page 99).

There are occasions when you want the same kind of sleeping behavior as with semaphores, but your test is more complex than just "Is v > 0?"

Condition Variables

Figure 6–7 shows a flow chart for a generalization on semaphores. Here the mutex is visible to the programmer and the condition is arbitrary. The programmer is responsible for locking and unlocking the mutex, testing and changing the condition, and waking up sleepers. Otherwise, it is exactly like a semaphore.

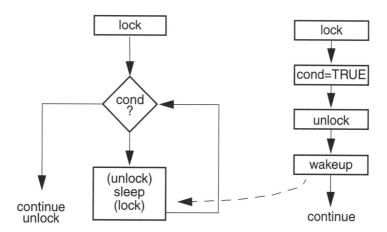

Figure 6–7   *Using a Condition Variable*

Perhaps you want a thread to execute some code only if X > 17, Y is prime, and grandmother is visiting next Thursday. As long as you can express the condition in a program, you can use it in a condition variable. A condition variable creates a safe environment for you to test your condition, sleep on it when false, and be awakened when it might have become true.

It works like this: A thread obtains a mutex (condition variables always have an associated mutex) and tests the condition under the mutex's protection. No other thread should alter any aspect of the condition without holding the mutex. If the condition is true, your thread completes its task, releasing the mutex when appropriate. If the condition isn't true, the mutex is released *for you*, and your thread goes to sleep on the condition variable. When some other thread changes some aspect of the condition (e.g., it reserves a plane ticket for granny), it calls `pthread_cond_signal()`,[7] waking up one sleeping thread. Your thread then reacquires the mutex,[8] reevaluates the condition, and either succeeds or goes back to sleep, depending upon the outcome. You *must* reevaluate the condition! First, the other thread may not have tested the complete condition before sending the wakeup. Second, even if the

---

[7]The term "signal" here is distinct from UNIX signals (SIGINT, etc.). "Wakeup" might be a better term.

[8]Obviously, when a thread sleeps on a condition variable, the mutex must be released (so other threads can acquire it) and reacquired upon waking. All of this is handled for you by `pthread_cond_wait()`.

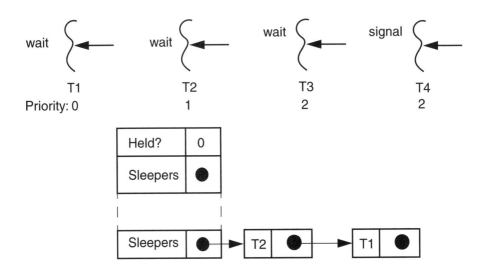

Figure 6–8   *A Condition Variable in Use*

condition was true when the signal was sent, it could have changed before your thread got to run. Third, condition variables allow for spurious wakeups. They are allowed to wakeup for no discernible reason whatsoever![9]

In Figure 6–8, T1, T2, and T3 all evaluated the condition, determined it to be false, and went to sleep on the condition variable. T4 then came along and changed the condition to true, and woke up the first of the sleeping threads. T3 was awakened, reevaluated the condition, found it to be true, and did its thing, releasing the mutex when done. We'll assume that T3 also changed the condition back to false, so there was no reason to wake any other threads. If T3 hadn't changed the condition, then it should have woken up another thread.

Depending upon your program, you may wish to wake up all the threads that are waiting on a condition. Perhaps they were all waiting for the right time of day to begin background work, or were waiting for a certain network device to become active. A `pthread_cond_broadcast()` is used exactly like `pthread_cond_signal()`. It is called after some

---

[9]Due to some arcana in the hardware design of modern SMP machines, it proves to be highly convenient to define them like this. The hardware runs a little faster, and the programmer needed to reevaluate the condition anyway.

aspect of the condition has changed. It then wakes all of the sleeping threads (in an undefined order), which then must all hurry off to reevaluate the condition. This may cause some contention for the mutex, but that's OK.

Presumably you are calling signal or broadcast any time that the condition has been changed such that it may have become true. In most cases you will have completely evaluated the condition before you signal or broadcast, but you do not have to. You certainly would want to signal any time that the condition became true.

There are several things you can do with condition variables that the compiler won't complain about, but are guaranteed trouble. You could use the same condition variable with different mutexes. You could have several functions that use one condition variable, but that evaluate different conditions. You could initialize the condition variable to be cross-process, but not the mutex; or vice versa. *Don't do that!*

Condition variables also allow you to limit the sleep time. By calling `pthread_cond_timedwait()`, you can arrange to be awakened after a fixed amount of time, in case you're the impatient type. Should you know the condition ought to change within some time frame, you can wait for that amount of time, and then figure out what went wrong.

You can also use it simply as a thread-specific timer, although the standard timer functions (`sleep()`, `nanosleep()`) are more appropriate and easier to use. Be aware that the system clock will limit the precision of the wakeup. A 10ms quantum is typical. If you want 100µs precision you'll probably have to use something highly vendor-specific and you may have trouble getting such precision at all.

Once the wait time expires, the sleeping thread will be moved off the sleep queue and `pthread_cond_timedwait()` will return ETIMEDOUT. It doesn't make any difference should another thread signal the sleeper 1ms later. It also makes no difference should it subsequently take the ex-sleeper 16 hours to become active or get the mutex. Counterwise, once the sleeper is signaled, it is taken off the sleep queue and the timer is turned off. If it takes another week before `pthread_cond_timedwait()` returns, too bad. You will not get a timeout.

Neither of the wait functions will ever return without the mutex being locked—not on normal wakeups, not on timeouts, not on spurious wakeups, not even on cancellation. It is possible that right after waking up, a thread must go back to sleep because the mutex is held by another thread!

Thread 1	**Thread 2**

```
pthread_mutex_lock(&m);
while (!my_condition)
  pthread_cond_wait(&c, &m);
                                   pthread_mutex_lock(&m);
... sleeping ...                   my_condition = TRUE;
                                   pthread_mutex_unlock(&m);
                                   pthread_cond_signal(&c);
do_thing();
pthread_mutex_unlock(&m);
```

Code Example 6–9:   *Using a Condition Variable*

Because of the kind of interaction that exists between the condition variable and its associated mutex, it is possible to get some unwanted contention for the mutex. This is most evident when calling broadcast. Unfortunately there is not much you can do about it, and your program may well suffer dozens of microseconds in wasted mutex blocks.

Figure 6–9 illustrates the problem. In the "Desired Behavior" case, the little bit of extra time it takes T2 to wake up and try for the mutex is just long enough for T1 to release it. In the "Possible Behavior" case, the waiting threads wake up, try for the mutex, and have to go right back to sleep because the mutex hasn't been released yet. The most obvious solution for at least some of this problem is to make the call to signal or broadcast outside of the critical section. This is what all of our code does.

Both Win32 and OS/2 implement what they call *event objects (event semaphores)*, which are similar to condition variables and serve the same purpose (see *Event Objects* on page 117).

The Lost Wakeup

If you simply neglect to hold the mutex while testing or changing the value of the condition, your program will be subject to the fearsome *lost wakeup* problem. This condition occurs when one of your threads misses a wakeup signal because it had not yet gone to sleep. Of course,

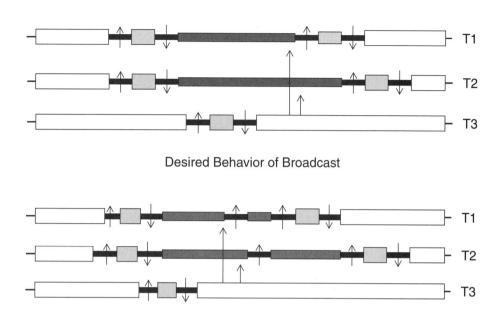

Desired Behavior of Broadcast

Possible Behavior of Broadcast

Figure 6–9 *Extra Contention: When the Mutex Is Held by a Different Thread*

if you're not protecting your shared data correctly, your program will be subject to numerous other bugs, so this is nothing special.

There is a point of confusion surrounding the lost wakeup that should be clarified. In much of Sun's documentation, it is described incorrectly as a problem that occurs when calling broadcast or signal outside of the critical section. That is not the case. The explanation was simply written down incorrectly. This should be fixed when Solaris 2.6 documentation comes out.

Controlling the Queue Length

So how do we prevent the queue from growing in the Producer/ Consumer example? The simplest way is to initialize a second semaphore to the maximum allowed length and count it down. (One way to imagine this inverse use of a semaphore is to consider the queue to have some number of available slots in it. The semaphore encodes this number. When a producer places a new request onto the queue, there is one less available slot, so we decrement the semaphore. When a consumer takes a request off, there is one more, so we increment it.)

```
producer()
{request_t *request;
 while(1)
    {SEM_WAIT(&requests_slots);
     request = get_request();
     add(request);
     sem_post(&requests_length);
    }
}

consumer()
{request_t *request;
 while(1)
    {SEM_WAIT(&requests_length);
     request = remove();
     process_request(request);
     sem_post(&requests_slots);
    }
}
```

Code Example 6–10:   *Producer/Consumer with Bounded Length (Using Semaphores)*

This particular design is nice because it separates the producer from `add()`, the code that inserts the new request onto the queue. This works quite well for simple programs.

Sometimes you will find that you have more extensive demands on the program and will need to use a condition variable. Code Example 6–11 shows this situation. We use the mutex `requests_lock` to protect both `length` and the list itself, so we move it out of `add()` and `remove()`. (The list and `length` must be changed together, automatically, for this to work, so we must use the same mutex.)

```
void *producer(void *arg)
{request_t *request;

 while(1)
   {request = get_request();
    pthread_mutex_lock(&requests_lock);
    while (length >= 10)
      pthread_cond_wait(&requests_producer, &requests_lock);
    add(request);
    length++;
    pthread_mutex_unlock(&requests_lock);
    pthread_cond_signal(&requests_consumer);
   }
}


void *consumer(void *arg)
{request_t *request;

 while(1)
   {pthread_mutex_lock(&requests_lock);
    while (length == 0)
      pthread_cond_wait(&requests_consumer, &requests_lock);
    request = remove();
    length--;
    pthread_mutex_unlock(&requests_lock);
    pthread_cond_signal(&requests_producer);
    process_request(request);
   }
}
```

Code Example 6–11: *Producer/Consumer with Bounded Length (Using Condition Variables)*

A Stoppable Producer/Consumer Example

Let's use the ideas above to deal with a more complex situation. Say you like the operation of the producer/consumer, but you want to be able to start and stop at will. Let's say there is a global variable, stop, which will control the threads. If it is TRUE, all the producers and consumers will finish what they're doing and exit. Let's further say that we don't want the queue to be emptied at stop time. When we decide to start up the producers and consumers again, we'll require that the consumers empty the queue before any producers are started.

The only tricky part to this exercise is that some of the threads may be sleeping at the time we set `stop` to TRUE, and we must ensure that they are awoken so that they can exit. We must also have the main thread sleep until the new consumers have emptied the queue. By having the threads wait on the condition `((length >= 10) && (!stop))`, they can be awakened on a change of state for either the length or `stop`.

```c
void *producer(void *arg)
{request_t *request;

  while(1)
    {request = get_request();
     pthread_mutex_lock(&requests_lock);
     while ((length >= 10) && (!stop))
       pthread_cond_wait(&requests_producer, &requests_lock);
     add_request(request);
     length++;
     if (stop) break;
     pthread_mutex_unlock(&requests_lock);
     pthread_cond_signal(&requests_consumer);
    }
  pthread_mutex_unlock(&requests_lock);
  sem_post(&barrier);
  pthread_exit(NULL);
}

void *consumer(void *arg)
{request_t *request;

  while(1)
    {pthread_mutex_lock(&requests_lock);
     while ((length == 0) && (!stop))
       pthread_cond_wait(&requests_consumer, &requests_lock);
     if (stop) break;
     request = remove_request();
     length--;
     pthread_mutex_unlock(&requests_lock);
     pthread_cond_signal(&requests_producer);
     process_request(request);
    }
```

Code Example 6-12:   *A Stoppable Producer/Consumer (`stop_queue.c`)*

```
  pthread_mutex_unlock(&requests_lock);
  sem_post(&barrier);
  pthread_exit(NULL);
}
```

Code Example 6–12: *A Stoppable Producer/Consumer (*`stop_queue.c`*)*

When we set `stop` to TRUE, we will need to wake up all threads that might be sleeping. In Code Example 6–13, we spawn a thread to set `stop` true after four seconds. After it's set, the thread calls `pthread_cond_broadcast()` to wake up all of the worker threads. We would do the same if it were a button we were using, or any other method. Notice that we must lock the mutex before changing the value of `stop`; otherwise we'll be subject to the lost wakeup problem.

```
void *stopper(void *arg)
{
  sleep(4);
  pthread_mutex_lock(&requests_lock);              /* REQUIRED! */
  stop = TRUE;
  pthread_mutex_unlock(&requests_lock);
  pthread_cond_broadcast(&requests_producer);
  pthread_cond_broadcast(&requests_consumer);
  pthread_exit(NULL);
```

Code Example 6–13: *Stopping the Producer/Consumer (*`stop_queue.c`*)*

Finally, in this bit of code from `main()` (Code Example 6–14), we see how we can synchronize on the exiting of the threads and the emptying of the queue. First we start them all up. Then we wait for all of the threads to complete their work (they'll probably exit immediately after they call `sem_post()`, however we don't really care). After they have all completed their work, we can set stop back to FALSE. (What if we didn't wait for all the threads to finish?) Then we create the consumers and wait for them to empty the queue. (Notice how we use the condition variable `requests_producer`.) Once the queue is empty, we start up the producers again.

A minor point: when we set `stop` = `FALSE`, we don't lock the mutex. Why can we get away with this?

```
for (j=0; j < 3; j++)
  {printf("Starting consumers. List length: %d.\n", length);
  for (i=0; i<N_CONS; i++)
    PTHREAD_CREATE(&tid, &attr, consumer, NULL);
  pthread_mutex_lock(&requests_lock);

  while (length != 0)
    pthread_cond_wait(&requests_producer, &requests_lock);

  printf("Starting producers.\n");
  pthread_mutex_unlock(&requests_lock);
  for (i=0; i<N_PROD; i++)
    PTHREAD_CREATE(&tid, &attr, producer, NULL);

  PTHREAD_CREATE(&tid, &attr, stopper, NULL);
  thread_single_barrier(&barrier, N_PROD+N_CONS);
  stop = FALSE;                         /* Lock not required! */
  printf("All exited. List length: %d.\n", length);
  sleep(4);
  }
```

Code Example 6–14:   *A Stoppable Producer/Consumer (Starting Up and*
                          Shutting Down in `main()`*)*

Summary

The main issue in writing MT programs is how to get threads to work together. Locks and condition variables are the fundamental building blocks from which anything can be built. Although there are many non-intuitive aspects of synchronization, most of them can be ignored, as things "just work."

7

Complexities

In which a series of more complex synchronization variables and options are presented and the trade-off between them and the simpler ones are discussed. Synchronization problems and techniques for dealing with them conclude the chapter.

Complex Locking Primitives

There are times when a simple mutex does not provide enough functionality. There are situations in which you can improve your program's efficiency or fairness by implementing more complex locking primitives. Keep in mind that the locks described below are more complex and therefore slower than normal mutex locks, generally by a factor of two or more. They are not generally useful, so be advised to consider your requirements closely before using them.

Readers/Writer Locks

Sometimes you will find yourself with a shared data structure that gets read often, but written only seldom. The reading of that structure may require a significant amount of time (perhaps it's a long list through which you do searches). It would seem a waste to put a mutex around it and require all the threads to go through it one at a time when they're not changing anything. Hence, readers/writer locks.

With an RWlock, you can have any number of threads reading the data concurrently, whereas writers are serialized. The only drawback to RWlocks is that they are more expensive than mutexes. So, you must consider your data structure, how long you expect to be in it, how much contention you expect, and choose between a mutex and an RWlock on those bases.

As a rule of thumb, a simple global variable will always be locked with a mutex, while searching down a 1000-element, linked list will often be locked with an RWlock.

The operation of RWlocks is as follows: The first reader that requests the lock will get it. Subsequent readers also get the lock, and all of them are allowed to read the data concurrently. When a writer requests the lock, it is put on a sleep queue until all the readers exit. A second writer will also be put on the writer's sleep queue in priority order. Should a new reader show up at this point, it will be put on the reader's sleep queue until all the writers have completed. Further writers will also be placed on the same writer's sleep queue as the others (hence, in front of the waiting reader), meaning that writers are always favored over readers. (Writer priority is simply a choice we made in our implementation; you may make a different choice.)

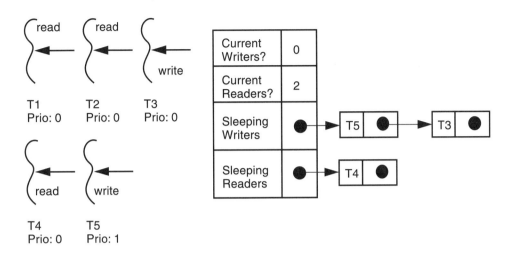

Figure 7–1   *How Reader/Writer Locks Work*

The writers will obtain the lock one at a time, each waiting for the previous writer to complete. When all writers have completed, the entire set of sleeping readers are awakened and can then attempt to acquire the lock. Readers' priorities are not used.

In Figure 7–1, five threads all need an RWlock. They have different priorities, which determine the order in which they go onto the *writers'* sleep queue. The threads have requested the lock in the order: T1, T2, T3, T4, T5. T1 and T2 own the lock, and T5 will be awakened as soon as they both release it, even though T3 and T4 requested the lock before T5. In Figure 7–2, we see exactly this happening. Note the overlapping read sections for T1 and T2.

You will be disappointed to discover that none of the three libraries define RWlocks. However, all is not lost. They can be built out of the primitives already available to you—mutexes and condition variables. We build them in our extensions library. Some of these are also defined in specific implementations as non-portable extensions (see *Pthread Extensions* on page 187).

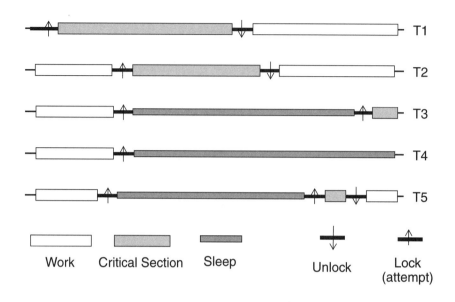

Figure 7–2 *Execution Graph for Reader/Writer Locks*

Priority Inheritance Mutexes

Should a high-priority thread (T2 in Figure 7–3) be blocked, waiting for a lock that is held by another thread of lower priority (T1), it may have to wait a longer time than seems reasonable, because a third thread (T3) of middling priority might be hogging the CPU. In order to do justice to overall system performance, it would be reasonable to elevate the scheduling priority of T1 to the level of the blocked thread (T2). This is not done for normal Pthread mutexes, so user programs may suffer from *priority inversion*. In POSIX, priority inheritance is an option during mutex initialization *for realtime threads only*. (Calling a PI mutex from a non-realtime thread is simply not defined in POSIX. Consult your vendor's documentation.)

POSIX defines two types of priority-inheritance mutexes. In the first, a *Priority Ceiling Mutex*, you declare a ceiling priority level for the mutex and any thread that locks the mutex automatically gets that priority. In *Priority Inheritance Mutexes*, a thread may lock a mutex without any change in priority level. When a second thread then goes to sleep, waiting for the mutex, the owner is given the priority of the sleeper,

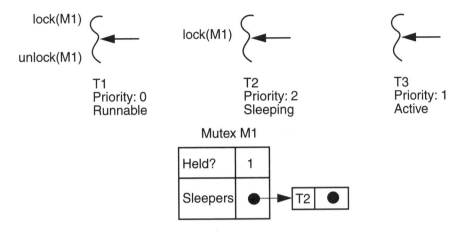

Figure 7–3 *Priority Inversion*

should the sleeper have a higher priority. Additional sleepers may cause additional changes in priority level of the owner. Upon release, the owner regains its previous priority level.

It is not terribly difficult to build basic priority-inheritance mutexes in the other libraries or for non-realtime POSIX threads, but it's not often of much value. To build them one hundred percent correctly and efficiently is tough.

FIFO Mutexes

Every now and then, you come upon a program where you want to ensure that the thread that is blocked on a mutex will be the next owner of the mutex—something which is not in the definition of simple POSIX mutexes. Typically, this situation occurs when two threads both need a mutex to do their work: they hold the mutex for a significant length of time; they do their work independently of each other; and they have very little to do when they don't hold it. Thus, what happens is (see Figure 7–4) that T1 grabs the mutex and does its work, while T2 tries for the mutex, and blocks. T1 then releases the mutex and wakes up T2. Before T2 manages to obtain the mutex, T1 reacquires it. This is illustrated in case 2.

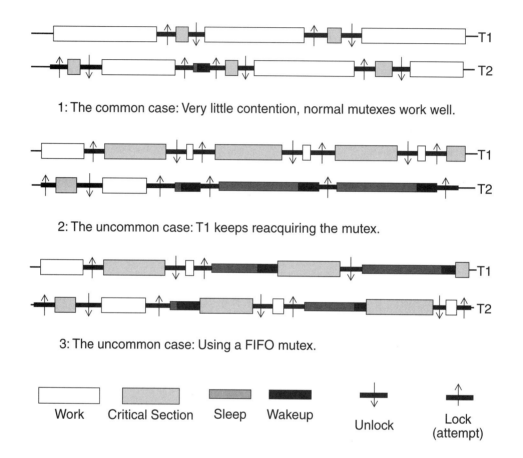

1: The common case: Very little contention, normal mutexes work well.

2: The uncommon case: T1 keeps reacquiring the mutex.

3: The uncommon case: Using a FIFO mutex.

Work   Critical Section   Sleep   Wakeup   Unlock   Lock (attempt)

Figure 7–4   *When FIFO Mutexes Are Valuable*

Case 3 assumes that you have implemented FIFO mutexes, where the owner of the mutex automatically hands ownership over to the first waiter when releasing the mutex.

This is a rare situation, and it merits reconsidering your algorithm before dealing with it. (If you contrast case 2 and case 3 against case 1, you will notice that the two threads are spending a lot of time sleeping on the job. This might run better with fewer threads!) But should you find yourself stuck with this kind of problem, it is a simple programming effort for you to implement guaranteed FIFO mutexes yourself.

Recursive Mutexes

Win32 and OS/2 mutexes are recursive—they can be locked multiple times from the same thread without deadlocking. POSIX mutexes cannot. Building a recursive mutex with POSIX is not at all difficult (an excellent exercise!) and we even include a definition in `thread_extensions.c`. The real question is not if you can build them, but whether it's a good idea.

The chances are very high that if you have a situation where you want to use recursive mutexes, you'd be better off redesigning your code so that you don't need them. Why are you locking this mutex? To protect some shared data. Once you've done so, why would you ever want to lock it again? Because your code is structured poorly. Fix your code.

Once you've locked a recursive mutex three times, you will need to unlock it three times before any other thread can lock it. You *could* write an "unlock_all" routine, but it would probably just make your code even more confusing.

Now that we've so thoroughly denigrated recursive mutexes, we'll take a small step backwards and admit that there are "special situations." Your situation might be one of them. If so, use 'em. Just be very careful to make sure you're correct.

Non-Blocking Synchronization

All of the synchronization variables have non-blocking calls associated with them. (For POSIX, `pthread_mutex_trylock()` and `sem_trywait()`. In Win32 and OS/2 there are time-outs associated with each call.) These functions can be used for things such as spin locks and complicated methods of coordinating threads while avoiding deadlock when you are unable to establish a lock hierarchy. It is very rare to ever use these functions. (See *Making malloc() More Concurrent* on page 210.)

Debug Mutexes

Sometimes it is difficult to debug a program because you don't know the owner of a mutex. Even though you don't need to know the owner for the production code, it can be very nice while debugging. Building a mutex that meets these requirements is fairly simple and easy to do. Some of the vendors supply debugging environments (e.g., Digital UNIX and HP-UX). In Code Example 7–1, we show such a mutex (pthread_dmutex_t), one that keeps track of its owner, shows how many times it was locked, how many times a thread tried to lock it, and aborts the program should the wrong thread try to unlock it. You would use this mutex while debugging, then do a global replace of "dmutex" with "mutex" to use normal mutexes in your code for final testing and release. Some vendors also supply some type of debug mutex.

```
pthread_dmutex_t lock1, lock2, lock3;

void *test3(void *arg)
{int i = (int) arg;

 pthread_dmutex_lock(&lock3);
 printf("%s in critical section 3\n", thread_name(pthread_self()))
 print_dmutexes();
 pthread_dmutex_unlock(&lock3);
 return;
}

main()
{...
 PTHREAD_CREATE(&tid, &attr, test3,  NULL);
 ...
 printf("Now crash with a self-deadlock...\n");
 pthread_dmutex_lock(&lock3);
 pthread_dmutex_lock(&lock3);/* Comment out for next error */
 printf("Now crash with a non-owner unlock...\n");
 pthread_dmutex_unlock(&lock1);
}
```

OUTPUT

```
T@8 in critical section 3
&lock3 T@10   Times locked:  14,  failed:  10.  Sleepers: ( )
&lock2 ----   Times locked:   0,  failed:   0.  Sleepers: ( )
&lock1 T@8    Times locked:  13,  failed:  15.  Sleepers: ( T@6 T@7 )

Now crash with a self-deadlock...
Error! T@1 deadlocking dmutex &lock3.
Abort
```

Code Example 7–1:   *Using a Debug Mutex (from* test_dmutex.c*)*

Monitors

If you chose to encapsulate the shared data with the locking required for its use, you would have a monitor. This encapsulation can be done informally in C by simply declaring everything to be local to the access functions (as in Code Example 7–2), or formally in an object-oriented language such as C++ or Java by creating a class that does this for you. In Java, monitors are already defined as part of the base language. In C++ you can define them yourself (see *C++* on page 232) or use one of the commercial libraries (see *Commercial Products* on page 238).

In many situations, monitors are an excellent synchronization technique. Forcing the programmer to manipulate shared data via monitored code ensures that there can never be a failure to lock its use, and that the access methods will be well defined. Monitors cannot handle all types of locking situations, however. When you need to acquire and release locks in an overlapping fashion (as in *One Local Lock* on page 220), or when you want to use the "trylock" functions, you must use regular mutexes.

There's no great magic here. Where monitors make the most sense, use them. When simple mutexes are required, use them. With a sufficiently intelligent compiler, a monitor will be just as fast as regular mutexes.

```
void count_things(int i)
{static int count=0;
 static pthread_mutex_t count_lock = PTHREAD_MUTEX_INITIALIZER;

 pthread_mutex_lock(&count_lock);
 count += i;
 i = count;
 pthread_mutex_unlock(&count_lock);
 return(i);                      /* Cannot return count outside the CS! */
}
```

Code Example 7–2: *Monitor Style Encapsulation in C*

Code Example 7–2 shows encapsulation in C. This is nice, though it doesn't prevent you from forgetting to releasing the mutex, and you would need a separate function for each data item. In C++ and Java, these little shortcomings are covered. In Code Example 7–3, the destructor for `Monitor` will be called any time that `bar()` returns, insuring that the mutex will be released.

```
class Monitor
{pthread_mutex_t *mutex;

 public:
 Monitor(pthread_mutex_t *m);
 virtual ~Monitor();
};


// Monitor constructor
Monitor::Monitor(pthread_mutex_t *m)
{ mutex = m;
  pthread_mutex_lock(mutex);
}


// Monitor destructor
Monitor::~Monitor()
{pthread_mutex_unlock(mutex);}



void bar()
{Monitor m(&data_lock);
 int temp;

 ...
 /* Now the destructor gets called to unlock the mutex */
}
```

Code Example 7–3:   *A Monitor in C++*

Spin Locks

Normally, you should hold a lock for the shortest time possible, to allow other threads to run without blocking. There will occasionally be times (few and far between) when you look at the blocking time for a mutex (about 42 μs on an SS4, see Appendix C, *Timings*) and say to yourself "42 μs?! The other thread is only going to hold the mutex for 5 μs. Why should I have to block, just 'cause I stumbled into that tiny window of contention? It's not fair!"

You don't. You can use a *spin lock* and try again. It's simple. You initialize   a   counter   to   some   value,   and   do   a `pthread_mutex_trylock()`—that takes about 2 μs. If you don't get the lock, decrement the counter and loop. Another 2 μs. Repeat. When the counter hits zero, then give up and block. If you get the mutex, then you've saved a bunch of time. If you don't, then you've only wasted a little time.

In Code Example 7–4, we show the construction of a simple spin lock. Although this is a good description of a spin lock, it's actually a poor implementation. We will discuss the issues and show a better implementation in Chapter 17, *Hardware*.

```
                        /* Don't use this code! */
spin_lock(mutex_t *m)
{int i;
    for (i=0; i < SPIN_COUNT; i++)
       {if (pthread_mutex_trylock(m) != EBUSY)
           return; }             /* got the lock! */
    pthread_mutex_lock(m);       /* give up and block. */
    return; }                    /* got the lock after blocking! */
```

Code Example 7–4: *A Simple Spin Lock*

Spin locks can be effective in very restricted circumstances. The critical section *must* be short, you *must* have significant contention for the lock, and you *must* be running on more than one CPU. If you do decide you need a spin lock, test that assumption. Set the spin count to zero and time your standardized, repeatable test case (you must have one!). Then set the spin count to a realistic value, and time the test again. If you don't see a significant improvement, go back to regular mutex locks. Spin locks are almost always the *wrong* answer, so be careful!

Spin locks are not part of any of the libraries, but they are easily built in all of them. They are also included in the proposed extension to POSIX.

Adaptive Spin Locks

A refinement of spin locks, called *adaptive spin locks*, is used in many kernels. You can't build them yourself and they are not generally provided by the vendor, but you might be interested in knowing what they are.

If you could find out whether the thread holding the desired mutex was in fact currently running on a CPU, then you could make a more reasoned judgement as to whether or not to spin. An adaptive lock can do this. If the mutex owner is running, then the requestor spins. If the owner isn't, then the requestor doesn't.

Unfortunately, in the user-level threads library, you generally cannot find out which thread holds a mutex, and even if you could, the system call required to find out whether the thread in question was on a CPU would be more expensive than just blocking. A clever trick in some operating systems does make this possible.

A fair (and unanswered) question is "Will the time saved by not spinning make up for the extra time to use adaptive locks?" If you are using spin locks, you should know exactly how long a critical section can be held. It may well prove faster to spin for the known time and ignore run state entirely!

Other Synchronization Variables

Join

The join functions are similar to synchronization variables in that they allow you to synchronize threads on the event of another thread exiting. You almost never actually care when a thread exits, and almost everything you do with join, you can do with the other synchronization variables. (See *Don't Wait for Threads, Don't Return Status* on page 51.)

Barriers

A barrier allows a set of threads to sync up at some point in their code. It is initialized to the number of threads to be using it, then it blocks all the threads calling it until it reaches zero, at which point it unblocks them all. The idea is that you can now arrange for a set of threads to stop when they get to some predefined point in their computation and wait for all the others to catch up. If you have eight threads, you initialize the barrier to eight. Then, as each thread reaches that point, it decrements the barrier, and then goes to sleep. When the last thread arrives, it decrements the barrier to zero, and they all unblock and proceed.

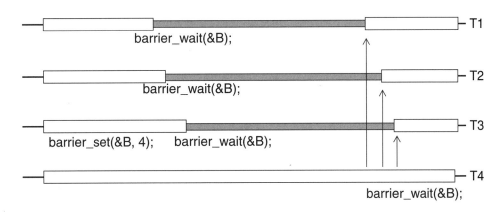

Figure 7–5 *Barriers*

Barriers are not part of any of the libraries, but they are easily implemented. They are also implemented in our extensions package and part of the proposed extensions to POSIX.

Event Objects

Both Win32 and OS/2 define event objects (called *event semaphores* in OS/2), which are really condition variables by a different name. (Their APIs are different, but they're used in the same way: to wait for complex events.) Win32 objects are either in a *signaled* state (meaning a thread will not have to wait when it calls `WaitForSingle-Object()`), or in a *nonsignaled* state (meaning a thread will have to wait). Thus a signaled mutex is an unlocked mutex, a signaled semaphore has a positive value, and a signaled event object will not delay you.

There are two versions of Win32 events objects. The *automatic reset* version wakes up one sleeper at a time. The thread calls `WaitForSingleObject()` and goes to sleep until another thread calls `PulseEvent()` or `SetEvent()`. The first wakes up one sleeper (if any) and leaves the object nonsignaled. The second wakes up one sleeper (if any) and leaves the object signaled (until a thread calls `ResetEvent()`).

The other type, *manual reset* events objects, are quite similar, save they wake up all sleepers.

Win32's wait function, `WaitForSingleObject()`, does not release the associated mutex for you. You must unlock the mutex, wait, then relock the mutex yourself. This is problematical. Because you are unlocking the mutex yourself, it is possible for a event pulse to arrive in between the unlocking and the going to sleep—the lost wake-up problem! Don't use `PulseEvent()` as you would `pthread_cond_signal()`.

When an object is signaled, any thread calling `WaitForSingleObject()` will *not* go to sleep but simply continue and loop back to retest the condition as long as the object remains signaled. Thus, you are responsible for resetting the event explicitly.

Thread 1	**Thread 2**

```
WaitForSingleObject(mutex)
while (!condition)
   {ResetEvent(event);
    ReleaseMutex(mutex);
    WaitForSingleObject(event)
    WaitForSingleObject(mutex)
   }
                              WaitForSingleObject(mutex)
                              condition = TRUE;
                              ReleaseMutex(mutex);
                              SetEvent(event);
```

Code Example 7–5: *Using Event Objects*

OS/2 event semaphores work in a fairly similar fashion, save that they must be reset to the "not posted" state explicitly.

OS/2 Critical Sections

OS/2 defines a rather extreme version of synchronization under the name *critical section*. Between calls to `DosEnterCritSec()` and `DosExitCritSec()`, all other threads are stopped. It is possible to build such calls from POSIX primitives, but it does not seem a terribly useful idea. Indeed, we have yet to come up with a single example of where these calls would work better than using mutexes, etc.

Win32 Critical Sections

In Win32, the term *critical section* is used to describe a simple mutex. The major distinction between Win32's mutexes and Win32's critical sections is that the former can be defined to be cross-process, while the latter cannot. All of the Win32 synchronization variables other than critical sections are kernel objects. Their handles must be closed before the kernel structures are released. They are also much slower than critical sections by about two orders of magnitude(!).

Multiple Wait Semaphores

In Win32, it is possible to wait for (a) any one of a set of synchronization variables, or (b) all of that set. In POSIX, you would write the program differently, and simply have a condition variable waiting on a complex condition.

Interlocked Instructions

In Win32, several special functions are defined: `Interlocked-Increment()`, `InterlockedDecrement()`, and `Interlocked-Exchange()`. As their names suggest, they perform their tasks automatically without the need of an explicit lock. This makes them quite fast, but limits their usefulness greatly. (Sure, you've incremented the value, but you don't know if someone else also incremented it a microsecond later.) These are implemented by the Digital UNIX compiler as intrinsics using LockedLoad/StoreConditional instructions (see *Load-Locked/StoreConditional and Compare and Swap* on page 291).

The things you can do with them include reference counting, semaphores, and not much else. These types of operations are not part of POSIX, and the requisite instructions are not on all CPU architectures.

Message Queues

A question fairly often asked is how can one build message queues for threads—queues where one thread can line up requests for another thread to process. If this is truly what you need in your program, the answer is quite simple: build a producer/consumer model with a queue as previously shown. This gives you both complete control over your program and a simple programming model. What more could you ask for?

Win32 implements a kernel-level message queue that you can use for the same purpose. As it is part of the Win32 library, it makes sense to use it for cross-process communication, especially when you don't have control over all the source code. Otherwise, in a single process, it simply imposes too heavy a burden, both in CPU time and code complexity.

The ability to interrupt a thread and change what it's doing is a much different requirement and a far more difficult one to achieve. If you are thinking along these lines, reconsider your objectives very carefully! Why do you want to interrupt this particular thread? Could you get your work done by either (a) polling from this thread, (b) waiting for this thread to complete its present task and then look at a queue, or (c) simply creating a new thread to execute the task at hand? There is probably a simpler means of doing what you want. Find it.

If you *really* want to interrupt a thread (other than killing it), then there is only one method of doing so—UNIX signals. We'll look at those later.

Win32 I/O Completion Ports

An I/O completion port is Win32's answer to the producer/consumer problem. You create a completion port with a file handle and then have a number of threads waiting on that completion port. When a packet arrives on that handle, one of the waiting threads is woken up and given the packet to work on. Upon completion, the thread sends any reply it needs to send and goes back to wait on the port again. Windows NT hackers love these things.

Cross-Process Synchronization Variables

Threads in different processes can synchronize with each other via synchronization variables placed in shared memory. This kind of synchronization works in all the libraries (it's an option in POSIX), even though threads in different processes are invisible to each other, as shown in Figure 7–6.

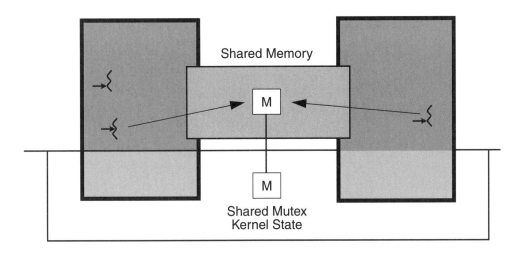

Figure 7–6 *Synchronization Variables in Shared Memory*

Both processes must know about the synchronization variable, and (exactly) one of them must initialize it to be cross-process. Then, both processes (or possibly more) can use it as a normal synchronization variable. The only difference between a single-process synchronization variable and a shared memory synchronization variable occurs when the requestor must go to sleep (e.g., a mutex is already locked). Then, the shared memory version will simply take longer (see Appendix C, *Timings*). There is no requirement that the processes themselves be multithreaded.

The implementation of blocking involves the unsuccessful thread making a system call, then going to sleep in the kernel. Thus, for locally scheduled threads, one LWP is effectively removed from the pool during this time. When another thread awakens the sleeper (e.g., via `pthread_mutex_unlock()`), the sleeping LWP is awakened. Once again, there is no *guarantee* that the newly wakened thread will succeed in its request on the synchronization variable, though the odds favor it.

Synchronization variables can also be placed in files and have lifetimes beyond that of the creating process. For example, a file can be created that contains database records. Each record can contain a mutex that controls access to the associated record. A process can map the file into its address space. A thread within this process can directly acquire the lock that is associated with the particular record to be modified. If any thread within any process that maps in the file attempts to acquire this lock, then that thread will block until the lock is released. Obviously, a process cannot be allowed to exit while it is still holding such a shared lock.

Initialization and Destruction

All synchronization variables have both initialization and destruction functions. The initialization functions take care of initializing the memory that the synchronization variables use, along with setting up kernel state should the synchronization variable be defined to be cross-process. It is legal for the initialization function to allocate additional memory for the synchronization variables or have other side effects, so initialization is required. The initialization functions are called once before the first use of the synchronization variable, and never again. You cannot use them to "reinitialize" a synchronization variable.[1]

The destructor functions mark the synchronization variables as being unusable, and free any memory that the initialization functions allocate. They do not do any kind of garbage collection for the synchronization variable itself. Destruction of a synchronization variable is not strictly required, unless you plan to free its memory. If you do build one from malloc'd memory, you probably will want to free it. If you do free it, you *must* call destroy first.

Destroying a synchronization variable and freeing its memory can be a bit tricky, as you must ensure that no thread ever accesses that variable again (e.g., there can be no sleepers). Either you must know that no other thread still has a pointer to it, or you must maintain some kind of list of valid dynamic synchronization variables. There are no particular differences between freeing memory used by synchronization variables and freeing memory used for other things. You just have to be careful in both cases. Code Example 7–6 (from *Manipulating Lists* on page 213) shows

---

[1]Once you call the destroy function, the variable reverts to its original status of being just undistinguished memory. You can initialize that memory to anything you want. It is *not* the same object as before and no previous references to it are valid.

the allocation and initialization of a mutex inside of a structure, and its eventual destruction and freeing.

```
void liquidate_person(person_t *p)
{person_t   *p1;
  ...
 pthread_mutex_lock(&(p1->lock));
 pthread_mutex_unlock(&(p1->lock));/* Must unlock before destroy */
 pthread_mutex_destroy(&(p1->lock));
 free(p1->name);
 free(p1);
}

void add_to_people(char *name)
{person_t *p;

 p = (person_t *) malloc(sizeof(person_t));
 p->name = name;
 pthread_mutex_init(&(p->lock), NULL);
  ...
}
```

Code Example 7–6: *Allocation, Initialization, Destruction, and Deallocation of a Mutex*

Notice that we lock `p1->lock` before destroying it. In this particular program, it is possible that some other thread is holding the lock and working on the structure when we decide to free that structure. So we must wait for it to finish. Once that thread releases the mutex, we know (because we wrote the code) that there is no possibility of any other thread ever accessing this structure and locking it again. This is a requirement. It must be *impossible* for any other thread to access the structure, if for no other reason than that section of memory might be reallocated for some other purpose.[2]

Synchronization Problems

A number of things can go wrong when you try to coordinate the interactions of your threads. Not using synchronization variables is the most

---

[2]One of the more "amusing" bugs we've seen occurred when a structure with a mutex in it was freed while a thread was still sleeping on it. That same area of memory was later reallocated as the same type of structure, *not initialized*, and the sleeping thread awoken. *Don't do that!*

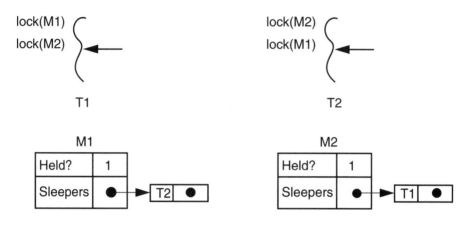

Figure 7–7 *A Typical Deadlock*

obvious and most common. But even when you've been careful to lock everything in sight, there are still other problems you may encounter. All of them have solutions, none of them have perfect solutions.

Deadlocks

A deadlock is a kind of Catch-22, in which one thread needs another thread to do something before it proceeds, and the other thread needs something from the first. So they both sit there, doing nothing, waiting for each other, forever. This is a bad thing.

A typical deadlock (Figure 7–7) occurs when thread T1 obtains lock M1, and thread T2 obtains lock M2. Then thread T1 tries to obtain lock M2, while thread T2 tries for lock M1. Although typically a two-thread problem, deadlocks can involve dozens of threads in a circle, all waiting for one another. They can involve a single thread that tries to obtain the same mutex twice, and they can involve a thread that holds a lock dying while another thread is waiting for it.

Deadlocks can always be avoided simply by using careful programming practices. If you declare a lock hierarchy and always acquire locks in the same order—A before B before C, etc.—then there is no chance of a deadlock. When you want to do out-of-order locking, you can use the trylock functions to see whether you can get all the locks you need, and if not, then release them all and try again later.

A typical instance of this out-of-order locking is the Solaris virtual memory system; which must lock access to pages. There is an official hierarchy that says page #1 must be locked before page #2, etc. Occasionally the VM system will lock page #2 and then discover that it also wants page #1. It will then execute a trylock on page #1. If that succeeds, then all is well and it proceeds. If it fails, then it releases the lock on page #2 and requests the locks in proper order.[3] This is a simple optimization that saves a bit of time in the normal case and is always correct.

```
pthread_mutex_lock(&m2);
...
        if (EBUSY == pthread_mutex_trylock(&m1))
            {pthread_mutex_unlock(&m2);
             pthread_mutex_lock(&m1);
             pthread_mutex_lock(&m2);
            }
do_real_work();                                         /* Got 'em both! */
}
```

Code Example 7–7: *Locking Mutexes Out of Order*

Race Conditions

Races are instances of indeterminacy in otherwise deterministic programs. The result a program will give in a race condition depends upon the luck of the draw—which thread happens to run first, which LWP happens to get kicked off its processor by the page daemon, etc. Race conditions are generally bad things, although there are times when they are acceptable. Certainly one would be upset if 1414.60/2.414 came out to be 586 on one run of a program, and 586.001 on the next.

Most commonly, race conditions come around in programs in which the programmer forgot to write proper locking protection around some shared data, or when locks were taken out of order. Still, it is certainly possible to write code that is perfectly correct, yet suffers from races. Consider Code Example 7–8, if v starts with the value one, then the result will either be one or zero, depending upon which thread runs first.

---

[3]Note that you must release lock m2. Just spinning, waiting for m1 to become available, will not work.

Thread 1	**Thread 2**
`pthread_mutex_lock(&m)`	`pthread_mutex_lock(&m)`
`v = v - 1;`	`v = v * 2;`
`pthread_mutex_unlock(&m)`	`pthread_mutex_unlock(&m)`

Code Example 7–8: *A Simplistic Race Condition*

It is worth noting that some instances of indeterminacy in a program are acceptable. If you write a program that searches for a solution to a chess problem by creating lots of threads to consider lots of different possible moves, then you may get different answers depending upon which thread completes first. As long as you get one good answer ("Checkmate in three!"), you don't really care if you move your pawn first or your rook.

Recovering from Deadlocks

A common question is "What if a thread that is holding a lock dies? How can I recover from this?" The first answer is "You can't." If a thread was holding a lock, then it could legitimately have changed portions of the data that the lock protected in ways impossible to repair. If it was in the midst of changing the balance of your bank account, there is no inherent way for you to know whether it had credited the deposit it was working on or not. This, of course, is a very bad thing.

Pthreads makes no provision for this situation. Only the owner of a mutex can release it, and should that owner die, the mutex will never be released. Period. This is not really a problem for well-written programs. The only way for a thread to die is for the programmer to write the code that kills it. Thus, the proper answer here is "Fix your code!"

You can, however, build arbitrarily complex "recoverable" locks from the primitives in all of the libraries. Using them properly is the trick. Win32 mutexes do allow recovery, should the owner thread die. This is nice functionality if you need it, but it makes mutexes more expensive to use when you don't.

In a single-process, multithreaded program, recovering from deadlocks is not too much of an issue. You have complete control over your threads, and if your process dies, all the threads die with it. In a shared memory, multiple-process program, it is more problematic, as it is possible for one process to die, while leaving others running.

It is somewhat reasonable to consider recovering from a deadlock in the case of a process dying unexpectedly. In other deadlock situations, where threads are waiting for each other, you really shouldn't be looking at recovery techniques. You should be looking at your coding techniques.

System V shared semaphores do make provision for recovery, and they may prove to be the solution to your problem. They provide room for a system-maintained "undo" structure, which will be invoked should the owner process die, and they can be reset by any process with permission. They are expensive to use, though, and add complexity to your code.

Both Win32 and OS/2 mutexes have built-in "death detection" also, so that your program can find out that the mutex it was waiting for was held by a newly dead thread.

Still, just having undo structures that can reset semaphores does not solve the real problem. The data protected may be inconsistent, and this is what you have to deal with. It is possible to build arbitrarily complex undo structures for your code, but it is a significant task that should not be lightly undertaken.

Database systems do this routinely via "two-phase commit" strategies, as they have severe restrictions on crash recovery. Essentially, what they do is (a) build a time-stamped structure containing what the database will look like at the completion of the change; (b) save that structure to disk and begin the change; (c) complete the change; (d) update the time stamp on the database; and (e) delete the structure. A crash at any point in this sequence of events can be recovered from reliably.

Be very, very careful when dealing with this problem!

Summary

Deadlocks can always be avoided, race conditions are more problematical. More complex synchronization is possible, but probably not useful. Trying to recover from deadlocks is very, very tricky.

8

TSD

In which an explanation of thread-specific data is provided, its use and some of the implementation details. We note a few places where use of TSD could be made more efficient and a few other optimizations that can be made.

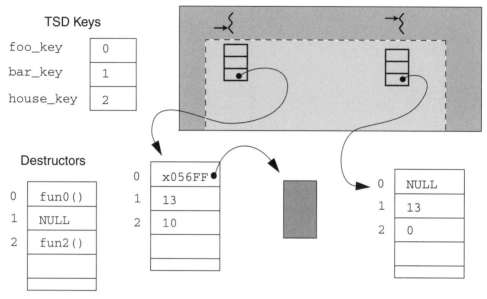

Figure 8–1   *Thread-Specific Data*

Thread-Specific Data

Sometimes it is useful to have data that is globally accessible to any function, yet still unique to the thread. Two threads that are printing out data, one in French and the other in Danish, would find it most convenient to have a private global variable, which they could set to the desired language. The example of errno also comes to mind. It sure would be a bummer if one thread made a system call, got an error, and just before it got the chance to look at errno, another thread also got an error on a system call and changed the value of errno (a race condition!).

TSD provides this kind of global data by means of a set of function calls. Essentially, this is done by creating an array of "key" offsets to "value" cells, attached to each thread structure (Figure 8–1).

To use POSIX TSD, you first create a new key, which is then added to the TSD arrays for all threads. Keys are just variables of type pthread_key_t (which are opaque data types, most commonly integers), and key creation ("initialization" is a more descriptive term) consists of setting the value of the key to the next location. Once the key has been created, you can access or change the value associated with the key via calls to pthread_getspecific() and pthread_setspecific().

The value cell is a (void *), which is a single word (typically either 32 or 64 bits). When the data you want to be thread specific is a structure, array, object, or anything larger than one (void *), you'll need to malloc the storage for that structure and place a pointer to it in the TSD array. To ease your programming burden when exiting the thread, you may declare a destructor function for each item. At key creation time, you can include a function that will be run on that item when the thread exits. If you malloc a structure and place a pointer to it in TSD, then the destructor will just be free().

TSD is typically used to declare all the keys globally, initialize (er, "create") them in main(), then create threads and start the program for real. If you are creating some TSD in a library, you must arrange for that library to do the initialization before use.[1]

In Code Example 8–1, bar() in the first thread will see root(2),[2] and in the second thread will see Π.

```
pthread_key_t house_key;

foo((void *) arg)
{
    pthread_setspecific(house_key, arg);
    bar();
}

bar()
{float n;
    n = (float) pthread_getspecific(house_key);
}

main()
{...
    pthread_keycreate(&house_key, destroyer);

    pthread_create(&tid, NULL, foo, (void *) 1.414);
    pthread_create(&tid, NULL, foo, (void *) 3.141592653589);
...}
```

Code Example 8–1: *Usage of POSIX TSD*

---

[1]SVR4 libraries have ".ini" sections in which you can define functions to be called before main() starts. In Win32, you can do this in the DLL.

[2]One of my best friends, a math wiz, purchased a small farm in rural Minnesota. His address was 1414, rural route 2.

POSIX allows you to delete (and presumably recycle) a TSD key with `pthread_key_delete()`. It is your responsibility to clean up any TSD data that needs it. The destructors will not be run. Deleting TSD keys sounds like a bad idea in general. You are also allowed to create a new key at any time. This also sounds like a bad idea.

Calling `pthread_getspecific()` in a thread when the value has not yet been set is legal and will return a value of NULL. You may use NULL as a legal value yourself; just be aware of this. In addition, TSD destructors will not be run on a NULL value.

In Win32 and OS/2 there are different versions of TSD. Win32 calls it *dynamic thread local storage* and the usage is virtually identical to TSD in POSIX. Other than the lack of destructors, you may use it in the same fashion as TSD.

```
key = TlsAlloc();
TlsSetValue(key, data);
data = TlsGetValue(key);
```

Code Example 8–2: *Dynamic TLS in Win32*

In OS/2, the design is simpler and the usage more awkward. You are provided with one (`void *`) for each thread. You then store whatever value you want into that (`void *`). Typically this will be a pointer to a structure which you have allocated yourself to hold the actual values of interest.

```
foo()
{...
   my_data_pointer = (my_data_struct **) _threadstore();
   *my_data_pointer = malloc(sizeof(my_data_struct));
   (*my_data_pointer)->key = data;
...}

bar()
{...
   my_data_pointer = (my_data_struct **) _threadstore();
   data = (*my_data_pointer)->key;
...}
```

Code Example 8–3: *TSD in OS/2*

The actual implementation of TSD is different from vendor to vendor, but in general they're all the same. When accessing a TSD item, we

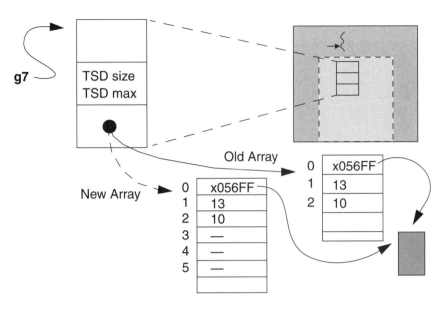

Figure 8–2   *Expanding a TSD Array*

first need to know which thread we're running on. Think about this for a moment. How does a thread find out who it is? How does it find its own thread structure? On SPARC machines, there is one register (g7) reserved for special use. Compiler writers are instructed not to use it. Here the threads library places a pointer to the thread structure of the running thread. As shown in Figure 8–2, the thread first dereferences g7 to find the structure, then it dereferences an element of the structure to find the TSD array. Finally it looks up the appropriate element in the array.

In some implementations the TSD array may be dynamically expanded. If it starts with 32 elements and you create a 33rd key, then when you try to set that element, the library will copy the current array into a larger array, adding a 33rd value to it. According to the spec, a library need support only 128 TSD elements, so a portable program should not assume more. (See *Constants Comments* on page 184.)

So, how does errno work? It's a hack. Essentially, it is a thread-specific data item. In multithreaded programs, all system calls change the TSD value instead of the global value. Then, when you reference errno in your program, there is a #define in the errno.h header file that conditionally redefines errno to be a call to a thread-specific value.[3]

Clever, eh? (See :   *The Actual Definition of errno in errno.h (Solaris)* on page 200.)

TSD is simple but somewhat expensive when compared to accessing a global variable. Each call to a TSD function requires a function call, then a series of offsets: first to the array pointer in the thread structure, then from the array to the key value. TSD requires about 40 instructions, while a simple global reference requires just one load instruction. It is a useful feature, but you clearly want to restrict its use to when you really need it.

The best answer to the problems of TSD is to write good, clean code that eschews the excessive use of globals. Unfortunately, far too many programs have preexisting conditions, and they seem to demand TSD. It is worthwhile to consider a couple of tricks to avoid excessive use of TSD. *Don't even consider any of this stuff until you are sure you have a problem!*

One thing you can do is to cache TSD data in a local block of its own, where you know it's safe.

Not this:

```
for (i ...)
    {v = pthread_getspecific(v_key);
     s+=f(v);
    }
```

Code Example 8–4:   *Normal Use of TSD*

but rather:

```
v = pthread_getspecific(v_key);
for (i ...) s+=f(v);
```

Code Example 8–5:   *Cached Use of TSD*

The other thing you can do is to create your own personal version of lexical scoping. Create a structure that contains all the data you wish to be thread specific and pass that structure to every function that is going to access it.

---

[3]Actually, POSIX defines the implementation slightly differently. If you look at errno.h, you'll see that the definition of errno is ___errno(). The effect is the same as if TSD had actually been used.

```
struct MY_TSD
{   int a
    int b;
}

start_routine()
{struct MY_TSD *mt;

    mt = malloc(sizeof(MY_TSD));
    mt->a = 42; mt->b = 999;
    foo(x, y, z, mt);
    bar(z, mt);
    ...
}

void foo(x, y, z, struct MY_TSD *mt)
{int answer = mt->a;
...}
```

Code Example 8–6: *Passing Structures Instead of Using TSD*

No, this isn't pretty. However it is clean, safe, and relatively efficient.

Thread Local Storage

TLS is an alternate method of providing the functionality of TSD. It allows you to declare a set of global variables to be "thread local." These variables can then be treated exactly like normal global variables (except that you don't have to lock them). Unfortunately, TLS has a number of severe limitations. It requires either a change to the compiler or some tricky memory map manipulations. It cannot dynamically allocate new keys—the TLS segment is fixed at link time—and it is not portable.

The Pthreads committee couldn't require compiler changes, so chose to specify TSD instead. Win32 implements TLS in addition to TSD. It's called *static TLS*, and it does indeed require compiler support.

Global Variables, Constants, and Cheating

Now a little detail to consider: a TSD key is a shared global variable. We say you should always lock shared data when using it. Here's the exception. If you can *guarantee* that a global will never be changed (and changing the value of a key would be a *bad* idea), then you can safely get away without putting a lock around its use. This guarantee effectively means that the key is really being treated like a constant, not a variable.

The same is true for any globally declared variable that is used as a constant. If you are doing this kind of "cheating," you must be certain that you set the variable from only one thread (presumably the initial thread). You must do so before creating any other threads. It absolutely must be used as a constant and *never* changed. Any deviation from this will cause you no end of problems. *A Cancellation Example* on page 142 addresses this issue.

The other time when you may wish to deal with shared data outside a critical section is when you don't need the value to be correct. If you are content to test a variable, then do something on the basis of its *probably* being correct, then you can do so. The actual definition of spin locks does this (see : *Spin Locks Done Better* on page 290). This kind of "cheating" is a very rare thing to do, and it's easy to do it wrong.

Summary

We described the basic design of thread-specific data storage, its use, and some of the implementation details. We noted a few places where use of TSD could be made more efficient.

9

Cancellation

In which we describe the acrimonious nature of some programs and how unwanted threads may be disposed of. The highly complex issues surrounding bounded time termination and program correctness are also covered. A simple conclusion is drawn.

What Cancellation Is

Sometimes you have reason to get rid of a thread before it has completed its work. Perhaps the user changed her mind about what she was doing. Perhaps the program had many threads doing a heuristic search, and one of them found the answer. In such cases you want to be able to have one thread kill the other threads. This is known as *cancellation* (POSIX), *termination* (Win32), and *killing* (OS/2).

No matter how you choose to deal with the issues of cancellation, be it in OS/2, Win32, or POSIX threads, the primary issues remain the same. You must ensure that any thread that you are going to cancel is able to release any locks it might hold, free any memory it may have allocated for its own use, and leaves the world in a consistent state.

The fundamental operation is quite simple: you call the cancellation function with the target TID, and the target thread dies sometime "soon." The ramifications of doing this are, however, quite complex, making cancellation one of the most difficult operations to execute correctly.

In Win32 and OS/2, there is a single, simple method of cancellation—you call it, the target thread dies. Unfortunately, should that thread own some resource, hold some lock, or have malloc'd some memory, your program will be in trouble. This type of cancellation is known as unrestricted *asynchronous cancellation* and it is the responsibility of the killer to know that the victim can be safely eliminated at the time of cancellation—a difficult task at best, impossible at worst.

POSIX has a more elaborate version of cancellation. It defines a *cancellation state* for each thread that will enable or disable cancellation for that thread. Thus you can disable cancellation during critical sections and reenable it afterwards. Neither Win32 nor OS/2 define this state, although it would not be too difficult for you to write it yourself. Cancellation state makes it feasible to use asynchronous cancellation safely, although there are still significant problems to be dealt with. For example, if your thread has malloc'd some storage and is then cancelled, how do you free that storage?

In Win32 there is an additional problem facing cancellation: system-wide active handles and runtime library private data, which are not freed upon cancellation, along with the thread stack and attached DLLs. As you have no control over this, it is nearly impossible to use Win32's cancellation at all.[1]

---

[1]From the Microsoft documentation: "TerminateThread is a dangerous function that should only be used in the most extreme cases." In other words, expect your program to hang after you call it!

The other type of cancellation, defined only in POSIX, is known as *deferred cancellation*. In this type of cancellation, a thread only exits when it polls the library to find out if it should exit, or when it is blocked in a library call which is a *cancellation point*. This polling is done by calling the function `pthread_testcancel()`, which in turn just checks to see if a bit has been set. If a request is pending, then `pthread_testcancel()` will not return at all, and the thread will simply die. Otherwise, it will return, and the thread will continue. You may call `pthread_testcancel()` in your own code. POSIX also defines a set of standard library functions that must call it (see *Defined Cancellation Points* on page 141).

In deferred cancellation, a thread may run for an arbitrary amount of time after a cancellation has been issued, thus allowing critical sections to execute without having to disable/enable cancellation. The disadvantage of this is that you must do extra work if you wish to ensure bounded cancellation times. A thread in deferred state might go off and run in a loop for hours before hitting a cancellation point. Of course, this might be OK.

There is no pat answer to these issues and you, as the responsible programmer, must resolve them on a program by program basis. You may select asynchronous for one program, deferred for a second, and a mixture of both for a third. All Pthreads start life with deferred cancellation enabled.

Although neither Win32 nor OS/2 define deferred cancellation, it would not be terribly difficult for you to define the polling part yourself. To make it possible to cancel threads blocked in system calls, you would really have to wrap every such call with a wrapper function—a bit much to ask for.

Cancellation Cleanup Handlers

When a thread is cancelled, Pthreads provides a way to clean up the thread's state through a set of cleanup handlers that are called upon the exiting of a thread. These are functions of one argument, which you define and then push onto a thread's cleanup stack.[2] Should the thread exit (either via cancellation or a call to `pthread_exit()`), the functions on the stack will be run on the argument you supplied. Should

---

[2]The cleanup stack is probably not implemented as a separate stack (as in our picture). It is probably just entries on the call stack.

the thread not be cancelled, then you may pop the functions off when they are no longer required.

If `pthread_cleanup_pop()` is invoked with a non-zero argument, then the top handler function will be popped off the stack and executed. If the argument is zero, then the top handler will be popped off the stack, but not executed.

The calls `pthread_cleanup_pop()` and `pthread_clean-up_push()` (Figure 9–1) are typically implemented as macros emphasizing that they must be paired (one push, one pop) at the same lexical level. Jumping out of the push/pop block may compile, but it would leave the cleanup handlers on the stack. Jumping into a block will probably crash the program as soon as the pop is executed. *Don't do this.*

Correct:

```
pthread_cleanup_push(free, pointer);
...
pthread_cleanup_pop(1);
```

Incorrect (won't compile):

```
  pthread_cleanup_push(free, pointer);
  ...
 }
pthread_cleanup_pop(1);                 /* Outside the code block */
```

Code Example 9–1:   *How Cleanup Handlers Are Used*

The general idea for cancellation is that programmers will write their programs such that sections of code that allocate resources, obtain locks, etc., are immediately preceded (or followed) by cleanup handler pushes. The cleanup handlers will be responsible for freeing resources, reestablishing data invariants, and freeing locks.

These sections of code must be performed atomically with respect to cancellation. Then the body of the code that uses that resource is run with cancellation allowed. Upon completion, the resource is freed and the handler popped off the stack atomically. If there are cancellation points (e.g. `sem_wait()`) in the middle of the allocation or deallocation sections, then cancellation must be disabled during that period.

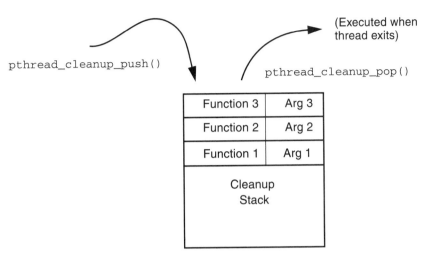

Figure 9-1 *Cancellation Cleanup Handler Functions*

Defined Cancellation Points

POSIX *requires* that the following set of library functions must be cancellation points and that they must be interruptible should they be blocked at cancellation time. They are *required* to test for cancellation even if they don't block.

```
aio_suspend(3R), close(2), creat(2), fcntl(2),   fsync(3C),
mq_receive(3R), mq_send(3R), msync(3C), nanosleep(3R),
open(2), pause(2), pthread_cond_timedwait(3T),
pthread_cond_wait(3T), pthread_join(3T), pthread_testcancel,
read(2), sem_wait(3R), sigwaitinfo(3R), sigsuspend(2),
sigtimedwait(3R), sigwait(2), sleep(3C), system(3S),
tcdrain(3), wait(2), waitpid(2), write(2).
```

POSIX allows these functions to be cancellation points (they may well call one of the functions above), but leaves it to the vendor's discretion:

```
closedir(3C), ctermid(3S), fclose(3S), fcntl(2), fflush(3S),
fgetc(3S), fgets(3S), fopen(3S),   fprintf(3S), fputc(3S),
fputs(3S), fread(3S), freopen(3S), fscanf(3S), fseek(3S),
```

```
ftell(3S), fwrite(3S), getc(3S), getc_unlocked(3S),
getchar(3S), getchar_unlocked(3S), getcwd(3C), getgrgid(3C),
getgrgid_r(3C), getgrnam(3C), getgrnam_r(3C), getlogin(3C),
getlogin_r(3C), getpwnam(3C), getpwnam_r(3C), getpwuid(3C),
getpwuid_r(3C), gets(3S), lseek(2), rename(2), opendir(3C),
perror(3C),    printf(3S), putc(3S), putc_unlocked(3S),
putchar(3S),   putchar_unlocked(3S), puts(3S), readaddr(3C),
remove(3C), rewind(3S), rewinddir(3C), scanf(3S),
tmpfile(3S), ttyname(3C), ttyname_r(3C), ungetc(3S),
unlink(2).
```

Unexpected Cancellation Points

Because POSIX allows vendors to implement different cancellation points, it is possible for a thread to exit in different code on different platforms. In particular, you might have tested your program on Solaris, knowing that gets() was not a cancellation point. Perhaps it is one on AIX. If you had a locked mutex while calling gets(), then your program would work fine on Solaris, but deadlock on AIX. This would be a bad thing.

For code that will run on a single platform, it is easy enough to look up all the library calls that are cancellation points. For multi-platform code, you will either need to look up all the calls that are cancellation points on all of the platforms, or assume that all of the above functions are, but also verify your code where only the first group is.

In writing your own libraries, it would be nice to have all of your functions deferred-cancellation safe. You can assure this by never calling any of the functions above, or by properly handling cancellation when you do. You might simply turn off cancellation while your function runs. You might need to install cancellation handlers. You might not need to do anything. You do have to figure it out.

A Cancellation Example

The program below uses cancellation to get rid of unneeded search threads. This program has the objective of finding a certain number by using a heuristic. The desired number is the process ID, and the heuristic is to generate random numbers, checking to see if they happen to be the PID. Admittedly this is not a very clever heuristic, but the concept is solid. You can reasonably replace the problem and heuristic with more meaningful ones, such as a chess position and an Alpha-Beta search. The cancellation issues won't change.

The main thread gets the PID and creates 25 threads to search for it. Each of the searcher threads enables deferred cancellation. Then each searcher proceeds to generate a random number, checking to see if that happens to be the PID. When one thread finds the number, it decrements a semaphore that is acting as a lock (1), and then sends a cancellation request to all the other threads (2). Instead of calling `sem_trywait()` at (1), we could have simply called `sem_wait()` and slept there until cancelled. We just wanted to illustrate this version here.

Each of the searcher threads calls `pthread_testcancel()` at several points during the loop, so there is no concern about them never seeing the cancellation. On the off chance that a second thread also finds the number before it gets cancelled, it also tries to decrement the semaphore. Because the semaphore is zero, this thread knows that it's about to be cancelled, and it simply exits (3). When the successful searcher thread tries to cancel the exited thread, `pthread_cancel()` simply returns ESRCH (2).

Each searcher needs to use some memory. When it mallocs that memory, it also places a cleanup handler on the stack (4) to be run in case a cancellation request comes in before that memory is freed (5). Note that asynchronous cancellation would not work here (6).

The main thread looks for the result in the global variable `answer`. It prints out its success, noting the number of attempts required, then waits for all of the searchers to exit. When they have all exited, it repeats the process. Simple? Well...

```
/*
    This program does a heuristic search for an integer, then cancels
    all threads that didn't find it.  The actual heuristic is silly
    (it calls rand_r()), but the technique is valid.

    All of the calls to delay() are there to slow things down and
    make different contention situations more likely.

    A couple of simple cleanup handlers are included.  In a real
    program, these would be even more complex.
```

Code Example 9–2:   *Cancellation in the Heuristic Search Program*
cancellation.c

```
        NB: sem_trywait() -> EBUSY in Solaris 2.5 is a bug.
        It *should* be EAGAIN (fixed in 2.6).
*/

/*
cc -o cancellation cancellation.c -L. -R. -g -lpthread -lthread
    -lthread_extensions -lposix4
*/

#define _POSIX_C_SOURCE 199506L
#include <stdio.h>
#include <stdlib.h>
#include <unistd.h>
#include <pthread.h>
#include <semaphore.h>
#include <errno.h>
#include "thread_extensions.h"

#ifdef __sun                     /* This is a bug in Solaris 2.5 */
#define MY_EAGAIN EBUSY
#else
#define MY_EAGAIN EAGAIN    /* Correct errno value from trywait() */
#endif

#define NUM_THREADS 25      /* the number of searching threads */

pthread_attr_t    attr;
pthread_t         threads[NUM_THREADS];
pthread_mutex_t   threads_lock = PTHREAD_MUTEX_INITIALIZER;
pthread_mutex_t   wait_lock    = PTHREAD_MUTEX_INITIALIZER;
pthread_mutex_t   rand_lock    = PTHREAD_MUTEX_INITIALIZER;
sem_t             death_lock;/* I'm using it like a lock */
pthread_mutex_t   count_lock   = PTHREAD_MUTEX_INITIALIZER;
pthread_cond_t    wait_cv      = PTHREAD_COND_INITIALIZER;

int answer;                     /* Protected by death_lock */


void count_tries(int i)     /* Note the encapsulation */
{static int count=0, old_count=0, max_count = 0;
 static pthread_mutex_t count_lock = PTHREAD_MUTEX_INITIALIZER;

 pthread_mutex_lock(&count_lock);
 count += i;
```

Code Example 9–2:   *(cont.) Cancellation in the Heuristic Search Program*
                          cancellation.c

```
  if (i == -1) printf("Total attempt count: %d\n", max_count);
  if (count > max_count)
    max_count = count;
  pthread_mutex_unlock(&count_lock);
}


void cleanup_count(void *arg)
{int *ip = (int *) arg;
 int i = *ip;
 pthread_t tid = pthread_self();
 char *name = thread_name(tid);

 count_tries(i);
 printf("%s exited (maybe cancelled) on its %d try.\n", name, i);
 /* Note that you can't tell if the thread exited, or was cancelled*/
}


void cleanup_lock(void *arg)
{pthread_t tid = pthread_self();
 char *name = thread_name(tid);

   printf("Freeing & releasing: %s\n", name);
   free(arg);
   pthread_mutex_unlock(&rand_lock);

}


void *search(void *arg)
{char *p;
 unsigned int seed;
 int i=0, j, err, guess, target = (int) arg;
 pthread_t tid = pthread_self();
 char *name = thread_name(tid);
 seed = (unsigned int) tid;

 pthread_setcanceltype(PTHREAD_CANCEL_DEFERRED, NULL);
 pthread_setcancelstate(PTHREAD_CANCEL_ENABLE, NULL);
 pthread_cleanup_push(cleanup_count, (void *) &i); /* Q: Why &i ? */

 while (1)
   {i++;
```

Code Example 9–2: *(cont.) Cancellation in the Heuristic Search Program*
cancellation.c

```
        /* Extra stuff to make it more realistic and complex. */
        pthread_mutex_lock(&rand_lock);
        p = (char *) malloc(10);              /* Must free this up! */
        /* Q:  What if you allow cancellation here? */
        pthread_cleanup_push(cleanup_lock, (void *) p);      /* 4 */
        guess = rand_r(&seed);
        delay(0, 10);
        pthread_testcancel();                                /* 5 */
        pthread_cleanup_pop(0);
        /* Q:  What if you allow cancellation here? */       /* 6 */
        free(p);
        pthread_mutex_unlock(&rand_lock);

        delay(0, 10);

        if (target == guess)
         {printf("%s found the number on try %d!\n", name, i); /* 7 */
          /* I could also simply do sem_wait() & let cancellation work */
            while (((err = sem_trywait(&death_lock)) == -1) /* 1 */
                  && (errno == EINTR)) ;
            if ((err == -1) && (errno == MY_EBUSY))

         {printf("%s Exiting...\n", name);
           pthread_exit(NULL);                               /* 3 */
         }
            count_tries(i);
            answer = guess;
            delay(5000, 0);/* Encourage a few more threads to find it. */
            pthread_mutex_lock(&threads_lock);
            for (j=0;j<NUM_THREADS;j++)
               if (!pthread_equal(threads[j], tid))
                   if (pthread_cancel(threads[j]) == ESRCH)   /* 2 */
                       printf("Missed thread %s\n",
                                      thread_name(threads[j]));
            pthread_mutex_unlock(&threads_lock);
            break;/* Cannot release death_lock yet! */
         }
        pthread_testcancel();/* Insert a known cancellation point */
  }
 pthread_cleanup_pop(1);
 pthread_exit(NULL);
}
```

Code Example 9–2:   *(cont.) Cancellation in the Heuristic Search Program*
                          cancellation.c

```
start_searches()
{int i, pid, n_cancelled=0, status;
 pthread_t tid;

 pid = getpid();

 while (pid > RAND_MAX)
     pid /= 2;

 printf("\n\nSearching for the number = %d...\n", pid);

 pthread_mutex_lock(&threads_lock);
                              /* Q: Why do we need threads_lock ? */
 for (i=0;i<NUM_THREADS;i++)
   PTHREAD_CREATE(&threads[i], &attr, search, (void *)pid);
 pthread_mutex_unlock(&threads_lock);

 for (i=0;i<NUM_THREADS;i++)
   {pthread_mutex_lock(&threads_lock);
    tid = threads[i];                        /* Actually a constant now
    pthread_mutex_unlock(&threads_lock);/* Q: Why like this? */
    pthread_join(tid, (void **) &status);              /* 9 */
    if ((void *)status == (void *)PTHREAD_CANCELED) n_cancelled++;
    /* Casts required due to bugs in Solaris vs. Irix */
  }
 sem_post(&death_lock);             /* Cannot release any earlier! */
 count_tries(-1);
 printf("%d of the threads were cancelled.\n", n_cancelled);
 printf("The answer was: %d\n", answer);
}

main()
{int i;

 PTHREAD_ATTR_INIT(&attr);
 pthread_attr_setscope(&attr, PTHREAD_SCOPE_SYSTEM);
 pthread_attr_setdetachstate(&attr, PTHREAD_CREATE_JOINABLE);
 SEM_INIT(&death_lock, NULL, 1);

 for (i=0; i<2; i++)
   start_searches();

 pthread_exit(NULL);
}
```

Code Example 9–2: (cont.) *Cancellation in the Heuristic Search Program*
cancellation.c

Using Cancellation

You've seen the definition of cancellation. Now how can you use it effectively? The answer is "not easily!"

First, let us consider your objectives in using cancellation. You created some threads to accomplish a task and now you don't need them to work on it any longer. Perhaps the task has already been accomplished, or perhaps the user has changed her mind. Normally, we use cancellation to stop threads because we don't want them to waste time on something unnecessary. This is the best case. Sometimes we want to use cancellation to prevent threads from doing something that we no longer desire. This is harder.

In cancelling a thread, what do you want? Do you want to

1. Kill it instantly?
2. Kill it in bounded CPU time?
3. Prevent it from making any more global changes?
4. Prevent it from wasting CPU time?

Presumably you want #4, generally implying #2. After all, if you don't care whether the CPU time is bounded, why bother cancelling the thread at all?

If you think you need #1, you'd best do some rethinking. First, it isn't possible; second, it isn't even well-defined.[3] So, instead of #1, what is it that you really want?

If it was #3 you were thinking of, you're in much the same boat. It really isn't possible and not very meaningful. Now if you're satisfied with "not very many more global changes," then we can put that in with #4 and proceed.

Ensuring Bounded CPU Time

The exact time of cancellation is not guaranteed by POSIX. The target thread will become aware of a pending cancellation some time "soon" after `pthread_cancel()` has been called. If you are using asynchronous cancellation, then the thread will indeed spend very little

---

[3]If nothing else, special relativity denies the concept of objective synchronisity. Practically speaking, it will take at least 1μs to send an interrupt anyway.

extra time processing. No assurances here, but you can reasonably expect that it will be gone within a few milliseconds of CPU time (who knows how long it might sleep for!). With deferred cancellation, the timing situation is more complex. The main point is that you cannot rely upon the target thread exiting at any specific time. If you need to know when it has exited (you usually do!), then you must use some sort of synchronization.

As an example of long wall-clock delay in cancellation, consider the case of a low-priority target thread and a high-priority killer on one LWP. The cancellation will be sent, but as the high-priority thread continues to run, the target thread will not get a chance to exit any time soon. If the killer is running in realtime mode, the target might never exit! (Of course, in that case, you have lots of other problems to deal with.)

In asynchronous cancellation, you can expect the target thread to exit the next time it is scheduled onto a CPU. As long as your concerns are #2 and #4, you're fine. All you have to worry about is the cancellation safety issues below.

Deferred cancellation is a polling scheme when a thread is running, and more like async cancellation when the thread is blocked. For running threads, the polling is essentially the code below. Thread T2 cancels T1 by calling `pthread_cancel()`, which in turn sets a variable in the thread structure. When T1 enters a cancellation point such as `sem_wait()`, that function then checks to see if the thread has been cancelled, and exits if so.

```
       T2                    T1              Cancellation Point

                                             sem_wait(...)
die[T1] = TRUE;       sem_wait(...)          {...
...                   ...                        if (die[self])
                                                     pthread_exit();
                                             }
```

Code Example 9–3: *Deferred Cancellation as Polling*

In order to ensure bounded cancellation time with deferred cancellation, it is up to you, the programmer, to insert calls to cancellation points within every unbounded code path. In other words, for every loop that might run longer than your declared time limit, you must make sure that there is a cancellation point in that loop. The obvious method is simply to include a call to `pthread_testcancel()` in the loop.

In a tight loop, the overhead of `pthread_testcancel()` may prove excessive, even though it is very fast (~250ns on an SS4). Your options include:

1. Testing only once every N iterations:

```
for (i=0; i < N; i++)
   {a[i] = b[i];
    if (i%1000 == 0) pthread_testcancel();
   }
```

Code Example 9–4:   *Testing Once Every 1000 Iterations*

This is the best solution for most programs.

2. Changing your mind, and deciding that your time limit is greater than the maximum execution time of the loop (should it be a bounded loop).
This is a great solution if you can actually do it.

3. Using asynchronous cancellation for just that one portion. This is possible, if awkward. Almost certainly you will need to either disable cancellation during other portions of the program or to switch back and forth between deferred and asynchronous mode:

```
pthread_setcanceltype(PTHREAD_CANCEL_ASYNCHRONOUS, NULL);
   for (i=0; i<N; i++)
   ...                        /* Must be Async-Cancellation Safe! */
pthread_setcanceltype(PTHREAD_CANCEL_DEFERRED, NULL);
```

Code Example 9–5:   *Turning Async Cancellation On and Off*

So how long a latency can you afford for cancellation? That's a decision for you to make. Most likely the answer is going to be something like "I want the target thread gone within 10ms of CPU time after the call to cancel, with a probability of 99.999%."[4] With any sort of normal program, you'll have no problems. Analyze your program carefully, then test it.

What if you want bounded wall-clock time? Things get a bit stickier. We are now talking about realtime processing and a whole different set

---

[4]What if you want 100% probability? Forget it. Ain't no such beast. When the probability of program failure drops below the probability of the computer being hit by a meteorite (about 1E-11 per year) you can relax.

of issues. The basic answer is "Don't do that!" If you are going to do it, you'll need to know more than we do about realtime.

Cancelling Sleeping Threads

A thread which is waiting for a mutex to be unlocked is not at a cancellation point, and it will continue to sleep until that mutex is unlocked. Once it acquires the mutex, it then must proceed until it hits a cancellation point. This can be a serious sticking point when you are concerned about elapsed wall clock time. The best answer to this problems is *"Don't do that."*

Consider the code in Code Example 9–2. At (7), the thread has already found the number and now wishes to cancel all the other threads. Unfortunately, two threads can find the number at the same time and can both reach (1) at the same time. We only want a single thread to do the cancellation (imagine that there were multiple threads, all killing each other at the same time!), so we need to block out all the others as soon as one gets in. There are different methods of doing so. We could have used a lock as in the code, testing with trylock and exiting if it was owned. We could also block on a semaphore as below.

```
if {target == guess)
    SEM_WAIT(&s);        /* Allow only one thread to proceed */
```

Code Example 9–6: *Avoiding Blocking on Mutexes During Cancellation*

In this example we are not calling `pthread_exit()` ourselves (unlike the searcher code), but because `sem_wait()` is a cancellation point, the thread will be woken up when we cancel it. We could also have done something similar with a more complex condition using a condition variable (the condition wait functions are also cancellation points). What we can't do, is to sleep on a mutex. The mutex functions are not cancellation points.

What would happen if we just call `pthread_mutex_lock()` instead of trylock and exit in `search()`? Take the code, make the change. It deadlocks every now and then, right? *Don't do that.*

Cancellation in `pthread_join()`

If T1 is waiting for a T2 to exit, and T3 cancels T1, there will be a problem with the fact that no one is left waiting for T2. When T2 exits, it will then become a zombie and never have its structure freed. The easiest solution is simply never to cancel a thread that might call `pthread_join()`. Lacking that, you could have another thread also do a join on T2. (If two threads try to join the same thread, one of them will get a return value of ESRCH.) You could also write a cleanup handler that called `pthread_detach()` on T2.

By far the best solution is the first.

Cancellation in Condition Variables

While `pthread_cond_timedwait()` and `pthread_cond_wait()` are cancellation points, there is an additional issue that must be addressed. Upon a normal return, they always lock the mutex. Upon cancellation, they also lock said mutex! Any cancellation handlers will be run with the mutex held. You'd better make sure the mutex gets unlocked if you ever expect to use it again. Only the owner thread is allowed to unlock a mutex, so, by definition, the unlocking has to occur in a cleanup handler!

The code below shows how our cancellation example could have used condition variables with cleanup handlers instead of simply exiting as it does now. Note the required cleanup handler unlocking the mutex!

```
void cleanup_lock2(void *arg)
{
  printf("Freeing M: T@%s\n", thread_name(pthread_self()));
  pthread_mutex_unlock((pthread_mutex_t *) arg);
}


    if (target == guess)
      {printf("T@%d found the number on try %d!\n", tid, i);
       pthread_mutex_lock(&answer_lock)
       pthread_cleanup_push(cleanup_lock2, (void *) &answer_lock);
       while (!first_thread_to_find_the_answer)
          pthread_cond_wait(&cv, &answer_lock);
       pthread_cleanup_pop(0);
      }
```

Code Example 9–7: *Cancellation in Condition Variables*

The Morning After

Well, now that we've done all that, we're ready to get back to some useful work, right? Not quite....

Threads are rather particular about how they're treated after cancellation. They want to be pampered. They want to be joined or at least waited for after they clean up.

The point here is that you don't want to be starting up new threads until the old ones are truly gone. What if you have global variables that you need properly initialized? What if there is shared data that you don't want old and new threads sharing? If nothing else, it's nice to clean up memory before making new demands. (We're assuming that you'll run the same code again in your program. If you really only ran it once, you wouldn't need to be so careful.)

In the searcher example we have one global array of TIDs. It would not do to start filling in new TIDs while the successful searcher was still busy killing off the old losers. Instead we must wait for all of the threads to exit before we reinitialize and start over again.[5]

Instead of using join, the same effect could be accomplished by using a `thread_single_barrier()`. However we would not know if a thread had been cancelled or had exited voluntarily. (We may not care.) In this case, a new problem arises: TIDs for detached threads may be recycled! You must not cancel a detached thread unless you know it's alive. For our program, we can accomplish this by having the searcher threads block on `sem_wait(&death_lock)`. This program is on the web under the name `cancellation_detached.c`.

Another detail to note in this code is the joining code at (9). We first lock the mutex, then unlock it again before calling join. Why? Well try it! Just put the lock/unlock outside of the loop. Deadlock again! (The main thread is holding the mutex, blocking on a join, while the successful searcher needs to lock the mutex before it can cancel the other searchers.)

This is actually a very interesting bit of code. As soon as the main thread has created the last searcher thread and released the mutex, the array can be treated as a constant—no other changes will be made to it until all searcher threads exit. This means that the main thread, which knows that the array is a constant, could dispense with locking the array.

---

[5]We don't actually need the threads to exit. We merely need the threads to reach a point where they will never change any shared data and we will never use their TIDs again.

The searcher threads, which don't know when the array becomes a constant, must synchronize on that state somehow. The existing mutex is the most obvious (and fastest) method. (What if one of the searchers found the PID before the main thread had finished creating the rest? It might execute the cancellation loop and miss the not-yet-created threads.)

Cancellation Safety

What if a library function, say printf(), were to hold a lock just as it got cancelled? This would not be a good thing. Some functions are *Async Cancellation Safe*, some aren't. If you are going to use cancellation, you're going to have to worry about this.

Some functions are certainly going to be cancel-safe. Such functions as atoi() and sqrt(), which don't need locks or other shared data, are obvious examples. Unfortunately, unless they are actually listed as cancel-safe, you shouldn't assume it.

Mixing Cancellation Types

In a well-written, complex program using cancellation, you might well find yourself mixing things. You may disable cancellation during initialization, enable it deferred during the majority of the program, and enable it asynchronously during long-running, tight loops that make no library calls.

Changing State and Type in Libraries

It is legal for a function to restrict cancellation while running sensitive code, as long as it resets the cancellation state and type to their previous settings. A function may not make cancellation less restrictive.

Simple Polling

In a program of any complexity, using cancellation is very difficult. A program that will be ported to other platforms will be even harder to write correctly. A strict polling scheme such as in *A Stoppable Producer/ Consumer Example* on page 101 would be vastly superior in almost every respect, as long as we don't have to worry about blocked threads.

In the code for `cancellation_not.c` (web page), we see the same searcher program written using polling.

Summary

Cancellation is the method by which one thread can kill another. Because of issues surrounding shared resources, held locks, and dynamically allocated storage, cancellation is extremely difficult to use correctly.[6] In Win32 and OS/2, there is virtually no way to use cancellation correctly. Cancellation can be completely avoided by implementing a polling scheme in any of the libraries, as long as we don't have to worry about blocked threads. In POSIX, deferred cancellation combined with cleanup handlers make it merely difficult to use cancellation.

Avoid cancellation if at all possible.

---

[6]Just spelling cancellation is an issue! Webster's allows it to be spelled with either one "l" or two.

10

Signals

In which we deal with the various aspects of handling asynchronous events in a multithreaded program. The definitions are given, alternative designs are discussed, and a program illustrating the most complex case is shown.

Signals in UNIX

Signals were invented in UNIX to handle a series of issues related to asynchronous events. The basic question was "How can a program do what it's supposed to do while still being able to respond to unexpected events in a timely fashion?" For example, a program that does fancy 3D modeling spends massive amounts of time in simple calculation loops. That program also has to respond to unpredictable window events such as "open," "close," and "repaint." Having the program poll for external events would be slow and awkward.

Instead of polling, UNIX invented signals that will interrupt a program and send it off to execute some other code to handle whatever situation might have arisen. Thus our 3D program can do its calculations completely independent of any repainting code; hence the loops can be simple and fast. When a SIGWINCH ("window has changed") comes in, the loop will be interrupted, and the program will then repaint the window, returning to the calculation loop when complete.

The basic UNIX signal model is that a program gets to declare which code it wants to handle the different incoming signals. The program can also set a signal mask to indicate if it wants to see the different signals. (A program may wish to disallow a signal while a specific section of code is executing.) When a signal is generated (normally by an external process), the kernel looks at the signal mask and the dispatch table to decide what code to run (if any). The kernel will then interrupt the process, pushing the current state onto the stack and restarting it in the chosen signal handler. The signal handler may do anything at all. Normally it will do its job and return. It may decide to exit the process or it may even do a siglongjmp() to a different point in the execution.

If several of the same signal (say SIGUSR1) are sent to a process, UNIX guarantees that at least one signal will be delivered at some point in time after the last one was sent. Presumably the signal will be delivered quite quickly, but this is not guaranteed. In particular, if process 1 sends a SIGUSR1 to process 2 and then does it again, process 2 may not awaken soon enough to handle the first signal. In that case, process 2 will only see a single signal. This is an important detail: you cannot count signals. The logic is that a signal tells the program that something needs attention and it's up to the program to decide what that something is. Thus, should window 1 be obscured by both window 2 and window 3, and should they both be closed, then the window system will send two SIGWINCH signals to the process. If the process only sees one of them,

that's OK, because the process must check all of its repainting requirements upon receipt, and it will see that two different portions of window
1 need repainting.

UNIX signals are used for three different purposes: error reporting,
situation reporting, and interruption. In traditional, single threaded programs, these three purposes were mixed together and handled identically. Indeed, most UNIX programmers wouldn't even distinguish between
them. In multithreaded programming, the distinctions become important and the methods of dealing with them are different.

Error Reporting occurs when a program has executed an illegal instruction. Perhaps it tried to divide by zero, or perhaps it tried to reference unmapped memory. In such cases, the hardware itself takes a trap
on the illegal instruction, and then a trap handler is run by the kernel.
The kernel figures out what happened and sends a signal to the process
(e.g., SIGFPE for divide by zero). As the process has obviously halted at
that instruction, we can be certain that the signal handler will be run with
that as the return address. Signals which are generated by traps are
known as *synchronous* signals.[1]

Situation Reporting is asynchronous signal delivery when the objective is to inform the program that some situation has changed and needs
attention. SIGWINCH is an obvious example. In such cases you are happy with what the program is doing; you simply wish the program to do
something extra.

Interruption is asynchronous signal delivery when the objective is to
stop the program from what it's doing and give it something else to do.
For example, you have just invented an unreliable device and you wish
to call read() on it, but you don't want to lose control should the device
fail to respond. If there is no automatic time-out on your read() call,
you could set a timer to go off after ten seconds. That timer would send
a SIGALRM to the process, which would then run a signal handler, realize that the device has failed, and then deal with it. Perhaps it would do
a siglongjmp() and force the program out of the read() call.

In traditional programs, the three situations are all mixed together.
Indeed, there is no particular reason to separate them out. In multithreaded programs, each of these cases must be handled differently.
OS/2 and Win32 have completely different methods of dealing with
traps, so signals are not an issue for them.

---

[1]It is the *delivery* of the signal that is synchronous with the illegal instruction, not the signal itself. You
could send a SIGFPE asynchronously via a call to kill() yourself if you wanted to. *Don't do that.*

For *Error Reporting*, the library guarantees that the signal will be delivered to the offending thread. (It would be pretty dumb for thread 1 to do a divide by zero and for thread 2 to get the signal.) Thus, if you wish to handle these situations, you can declare a signal handler, and whichever thread executes an illegal instruction will run it.

For *situation reporting*, externally generated signals (the asynchronous ones) are directed to the process (not to the LWP, certainly not to the thread). As we have seen, the process structure contains a single dispatch table, so there can be only one set of signal handlers for the entire process (i.e., one handler for SIGUSR1, another for SIGUSR2, etc.). Normally, the library simply decides which user thread should receive the signal and arranges for that thread to run the user-installed signal handler. (Any thread in the process can run the signal handler, depending upon the state of its individual signal mask and how attractive it looks in terms of priority level, run-state, etc.) Which thread will run the handler is implementation-dependent and is not guaranteed to be the same each time. You cannot rely on it. The only control you have is to set the thread signal mask.

This definition works fine. It really doesn't make much difference which thread repaints a dirty window.

For *interruptions*, the POSIX definition really doesn't do what you want. A SIGALRM will be delivered to the process (not the thread that requested it), and there's no general, reliable method of ensuring that it then gets delivered to the proper thread. (Masking out the signal on all but one thread would work, but it wouldn't be general.) This poses a problem which we shall look at more.

Multithreading obviates most of the need for signals because multithreaded programs are already asynchronous, and they don't need much additional asynchronous behavior. A multithreaded program can simply spawn a new thread to wait for whatever events interest the programmer. There are still times when you will need to deal with signals, however. The most likely reasons are (a) the new program needs to deal with old programs that send signals, and (b) you really do want to be able to interrupt individual threads. Win32 and OS/2 don't have the first problem, but the second problem they have no general solution for.

Each individual thread has its own signal mask, and this is what determines which signals that thread will accept. When you are programming with threads, you will be concerned solely with the thread signal mask, and will never read, change, or even think about the kernel-level signal masks. You cannot control which thread will run the signal handler other than by setting the signal mask. The library will manage those details for you.

As the programmer, you can also send signals. You can even send them directly to individual threads inside your program by using `pthread_kill()`. These signals will behave exactly as if they had been sent from the outside, save that they are guaranteed to be delivered to the thread chosen. As is consistent with UNIX semantics, if they are masked out at the time, they will be queued as pending on the thread until such time as the mask is changed.

Async Safety

Just as you thought you had it all figured out, there's one more little detail. This is not an MT issue per se, but it bears mentioning here. Imagine you have just called `malloc()` from your thread, and a signal has come in. Now imagine that the signal handler also called `malloc()`. Well, most implementations of `malloc()` require it to lock some global data. If your thread's call to `malloc()` happened to hold that lock just when the signal came in, then trouble would be brewing. When the signal handler's call to `malloc()` tried to grab that same lock, it wouldn't get it. Deadlock! So, there's also a safety category known as *async safe* (or *signal safe*). The library routine `malloc()` is not async safe, nor for that matter are very many of the routines in any of the libraries.

Conclusion? Look at the manual page for every library call that you are planning to use. That will tell you if it's safe, if there's an alternate call to use, or if you have to do some hacking yourself. In practice, this will not be a very big issue for you, if you take our very good advice (below) and use `sigwait()` instead of installing signal handlers.[2] There are about 80 functions defined to be signal safe (consult your vendor's documentation).

The Solaris Implementation of Signal Handling

As we have said previously, we wish to keep implementation aspects separate from the specifications and talk about implementation only when necessary for clarity's sake. In the body of the text, we have told

---

[2]This is one of those rare instances where we actually take our own advice!

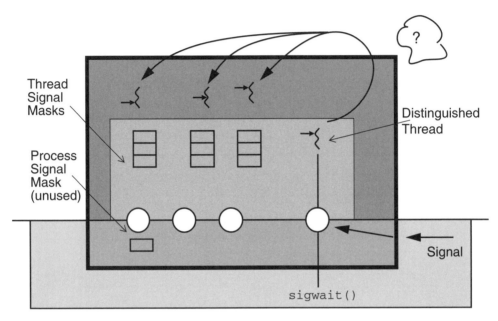

Figure 10–1   *Solaris 2.4 Signal Handler Implementation*

you everything you need in order to use signals correctly, and there is no need to say anything more. We include this section only because we know that bugs happen, and you are likely to run into this aspect of the implementation when debugging your program.

Once again, this is a peek under the covers. Do not base any of your programming upon what you read here!

The Solaris threads library has a distinguished bound thread of its own that handles all signal delivery issues (see Figure 10–1). This thread is created at start-up time and promptly calls `sigwait()`, which is a new POSIX function that simply waits for any signals you ask it to. The distinguished thread waits for all signals; hence it is assured that every signal will be delivered to it.

When a signal is delivered to the process, that thread then looks around at all the user threads, comparing thread signal masks and considering run-state (active, runnable, sleeping, etc.). It decides which thread is to run the signal handler. The chosen thread is interrupted, it runs the signal handler, then returns to whatever it was doing before (which could be sleeping!).

Should one of your threads call `sigwait()` itself, the threads library will interpose its own definition of `sigwait()`. This interposed function will simply inform the distinguished thread of your desires. When a signal comes in that your thread should receive in its `sigwait()` call, the distinguished thread will figure this out and cause the interposed function to return as if the signal had been delivered to `sigwait()` as specified.

Notice that you will *never* change the process signal mask. This is officially undefined in POSIX, and most likely `sigprocmask()` has been overwritten with an interposed function anyway.

By the way, this is the implementation that is being used in Solaris 2.4 and 2.5. A completely different implementation was used in Solaris 2.3 that did not rely on the use of `sigwait()` at all (it also didn't work very well). If somebody comes up with a better idea for Solaris 2.6, it could all change again. But no matter what kind of implementation is used, the specification will remain constant, so your programs will continue to work properly.

Don't Use Signal Handlers!

Now that you understand all the tricky details of how threads can receive signals and run signal handlers, we're going to suggest you avoid it all together. There will be some programs where you will want to have threads handle signals as we've just described, but not very many. What we suggest is that you designate one thread to do all of the signal handling for your program. This will simplify your programming, yet still give you all the functionality you need.

There are two ways of designating a signal-handling thread. You can mask out all asynchronous signals on all threads but one, then let that one thread run your signal handlers. You can just create the thread, and then immediately have it block. Even though it's sleeping, the library will still wake it up to run the signal handler.

```
pthread_sigmask(SIG_UNBLOCK, signal_set, NULL);
sigaction(signal_handler...)
SEM_WAIT(&s);                    /* Sleep forever */
```

Code Example 10–1: *Using a Sleeping Thread to Catch Signals*

The other, more recommended method, is to have this one thread call `sigwait()`. It will then go to sleep waiting for a signal to come in.

When one does, it will return from the `sigwait()` call with the signal, and you will decide how to act on it. Notice that you will have to block out the selected signals from all threads.

```
pthread_sigmask(SIG_BLOCK, signal_set, NULL);
sigwait(&signal_set, &signal);
switch(signal)
{   case SIGALRM:              run_alarm();
    case SIGUSR1               run_usr1();
}
```

Code Example 10–2: *Using a Sigwait Thread*

Per-Thread Alarms

Sometimes you will find the need to have an alarm sent to an individual thread. It's not terribly common, but it does happen. The canonical instance occurs when you have a specific thread doing I/O to an unreliable device, and you want the thread to time out if the device fails. Unfortunately, POSIX does not provide a good solution to this problem.

Some implementations did (or still do!) specify that certain kinds of alarms send their expiration signal directly to the calling thread (or LWP); however, this is not part of the POSIX standard, and it should not be relied upon.[3] So, what's a poor programmer to do?

We recommend that you write a thread-specific timer call-out queue yourself, depending upon the POSIX semantics for SIGALRM. That is, you write code that keeps track of which thread is waiting for the alarm, when that alarm is to go off, and you also take care of delivering that signal.

In Figure 10–2 we show the gist of how per-thread alarms can be built, demonstrating the use of `pthread_kill()` as we do.

First the waiter thread starts up during library initialization. It blocks all signals, sets up a handler for SIGUSR1, and enters a `sigwait()` loop. Then main starts up and spawns T1 and T2. T1 and T2 unblock only SIGUSR1, then call `thread_settimer()`, which arranges to set an alarm and also juggle any pending alarms. Then they both go to work.

---

[3]Solaris UI threads implemented SIGALRM in this fashion before POSIX had settled upon the standard. Solaris 2.5 and above will now implement SIGALRM according to the POSIX standard. There is a compiler flag, which will allow you to select per-LWP semantics for UI-compatibility. (*Don't do that!*)

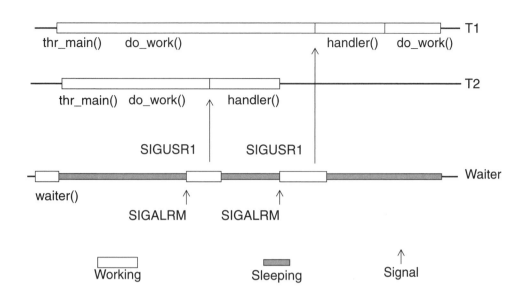

Figure 10–2 *Building a Per-Thread Alarm*

When the first alarm goes off, the waiter thread returns from `sig-wait()` with `SIGALRM`, figures out which thread requested that alarm, and sends a `SIGUSR1` to that thread. In this case that thread happened to be T2. T2 runs the handler, which decides to exit, and does.

As there is only one `SIGALRM`, the waiter thread must do some fancy footwork to keep track of which thread requested the alarm at what time, and it must also reset the alarm when required. We'll leave that bit as an exercise (it's in the extensions library).

Some time later, a `SIGARLM` comes in again, and the waiter thread figures out that it should be directed to T1. The scenario repeats; however the handler concludes that T1 should not exit, so when the handler is finished, T1 resumes where it was interrupted.

An important detail to notice is that this design for per-thread alarms requires the use of two signals. If we had tried to use `SIGALRM` when doing the `pthread_kill()`, then we would have had to have unblocked `SIGALRM` in the worker threads and we couldn't have guaranteed that the external `SIGALRM` would be delivered to the sigwaiting thread.

```
thr_main()                    waiter()
                              {
{                             int sig;
set_timer(5);                 sigset_t set;
do_work();
clear_timer();                    init_set(&set);
}
                                  while(1)
                                  {err = sigwait(&set, &sig);
                                   switch(sig)
                                      {case SIGALRM : tell_thr();
                                       case SIGUSR1 : do_usr1();
                                       default: etc...
                              }}}
```

Code Example 10–3:   *Implementing a Per-Thread Alarm (`callout.c`)*

Creating Threads for Events:
SIGEV_THREAD

A number of the functions in the POSIX realtime specification, POSIX.1b, allow for asynchronous I/O—you start an operation (e.g., `aio_read()`), but don't wait for it to complete. As part of this async I/O, you get to tell the operation what you would like it to do when it does complete. The common thing is for it to generate a signal, which you will then handle, presumably doing something with the data just read.

It is now possible to tell the library that you would like it to create a thread for you instead. The mechanism for doing this is straight-forward. You request that a function be run on an argument in a new thread.

```
struct sigevent                 event;

event.sigev_notify =            SIGEV_THREAD
event.sigev_value.sival_int =   100;
event.sigev_attributes =        attr;
event.sigev_notify_function =   handler

mq_notify(mesage_queue, &event);
```

Code Example 10–4:   *Setting up a SIGEV_THREAD Handler*

What advantages does this technique have over receiving the signal in `sigwait()` and then creating a thread? None we can think of. It's a little bit more complex, harder to debug, and gives you less control over your threads.

This is part of Pthreads and is supported by HP-UX 10.30, but not Solaris 2.5 or Digital UNIX 4.0 (a bug!). It is scheduled to be in Solaris 2.6 and Digital UNIX 4.0.1.

Summary

Signal handling has been extended to MT programs, however we will generally eschew the use of asynchronous signal handling in favor of waiting for signals directly. Per-thread alarms are the one exception where we will need signal handlers.

11

Details

In which the details of actually writing and compiling an MT program are reviewed. The defined constants are described and methods of dealing with errors are proposed. We note which vendors have made extensions to Pthreads, and where POSIX is headed.

Attribute Objects

The different threads APIs permit the programmer to create threads and synchronization variables with a variety of different attributes. For example, a thread can be created joinable or detached, and a mutex variable can be initialized to be interprocess or intraprocess. UI, Win32, and OS/2 control these states by using flags during the creation or initialization process. Pthreads uses a different approach. In Pthreads you use attribute objects, which contain the details for the desired attributes. The attribute object is then used as an argument to the creation (initialization) function.

In UI (using flags)

```
thr_create(NULL, NULL, foo, NULL, THR_DETACHED | THR_BOUND);
```

In POSIX (using attribute objects)

```
pthread_attr_t attr;

pthread_attr_init(&attr);
pthread_attr_setscope(&attr, PTHREAD_SCOPE_SYSTEM);
pthread_attr_setdetachstate(&attr,PTHREAD_CREATE_DETACHED);
pthread_create(&tid, &attr, foo, NULL);
```

Code Example 11–1:   *Creating a Detached, Bound Thread in UI and POSIX*

The state information in the attribute object is used only during creation (initialization). Once it is complete, a change in the attribute object will not affect the state of the thread (synchronization variable).

There are two major advantages to using attribute objects. The first is that it improves the readability of application code. A programmer can define all the attribute objects used in an application in one location. This allows all the initialization and state information for all the threads and synchronization variables in the application to reside in one piece of code. This also provides an easy way to modify the behavior of all the threads and synchronization variables in just a few lines of code.

The other advantage of attribute objects is that it now becomes possible to add new functionality to the library without changing the existing API. If UI designers decided to add a function to set a thread's signal mask at creation time, they would have to extend the `thr_create()`

call to have a new argument. In Pthreads, they can simply add a new attribute object function: `pthread_attr_setmask()`.

Although attribute objects provide an easy way to initialize threads and synchronization variables, they require memory to hold state information. This memory must be managed by the programmer. The memory is allocated when the attribute object is initialized, using the appropriate initialization function. This memory can be released by means of the related destructor function.

Although it is legal to allocate attribute objects dynamically, it probably isn't very practical. In all of our code we declare the attribute objects globally, initialize them, and use them. It would be convenient if attribute objects could be statically initialized the way that mutexes and condition variables can be. Unfortunately, that would mean exporting the implementation to the header file, making it impossible to extend the definition of attribute objects.

You may simply pass NULL to the creation (initialization) function instead of an attribute object, in which case the vendor-specific default values will be used.

Thread Attribute Objects

The attribute object used in creating a thread contains all the information needed to define the state of the new thread. This state information is the thread's:

- Scheduling scope
- Detach state
- Stack base address
- Stack size
- Other scheduling information

In most programs all threads will be created with identical attributes, so you'll declare one attribute object, initialize it, set its values, and use it everywhere. In almost all of our code we use globally scheduled, detached threads, and default synchronization variables. We don't use those other attributes at all.

Scheduling Scope
`pthread_attr_{set/get}scope()`

The scope determines whether the thread will have local or global scheduling. With scope set to PTHREAD_SCOPE_SYSTEM, the thread will be globally scheduled by the kernel in a one-to-one model. With scope set to PTHREAD_SCOPE_PROCESS, the thread will be locally scheduled by the library in a many-to-many model.

Detach State
`pthread_attr_{set/get}detachstate()`

The detach state determines whether the thread will be joinable from another thread and whether the thread can return exit status. A detach state of PTHREAD_CREATE_DETACHED means that a thread's resources and exit status will be discarded immediately. A detach state of PTHREAD_CREATE_JOINABLE (POSIX default) means the thread exit status and resources will be retained until the thread is joined by another thread.

Stack Size
`pthread_attr_{set/get}stacksize()`

The stack size in the attribute object defines the size of the stack, in bytes, for a thread. If the size of the stack is non-null, then the thread will use the stack size given in the attribute object. If a stack size is given, then it must be at least PTHREAD_STACK_MIN bytes in size (typically about 8k). If the size of the stack is NULL, then the system default stack size will be used (e.g., 64k on HP-UX, 1m on Solaris).

The default stack size is implementation dependent. For Solaris it is one megabyte, plus a *guard* page. A guard page is a page that is mapped invalid and will cause a SEGV when the stack overflows onto it. One megabyte is a huge stack and gives you plenty of room to do just about anything you want. Because it is mapped-in MAP_NORESERVE, none of the pages actually uses any physical memory or swap space unless they are accessed. Should you decide that you need more or less room for your stack, you may select a size, and the threads library will create for you a stack that size, plus guard page. It's up to you to figure out how much stack space you'll need. Window system calls can get nested pretty deeply, and if your thread might run a signal handler, you'll need room for that too.

Stack Address
`pthread_attr_{set|get}stackaddr()`

It is possible for you to manage the stack yourself. You can allocate the memory, create a guard page, then garbage collect the stack when the thread exits. When building realtime programs you might need to do this, otherwise forget it.

The stack address specifies the starting address of the stack you have allocated for the thread. If the value for the stack address is non-null, then the system will initialize the threads stack, starting at the given address. Obviously you would not want to have two threads sharing the same stack.

The default value for a thread stack address is NULL, which means the system will allocate the stack for the thread.

Scheduling Policy
`pthread_attr_{set|get}schedpolicy()`

The scheduling parameters define how the thread is scheduled for realtime threads. The policy may be: SCHED_OTHER, SCHED_RR, or SCHED_FIFO.

Scheduling Inheritance
`pthread_attr_{set|get}inheritsched()`

The scheduling parameters define how the thread obtains its scheduling information. Does it inherit those of its parents (PTHREAD_INHERIT_SCHED) or does it look at the rest of the information in the attribute object (PTHREAD_EXPLICIT_SCHED)?

Scheduling Parameters
pthread_attr_{set/get}schedparam()

The scheduling parameters define how the thread is scheduled and what its priority will be.

```
pthread_attr_t attr;

pthread_attr_init(&attr);                    /* Necessary */
pthread_attr_setdetachstate(&attr, PTHREAD_CREATE_DETACHED);
pthread_create(NULL, &attr, foo, NULL);
pthread_create(NULL, &attr, bar, NULL);
pthread_attr_setdetachstate(&attr, PTHREAD_CREATE_JOINABLE);
pthread_create(NULL, &attr, baz, NULL);
pthread_attr_destroy(&attr);                 /* Not necessary */
```

Code Example 11–2: *Using an Attribute Object in Thread Creation*

In Code Example 11–2, we create two detached threads with the default local scope and stack size. The third thread will be joinable and the change in the attribute object will not affect either of the first two threads.

Default Thread Attributes

When an attribute object is initialized, it is defined with a default state. The default state for a thread attribute object is largely implementation defined, so it would be wise to supply specific values yourself. Passing NULL instead of an attribute object will also give the defaults. In Table 11.1 we note what the POSIX spec says, and what we use in most of our programs. Individual vendor defaults will have to be looked up for each vendor.

Table 11.1 *Default Settings for Thread Attribute Objects*

Attribute	POSIX Default Setting	Our Defaults
Scope	PTHREAD_SCOPE_PROCESS	PTHREAD_SCOPE_SYSTEM
Detach State	PTHREAD_CREATE_JOINABLE	PTHREAD_CREATE_DETACHED
Stack Address	Implementation Defined	NULL
Stack Size	Implementation Defined	NULL

Table 11.1   *Default Settings for Thread Attribute Objects*

Attribute	POSIX Default Setting	Our Defaults
Parameter	Implementation Defined	NULL
Policy	Implementation Defined	SCHED_OTHER
Inheritsched	Implementation Defined	PTHREAD_EXPLICIT_SCHED

Synchronization Variable Initialization

Mutexes and condition variables in Pthreads use attribute objects to define the scope of the variable (process-local or cross-process) and the priority inheritance aspects of mutexes for realtime processing. Both of them may be initialized to the default state by passing NULL instead of an attribute object. They may also be statically initialized to the default values by setting them to a constant defined in the header file. In our code, you will see that static synchronization variables are always statically initialized when we want the default values (i.e., almost always).

In order for static initialization to work, the size of the object in question must be known at compile time. Thus, mutexes and condition variables cannot change size in future library releases. (A binary you compiled under IRIX 6.2 has to be able to run under 6.3.) Their *size* has become part of the public interface! By contrast, attribute objects cannot be statically initialized. Their sizes are not part of the public interface.

Mutex Attribute Objects

The static initializer is PTHREAD_MUTEX_INITIALIZER. It delivers the default values of non-shared, non-priority-inheriting mutex.

Cross-Process
pthread_mutexattr_{set|get}pshared()

If PTHREAD_PROCESS_SHARED, then the mutex will be sharable by other processes. If PTHREAD_PROCESS_PRIVATE (default), then not.

Priority Inheriting
`pthread_mutexattr_{set/get}protocol()`

For realtime threads, the thread owning such a mutex can either inherit the priority of the sleeping thread (PTHREAD_PRIO_INHERIT) or the predetermined "ceiling" priority of the mutex (PTHREAD_PRIO_PROTECT); otherwise it will not change its priority (PTHREAD_PRIO_NONE) (default).

Ceiling Priority
`pthread_mutexattr_{set/get}`
`prioceiling()`

For realtime threads, you can set the ceiling priority level.

Condition Variable Attribute Objects

The static initializer is PTHREAD_COND_INITIALIZER. It delivers the default value of non-shared condition variable.

Cross-Process
`pthread_condattr_{set/get}pshared()`

If PTHREAD_PROCESS_SHARED, then the condition variable will be sharable by other processes. If PTHREAD_PROCESS_PRIVATE (default), then not.

```
pthread_mutex_t       length_lock   = PTHREAD_MUTEX_INITIALIZER;
pthread_cond_t        length_cv     = PTHREAD_COND_INITIALIZER;
pthread_mutex_t       shared_lock;
pthread_mutexattr_t ma;

pthread_mutexattr_init(&ma);
pthread_mutexattr_setshared(&ma, PTHREAD_SHARED);
pthread_mutex_init(shared_lock, &ma);
```

Code Example 11–3:   *Static vs. Dynamic Initialization of Synchronization Variables*

Semaphore Initialization

Semaphore variables are not officially part of the Pthreads specification; they are actually part of the POSIX realtime specification (POSIX.1b). Hence they have a different protocol for their initialization. They cannot be statically initialized and use direct values instead of an attribute object. If the second argument is non-zero, then it will be a cross-process semaphore. The third argument is initial value.

```
sem_t      requests_length;

sem_init(&requests_length, TRUE, 10);
```

Code Example 11–4: *Semaphore Initialized to be Cross-Process with an Initial Value of 10*

POSIX Thread IDs

Although it's easy to miss this point, TIDs are opaque datatypes—you do not know how large they are, or what their structure is. In practice they are usually integers, either 32 or 64 bits long, but this is not part of the interface and you should not rely on it. The consequences of this include:

- You cannot compare TIDs with ==, you must use `pthread_equal()`.
- You cannot pass a TID to a function that expects a `(void *)`.
- You cannot print a TID.

```
if (tid == pthread_self()) ...
printf("T@%d", pthread_self());
pthread_exit((void *) pthread_self());
if (tid1 > tid2) ...
```

Code Example 11–5: *Incorrect Use of POSIX TIDs*

On the other hand, you can pass TIDs to functions that are expecting them (e.g., `pthread_equal()`), and you can set variables to TIDs with =. (You can copy any structure with =.)

You will notice in our library of "help" functions we have a function `thread_name()`, which maps a TID to a printable string. These strings have only coincidental association with the contents of the actual TID. We also cheat for known systems. We `#ifdef` more convenient (and non-portable) versions of `thread_name()` for known systems (Solaris, IRIX, Digital UNIX), which map our printed names onto the same printed names those systems use in their debuggers.

One last thing with TIDs that we find to be a bother is the fact that there is no "null" TID—nothing you can pass to a function to indicate that we have no TID to pass it. For example, it would be very nice to be able to pass `thread_name()` a null value, indicating that it should return the print name for the current thread, or to have a null value we could use for static initialization. Technically, we cannot do this. We *do* it, however (in just a few instances), defining `NULL_TID` to be `-1L`, which just happens to work on the known systems (notice that `NULL_TID` is the *last* element in the initializer shown in Code Example 11–6). We *are* cheating and we might get burned!

```
/* This NULL_TID may not work on all implementations! */
#define NULL_TID  (pthread_t) -1L

#define THREAD_FIFO_MUTEX_INITIALIZER \
{  PTHREAD_MUTEX_INITIALIZER, PTHREAD_COND_INITIALIZER, 0, \
   FALSE, NULL_TID}
```

Code Example 11–6: *Illegal (but very Useful) Use of POSIX TIDs*

One more little detail…, detached threads may have their TIDs reused.[1] Once a detached thread exits, you must not use its TID again. This affects only such things as `pthread_kill()` and `pthread_cancel()`.

---

[1]A pox on anyone who implements a library which recycles TIDs! There are better ways to deal with the problem than recycling TIDs.

Win32 Thread IDs and Thread Handles

In Win32 there are two references to thread objects, a thread handle that is local to the process (and most similar to a POSIX TID), and a thread ID that is a system-wide referent to the thread. Most functions use the handle, although the debugger and analyses use the TID. Both TIDs and handles are opaque, but they can be compared with == and passed as an `LPVOID`.

Initializing Your Data: `pthread_once()`

Normally, you will initialize all of your data before your program gets going "for real." You can use the ".ini" section in your libraries to run initialization functions there, and you can write an initialization function for your own main module. If, for some reason, you need to do initialization after the program has gotten going and there are multiple threads already in existence, then you'll have to be more careful. It certainly wouldn't do to have two threads both doing the initialization.

```
int epoch;

void initializer(void)
{epoch = now();}

#ifdef __sun
#pragma init (initializer)
#elseif __dec
__init_thread_timer()
{initializer;}
#endif
```

Code Example 11–7: *Initializing a Value in a Library's .ini Section*

The basic method of doing this initialization is to have the first thread calling your function lock a mutex, test to see if initialization is complete, and do the initialization if not. Any subsequent calls would have to wait until the first one completed. You could write all of this yourself, or you could use a special function designed for just this purpose.

The function `pthread_once()` does exactly what we've just described. It locks a mutex, tests to see if initialization is complete, then executes the initialization function if not. You use it like this:

```
int epoch;

void initializer(void)
{epoch = now();}

int time_since_epoch()
{static pthread_once_t initialized = PTHREAD_ONCE_INIT;

    pthread_once(&initialized, initializer);
    return(now() - epoch);
}
```

Code Example 11–8: *Using* `pthread_once()`

The one obvious drawback to this is that the data being initialized must be global, whereas in this example it might make more sense for epoch to be a static variable local to `time_since_epoch()`. The other drawback is that even just that little bit of testing does take time, about the time of locking and unlocking one mutex (~2μs). This is where you might pull one of those ugly little tricks...

```
  if (!done)
   pthread_once(&initialized, initializer)

void initializer(void)
{
  ...

  /* The last thing done should be to reset the flag. */
  done = TRUE;
}
```

Code Example 11–9: *Ugly little trick*

It's ugly because you're really duplicating the work of `pthread_once()`, but the cost of checking one global variable is very cheap (about 30 times faster) compared to calling a function, locking the mutex, etc. (If a few threads happen to get the wrong value for done, the worst that happens is you'll spend a few extra microseconds.)

If you can do load-time initialization, do!

POSIX Namespace Restrictions

In order to avoid conflicting names, POSIX strictly reserves the prefixes "PTHREAD_" and "pthread_" for the library functions. Vendors who add their own extensions to the library may use those prefixes as long as they add the suffix "_np" to indicate that the function in question is "non-portable." Hence, our naming scheme for the error-checking wrappers (PTHREAD_CREATE(), etc.) is pretty dicey. All of our other functions use the unreserved prefix "thread_".

Return Values and Error Reporting

All of the libraries make extensive use of return values to indicate errors. In general they do not set the value of errno and you should not look at it. It is possible that a thread function could call another library function that does set the value of errno, resulting in errno being set to a reasonable value, but you should not depend upon this. (E.g., pthread_create() might call malloc(), which would set errno to EAGAIN, should there be insufficient available free space. Then pthread_create() would return the value EAGAIN and errno would be coincidentally set to EAGAIN also.) The one exception to this is semaphores, which do set errno.

Pthreads also return error values when they detect programming bugs—something that you might well expect to be handled in a different fashion. For example, passing a semaphore to pthread_mutex_lock() is clearly a programming bug. Yet pthread_mutex_lock() is defined to return the value EINVAL![2] There is no realistic way for a running program to recover from a bug of this nature and for the vast majority of MT programmers, it may actually be a disservice to return an error value. We think it would be far more useful for the program simply to crash at that location so that it could be debugged.

Nonetheless, there is method to this madness. One of the groups heavily involved in the standardization effort was the realtime machine control crowd. These folks deal with such extremes as aircraft autopiloting, where "crash" takes on a whole new meaning. They wanted to

---

[2]If it notices, of course. It is always possible that one structure looks enough like another to fool any function. This error detection is optional.

include options in the standard that would allow them to recover from anything.

Well, that's the logic. If you are doing realtime control, you've probably thought a great deal about this kind of problem. The best advice we can give with respect to making such programming errors in the first place is *"Don't do that!"*

So how ought one deal with programming error? It makes for very heavy, ugly code to test for every error return value from every threads function, especially when you aren't going to do anything about these errors. You really have two choices: you can write good code and ensure you never run into these situations, or you can write wrappers that check for the return values and simply aborts the program.

In most of our programs, we do the former. In all of our calls to mutexes, for example, we assume that we have done a good job of programming, and in no instance do we ever get confused and cast a semaphore to a mutex.

One set of error values indicates a runtime error that we could not have programmed around—running out of free memory. In these instances it is best to take the second course of action. Code Example 11–10 shows are the full set of wrappers required to cover these runtime errors.

```
int PTHREAD_CREATE(pthread_t *new_thread_ID,
        const pthread_attr_t *attr,
        void * (*start_func)(void *), void *arg)
{int err;
 if (err = pthread_create(new_thread_ID, attr, start_func, arg))
   {printf("%s\n", strerror(err));
    abort();
  }}

int PTHREAD_ATTR_INIT(pthread_attr_t *a) ...

int PTHREAD_CONDATTR_INIT(pthread_condattr_t *a) ...

int PTHREAD_MUTEXATTR_INIT(pthread_mutexattr_t *a) ...

int SEM_INIT(sem_t *sem, int pshared, unsigned int value) ...
```

Code Example 11–10: *Error Detection Functions for Pthreads*
(thread_extensions.c)

There are a few more return values that are not really errors, but rather conditions with which you have to deal. They are the unsupported options and lack of permission. For the former, you must decide what to do for the specific platform you're on. Presumably you know what options are supported when you write the program and have already dealt with the situation. Very likely, your decision will be to ignore the missing option and run the program anyway. Presumably the program will still run correctly, just a little less efficiently.

For example, if the platform doesn't support priority inheritance mutexes, you'll just ignore that potential inefficiency. On the other hand, you might decide to write inheritance mutexes yourself. Once again, this would not be a runtime decision, but rather a porting-time decision.

A lack of permission results from a thread trying to do something with realtime scheduling when it is not running as root. On most systems, you cannot promote a thread into the realtime class, nor can you declare a mutex to be priority inheritance unless you are root. Presumably you'll avoid this altogether by checking for root permission as soon as your program starts up.

Finally there are a few return values that you'll only see if you are expecting them. These are not errors, but rather informational values. If you request a condition variable to time-out after a given period, `pthread_cond_timedwait()` will return `ETIMEDOUT`. The "try" function, `pthread_mutex_trylock()`, will return `EBUSY` if it cannot lock the mutex.

The functions that take a TID as an argument are legal to call even if the particular joinable thread has already exited. Thus `pthread_cancel()`, `pthread_kill()`, `pthread_getschedparam()`, `pthread_set-schedparam()`, and `pthread_join()` may all be called on joinable threads that don't exist, returning `ESRCH`. This is not true for detached threads, whose TIDs might be recycled. For them, you must be certain that they are still alive.

Not all compliant libraries are equal. Many do return different error values because (a) they interpreted the spec differently, (b) they chose different options, (c) they made a mistake(!).

Table 11.2 gives the complete list of return values from Pthreads functions and what we think you should do about them. There will be cases where you will want to do something more elaborate than what we suggest. These are only the defaults.

Table 11.2 *Pthread Function Return Values*

Value	Meaning	Handling Technique
EINVAL	Invalid argument	Don't
EFAULT	Illegal address	Don't
EINTR	Interrupted by a signal	Wrapper
EBUSY	A "try" function failed	Handle
ETIMEDOUT	A time limit has been reached	Handle
EPERM	No permission for operation	Don't
EAGAIN	Resource temporarily unavailable	Wrapper
ESRCH	No such thread	Ignore
EDEADLK	Program would have deadlocked	Don't
ENOSPC	No space on device	Wrapper
ENOMEM	Not enough memory	Wrapper
ENOTSUP	Unsupported option	Ignore
ENOSYS	Unsupported function	Don't

"Don't"   means write your program so this never happens. (It's a programming bug!)

"Wrapper"   means use one of the wrappers defined above.

"Ignore"   means run your program without the desired option, or don't worry if the thread has already exited.

"Handle"   means that this is a condition you specifically requested, so you'll obviously know how to handle it.

Constants Comments

Some of these constants are defined directly in the header files, some of them are either not defined at all, or defined as calls to runtime functions. For example, to get the value of PTHREAD_STACK_MIN in Solaris, you will see that it is defined to be:

```
#define PTHREAD_STACK_MIN _sysconf(_SC_THREAD_STACK_MIN)
```

in <unistd.h>	DEC 4.0D	IBM 4.2	SGI 6.2	Sun 2.5	HP 10.30
_POSIX_THREADS (Are threads implemented?)	X	X	X	1	X
_POSIX_THREAD_ATTR_STACKSIZE (Can you set the stack size?)	X	X	X	1	X
_POSIX_THREAD_ATTR_STACKADDR (User allocated the stacks?)	X	X	X	1	X
_POSIX_THREAD_PRIORITY_ SCHEDULING (Can you use realtime?)	X	X	X	1	X
_POSIX_THREAD_PRIO_INHERIT (Priority inheriting mutexes?)	–	–	–	–	–
_POSIX_THREAD_PRIO_PROTECT (Priority ceiling mutexes?)	–	–	–	–	–
_POSIX_THREAD_PROCESS_SHARED (Can SVs be cross-process?)	–	–	–	1	–
_POSIX_THREAD_SAFE_FUNCTIONS (MT-safe library calls?)	X	X	X	1	X

in <limits.h>

	DEC 4.0D	IBM 4.2	SGI 6.2	Sun 2.5	HP 10.30
PTHREAD_DESTRUCTOR_ITERATIONS (Iterations of TSD destructors)	4	4	4	4	4
PTHREAD_KEYS_MAX (Max TSD keys: implementation)	255	128	128	128	128
Actual runtime value				>1m	
PTHREAD_STACK_MIN (Smallest thread stack)	8k	8k	8k	1k	8k
Actual runtime value	24k			~8k	
PTHREAD_THREADS_MAX (Max threads: implementation)	64	64	64	64	64
Actual runtime value	>10k	>10k	>10k	>10k	>10k

Code Example 11–11: *Pthreads Constants*

Constant	Minimum Required Value (Actual)
PTHREAD_DESTRUCTOR_ITERATIONS	_POSIX_THREAD_DESTRUCTOR_ ITERATIONS (4)
PTHREAD_KEYS_MAX	_POSIX_THREAD_KEYS_MAX (128)
PTHREAD_STACK_MIN	0
PTHREAD_THREADS_MAX	_POSIX_THREAD_THREADS_MAX (64)

Code Example 11–12:   *Pthread Constants (Required Minimums)*

The "max" constants are a little bit confusing to read. The constant _POSIX_THREAD_THREADS_MAX represents the minimum number of threads every POSIX system must support. In other words, a compliant system may set the maximum number of threads to be 64, but no lower. This is the lower bound on the constant PTHREAD_THREADS_MAX, which is an implementation-dependent constant. It, in turn, tells you the minimum number of threads the *implementation* will support. The actual number may be higher.

Pthread Futures

The POSIX threads standard, POSIX.1c, was ratified in June '95. As with all standards, it is the product of a great many, very diligent, very hard working people with different needs and different objectives. Not everything that everyone thought valuable made the standard, and parts of the standard are less than perfect. Overall, it is a superb piece of work. The members of the group have done an excellent job. (Way to go, y'all!)

In addition to the various optional portions of the standard, there are a number of things that would have been nice to have, but which the members were unable to completely concur. There is work going on to resolve the differences and add these to a future version of Pthreads. Pthreads, the next generation, has two parts, neither is likely to emerge before 2000(?).

POSIX.1d (Realtime, part 2)

- Timed mutex lock
- Timed semaphore post

POSIX. 1j (Realtime, part 3)

- Relative wait functions (i.e., "In 10 minutes" vs. the current absolute wait functions, which say "At 10:15")
- Barriers
- Readers/Writer locks
- Spinlocks
- `pthread_abort()` (Forced cancellation, which ignores the disabled state.)

POSIX. 14

This working group is focused on clarifying how multiprocessor systems should deal with the optional portions of Pthreads, which should become required on MP systems.

Pthread Extensions

In addition to POSIX, X/Open has also written a number of extensions to Pthreads, as have a number of different vendors. In some cases, the naming scheme will include the suffix "_NP" ("_np") to indicate that they are additions to the standard. A great number of the extensions are easily written at user level and many are included in our extensions library.

Solaris Extensions

- `pread()` and `pwrite()`
- Readers/Writer Locks (via UI threads)
- `thr_setconcurrency()` (via UI threads)
- Debugger interface: `libthreaddb.so`

X/Open Extensions

X/Open has developed XSH5 (part of UNIX98 brand), which requires 1003.1b, 10031c, and adds some thread extensions.

The UNIX95 specification (aka Spec 1170) was an extension of POSIX where the vendors collected all of the library functions on all of the systems in order to make a truly usable specification. The XSH5 working definitions overlap with some of POSIX.1j, and it is likely that they will converge before ratification. They have included:

- Variable size guard pages
- Recursive mutexes
- Debug mutexes
- Readers/Writer locks
- pthread_setconcurrency()
- `pread()` and `pwrite()`
- Additional required cancellation points

AIX Extensions

- pthread_mutexattr_set{get}kind_np() for either fast or recursive mutexes.
- pthread_mutex_getowner_np()
- pthread_mutex_getunique_np()

Digital UNIX Extensions

- Much of the XSH5 extensions (with slightly different names): pread(), pwrite(), guardsize, different mutex types
- Full character names for objects (threads, mutexes, etc.)
- Debugger interface: `libpthreaddebug.so`
- Thread Independent Services—Pthread-like interfaces that are fast in nonthreaded processes, but vector to Pthread functions otherwise (instead of using stub functions in libc)

Comparing the OS/2, Win32, and POSIX Libraries

If we look at the specifications of the different libraries, we find a number of distinctions in their design philosophies, their functionalities, and some factors that affect the maximal efficiency of the implementations.

The POSIX thread specification is the most "primitive" of the libraries in the sense that it provides all of the base functionality but requires the programmer to construct the fancy stuff on top. This specification is good because these primitives are much faster than the fancy stuff, but it does require a bit more programming work in some cases. Of course, it also means that you are able to build exactly what you want.

OS/2 and Win32 both have much heavier libraries, containing more complex primitives. This complexity is good when that functionality is required, but your programs pay for it dearly in efficiency when it's not used. OS/2 and Win32 contain a built-in interdependency between windows and threads. Not just any thread can construct and use windows. OS/2 also has a system-wide limit of 256 (configurable to 4096) on the total number of threads.

In Table 11.3 we give a simple comparison of the four specifications. By "simple," we mean that the object is just about as small and fast as is possible to implement the functionality, whereas "complex" implies that it has other functionality that makes it more useful in limited circumstances, but it is also slower. "Buildable" means that such functionality is not part of the specification but is fairly simple to construct. "Difficult" means that it is humanly possible to construct from the supplied primitives but involves some tricky programming. It may not be possible to build all of that functionality, and it may require all programmers to do extra work, such as calling initialization functions when starting a thread. "Unusable" means that the API really can't be used, though you may be able to build a usable version yourself.

From our own, biased point of view, we find the simplicity and inherent speed of the POSIX threads specification most attractive. We think Win32 and OS/2 are too complex and slow, contain unreasonable limitations (the window system dependencies, the requirements for using system-wide handles), and in general do not seem to be as well thought-out as other parts of those systems.

Nonetheless, we recognize that you, the programmer, do not have a great deal of choice in the matter and must use the libraries supplied. To the largest degree, you can write any program with any of the libraries.

Table 11.3 *Comparing the Different Thread Specifications*

Functionality	POSIX Threads	Win32 Threads	OS/2 Threads
Design Philosophy (Simple Primitives?)	Simple	Complex	Complex
Scheduling Classes	Local/Global	Global	Global
Mutexes	Simple	Complex	Complex
Counting Semaphores	Simple	Complex	Buildable
R/W Locks	Buildable	Buildable	Buildable
Condition Variables	Simple	Complex	Complex
Multiple-Object Synchronization	Buildable	Complex	Complex
Thread Suspension	Difficult	Yes	Yes
Cancellation	Difficult	Unusable	Unusable
Thread-Specific Data	Yes	Yes	Difficult
Signal-Handling Primitives	Yes	n/a	n/a
Compiler Support Required	No	Yes	No

For the most part, even the design and construction of the programs will be identical. They have more in common than they have that which is different.

Summary

Pthreads uses attribute objects instead of flags for initialization. Many of the more exotic portions of Pthreads are optional, and system constants indicate their existence in an individual implementation. Most of the errors that POSIX functions return are best handled by aborting the program and fixing it. Several extensions to Pthreads are being worked on, and some vendors already provide their own extensions.

12

Libraries

In which we explore a variety of operating systems issues that bear heavily upon the usability of the threads library in actual programs. We examine the status of library functions and the programming issues facing them. We look at some design alternatives for library functions.

Multithreading is a fine and wonderful programming paradigm as we have described it thus far. However, it's not worth too much if it doesn't have the operating system support to make it viable. Most of the major operating systems are in a state of significant flux, so it would be difficult for us to say much about all of them. Instead we will stick with the issues that need to be considered and describe where the major systems are with respect to them.

The Threads Library

The threads library is an integral, bundled part of the operating system for some (Solaris, IRIX, AIX, Digital UNIX, UP-UX, Win95, NT, OS/2), but not all OSs. When it is bundled, you can write your program and not worry about whether the dynamic library will be there when you need it. As long as you write your programs legally, you will be able to move them across different machines and across different versions of the operating system without any problems at all.

All the system files you require in order to write and ship MT programs are bundled with the operating systems. The threads library is just a normal system library, so any legal compiler can be used, and there are plenty of them out there. Any legal debugger will work, although a debugger with MT extensions is to be vastly preferred.

Multithreaded Kernels

Many of the kernels are implemented using threads (Solaris, NT, OS/2, AIX, IRIX, Digital UNIX, HP-UX). The kernels use generally the same API that you have access to (Solaris kernel threads are very similar, Mach kernel threads are much lower level). There is no inherent connection between the kernel being multithreaded and the existence of a user-level MT library. Kernel programmers could have written the user-level library without the kernel being threaded, and they could have threaded the kernel without supplying a user-level library. They even could have built LWPs, made them realtime, SMP, and preemptable without the use of threads. Theoretically.

In practice, the same things that make MT so attractive to you also make it attractive to the kernel hackers. Because the kernel implements all internal schedulable entities as threads, it is much easier to implement SMP

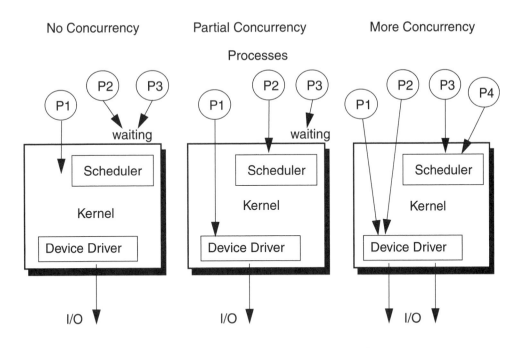

Figure 12–1   *Concurrency within the Kernel*

support and realtime scheduling, and make the kernel pre-emptable. So, LWPs are built on top of kernel threads. Interrupts are built with kernel threads. Creation, scheduling, synchronization, etc. of kernel threads works much the same way as for user-level threads.

The OS can be viewed as one gigantic program with many library calls into it (`read()`, `write()`, `time()`, etc.). Kernels are unusual in that they have always been designed for a type of concurrency. DOS is simple and allows no concurrent calls. If your program blocks while reading from disk, then everything waits. Multitasking systems, on the other hand, have always allowed blocking system calls to execute concurrently. The calls would get to a certain point (say when `read()` actually issues the disk request), save their own state, and then go to sleep on their own. This technique was non-pre-emptive, and it did not allow for parallelism. Code paths between context switching points can be very long, so few systems claimed any time of realtime behavior.

In the first case in Figure 12–1 (which is like SunOS 4.1.3 and most early operating systems), only one process can be in executing a system call at any one time. In the second case, locks are put around each major section of code in the kernel, so several processes can be executing system calls, as long as the calls are to different portions of the kernel. In the third case (like most current systems), the granularity of the locks has been reduced to the point that many threads can be executing the same system calls, so long as they don't use exactly the same structures.

Now, if you take these diagrams and substitute "processor" for "process," you will get a slightly different picture, but the results will be largely the same. If you can execute several things concurrently, with preemptive context switching, then you can execute them in parallel. A slightly different, but perfectly valid, way of looking at this is to consider it in terms of critical sections. In the "no concurrency" case, the critical section is very large—it's the whole kernel. In the "more concurrency" case, there are lots of little critical sections.

Symmetric Multiprocessing

SMP merely means that all processors are created equal and endowed by their designers with certain inalienable functionalities. Among these functionalities are shared memory, the ability to run kernel code, and the processing of interrupts. The ability of more than one CPU to run kernel code simultaneously is merely an issue of concurrency—an important issue, of course, but not a defining one.

All of the OSs discussed here were designed to run on uniprocessor systems and tightly coupled, shared memory multiprocessors. The kernel assumes that all processors are equivalent. Processors run kernel threads from the queue of runnable kernel threads (just as in user code). If a particular multiprocessor implementation places an asymmetric load on the processors (e.g., if interrupts are all directed to a single CPU), the kernel will nonetheless schedule threads to processors as if they were equivalent, not taking this asymmetry into account.

Are Libraries Safe?

Just because you write perfectly safe code that will run in a multithreaded environment with no problems doesn't mean that everyone else can. What would happen if you wrote a wonderful MT program, but then called a library routine that used a bunch of global data and didn't lock it? You'd lose. So, you must be certain that if you call a routine from multiple threads, it's *MT safe*. MT safe means that a function must lock any shared data it uses, it must use the correct definition of `errno`, and it must only call other MT safe functions.

Well, even programmers with the best of intentions find themselves with conflicting goals. "Make it fast," "Retain UNIX semantics," and "Make it MT safe" don't always agree. Some routines in some libraries will not be MT safe. It's a fact of life, and you have to deal with it. The manual page for each library call should indicate its level of "MT safeness." (Not all the documentation for all the systems are quite there yet. Ask your vendor.)

Libraries themselves are not safe or unsafe, per se. The *functions* in them are. Just to confuse things, there are libraries that contain some functions that are safe and some functions that aren't safe. Every time you use a function, you must make sure it's MT safe.

Some functions (e.g., `malloc()` and `printf()`) use global data structures internally. They need to lock the use of that data to become thread-safe. And that's exactly what they do. When a thread calls either `malloc()` or `free()`, it must acquire the lock first.

```
void *malloc(int size)
{pthread_mutex_t m = PTHREAD_MUTEX_INITIALIZER;

    pthread_mutex_lock(&m);
    ...
    pthread_mutex_unlock(&m);
    return(pointer);
}
```

Code Example 12–1:   *Making* `malloc()` *MT safe with a Mutex*

There are also functions that are defined to return global data. The function `ctime()`, for example, puts its data into a static string. There is no way to make this MT safe while retaining its semantics. (Even if we put a lock around the call, as soon as it returns and you try to use the data, some other thread can sneak in and change it. It's like the `errno` problem.) In this case, a new library call was written: `ctime_r()`, which operates just like `ctime()`, save that you must allocate a string to pass along with the call.[1] The results will be stored in this string. This is probably how

---

[1]A different solution would be to make that data thread-specific, which is exactly what Win32 does. Unfortunately, TSD would slow some functions significantly, and it would change the semantics, strictly speaking.

ctime() should have been defined in the beginning, but it's too late to change it now (too many programs depend upon its current behavior).

```
char *ctime(const time_t *clock)
{static char s[SIZE];

    ... Place the date string into s ...
    return(s);
}



char *ctime_r(const time_t *clock, char *s, int buflen)
{
    ... Place the date string into s ...
    return(s);
}
```

Code Example 12–2:   *The Unsafe* ctime() *and the MT safe* ctime_r()

Next there are a few functions that simply ran too slowly in their threaded version. The function getc(), for example, was actually implemented as a little macro. It ran very fast because it didn't even have to make a subroutine call. When the system programmers made it MT safe, they had to put a mutex lock around every call, and getc() became painfully slow. So, for non-threaded programs the original version of getc() is used. For threaded programs, the slower MT safe version is substituted in the header file. And for those MT programs where you plan to use the file descriptor from only one thread (or do the locking yourself), the original version of getc() is available under the name getc_unlocked(). (Note that we are locking the use of the particular file descriptor, not getc() itself.)

```
#ifdef (defined(_REENTRANT) || _POSIX_C_SOURCE >= 199506L)

extern int getc(FILE *);

#define getc_unlocked(p)(--(p)->_cnt < 0 \
                ? __filbuf(p) \
                : (int)*(p)->_ptr++)
#else /* _REENTRANT */

#define getc(p)(--(p)->_cnt < 0 ? __filbuf(p) : (int)*(p)->_ptr++)
```

Code Example 12–3:   *Definition of* getc() *(from* stdio.h*)*

```
#endif /* _REENTRANT */


/* Approximate implementation of MT safe getc() */
int getc(FILE *p)
{pthread_mutex_t *m = _get_lock(p);

    pthread_mutex_lock(m);
    c = (--(p)->_cnt < 0 ? __filbuf(p) : (int)*(p)->_ptr++)
    pthread_mutex_unlock(m);
    return(c);
}
```

Code Example 12–3: *Definition of* `getc()` *(from* `stdio.h`*)*

The calls `read()` and `write()` are technically MT safe, inasmuch as you can call them from multiple threads and get correct results. Unfortunately, they both move a pointer associated with the file descriptor. You'd have to keep track of that pointer yourself. In practice, if you perform concurrent operations from different threads on the same file descriptor, you're likely to get very confused. For this reason, there is a pair of calls (Figure 12–2): `pread()`[2] and `pwrite()`, which operate exactly the same way, except that you have to pass an explicit file position pointer along with them. Although not part of the Pthreads, these calls are part of the pending UNIX98 and can be found on many platforms (Solaris, HP-UX, Digital UNIX).

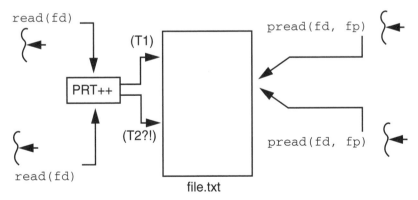

Figure 12–2 *Using* `pread()` *and* `pwrite()` *to Keep Track of the File Pointer*

---

[2]"Parallel read" and "parallel write." Why not `read_r()`? Well...

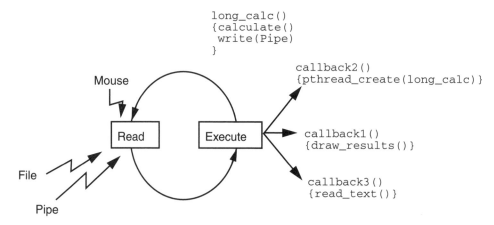

Figure 12–3   *Threads Using Pipe Callbacks with the Window Toolkit*

XView™ and CDE Motif are two of the most important libraries that are not MT safe.[3] The amount of global state associated with the windows, the widgets, etc., made it difficult to sanitize. Because they are designed around the concept of having an "event loop" waiting for window events, the only way to use them in an MT program is to execute all window calls from one thread. You can then have the event loop dispatch work to other threads that it will subsequently collect for display.

As the window toolkit thread will be in the event loop all the time (Figure 12–3), the only way for a thread to communicate with it is either (a) to pretend to send an X event, which will cause the event loop to run the callback for that particular event (see XCreateEvent() in an X programming manual), or (b) to open a pipe down which the worker thread will send notification, also causing the event loop to run the callback for that pipe.

Code Example 12–4 is from the program ThreadWin (see *Threads and Windows* on page 298) and shows callbacks being added for the buttons and the pipe, the function that runs when you push a button (which just creates a thread and returns), the work function (which does its work, then writes to the pipe), and the display function (which is run when the pipe is written to).

---

[3]The CDE 2.1 release is scheduled to be MT safe and will begin appearing in systems in late 1997.

```
main()
{
 ... initialize stuff ...
 pipe(msg);                                  /* Open a pipe */

/* Add callbacks for the pipe and the buttons */
 XtAppAddInput(app, msg[READ], XtInputReadMask, WorkComplete, 0);
 XtAddCallback(button[i], XmNactivateCallback, ButtonPushed, MT);
 XtMainLoop();/* Remain in the event loop forever */
}


DoWork(void *arg)
{
 ... do work ...
 write(message[WRITE], &w, sizeof(w)
 pthread_exit(NULL);
}


ButtonPushed(Widget w, XtPointer MT)
{
 pthread_create(&tid, &pt_attr, DoWork, w);
}


WorkComplete()
{
 read(msg[READ], &w, sizeof(w));
 ... redisplay whatever ...
}
```

Code Example 12–4: *Threads Using Pipe Callbacks with the Window Toolkit*

As XView is not one of the toolkits of the future, Sun has no plans to ever make it MT safe. The future of X Window System™ toolkits is CDE™ Motif, and these libraries will be made MT safe, presumably in the near future.

On top of all these details, there's the question of whether a library contains calls that are even consistent with an MT environment. Remember errno? And how there is a #define to turn it into a call to a distinguished TSD value? Well, it would be a disaster if some library were used in an MT program that didn't know about this trick. Even if it were only called from one thread, it would still be incorrect. This and several similar #define calls are enabled by a flag to the compiler.[4] All libraries that will be used in an MT program *must* be compiled with this flag.

```
#if (defined(_REENTRANT) || _POSIX_C_SOURCE >= 199506L)
extern int *___errno();
#define errno (*(___errno()))
#else
extern int errno;
#endif/* defined(_REENTRANT) || _POSIX_C_SOURCE >= 199506L */
```

Code Example 12–5: *The Actual Definition of* `errno` *in* `errno.h` *(Solaris)*

There is a clever hack (Solaris) that allows you to use a library compiled non-reentrant. By defining the location of the main thread's TSD `errno` to be the same as the global location for `errno`, you can safely use calls to these "MT Illegal" libraries from the main thread only.

Whew! That gives us five categories for library calls:

Table 12.1   *Categories of MT Library Calls*

Category	Meaning
MT safe	A function may be called concurrently from different threads.
MT hot	An MT-safe function that is also "fast" (perhaps it spawns threads; perhaps it uses no global data, perhaps it just uses a tiny bit of global data, reducing locking contention). (Marketing loves this name!)
MT unsafe	A function that is legal in an MT program but cannot be called concurrently.
Alternative	A function that is MT unsafe, but there is an MT-safe equivalent function that you can use (e.g., `ctime_r()`)
MT illegal	A function that wasn't compiled with the reentrant flag and may be called only from the main thread.

Of these, only the terms MT safe and MT unsafe are ever used in the man pages.[5]

---

[4]The flag is `_REENTRANT` for UI threads and earlier POSIX drafts (e.g., DCE threads), and `POSIX_C_SOURCE>=199506L` for POSIX (June 1995 is the date of Pthreads ratification).

[5]In Solaris 2.4 and 2.5 you will see a distinction made between "Safe" and "MT safe." You may treat them as being synonymous.

Stub Functions in libc

Some library functions, such as printf() and malloc(), need local mutexes to protect their internal data structures and other resources. This is all fine and well, but it means that all of these functions need the threads functions defined. If you're linking in libpthread.so anyway, that's not a problem. But what about all those primitive, uncouth single threaded programs out there? Do they have to use a different version of libc? Do they have to link in threads?

Neither! There are several different tricks used to solve this problem on the different OSs, all of which have the same consequences. In Solaris' libc.so, there are stub functions for mutexes and condition variables. These functions do nothing (they just return –1) and will be overridden if libpthread.so is linked in. This way printf() will use the real definition for mutexes in multithreaded programs and the stub version in single threaded programs. This is also why libpthread.so must be linked in after libc.so. (Other OSs accomplish the same thing by different methods.)

UI threads worked in a similar fashion, save that all of the thread functions had stubs. So what do you do if you want to include a call to pthread_create() (which has no stub) in a library that must be linkable non-threaded? First you should think carefully about whether or not you really want to do this. Then....

Use a new Solaris[6] pragma, weak. This pragma gives a symbol a value of zero while allowing it to be used as a function. It will be overridden if the symbol is defined by another library at run time. Thus you can write this code:

```
#pragma weak pthread_create

if (pthread_create == 0)
    do_work();                              /* No threads! */
else
    pthread_create(&tid, NULL, do_work, NULL);/* Threads! */
```

Code Example 12–6: *Using a Pragma for Undefined Functions*

---

[6]Other systems have other methods of dealing with the same problem.

New Semantics for System Calls

Several of the UNIX system calls have new semantics when used in a multithreaded program. The choices of how to handle these new semantics are not uniform between early POSIX drafts (e.g., DCE), UI, and POSIX, although in any realistically normal program, the differences will not be noticed.

Forking New Processes

According to the old definition of `fork()`, the kernel is to duplicate the entire process completely. With threads, the question comes up, "Should it duplicate all of the threads and LWPs?" The most common usage of `fork()` is to follow it immediately with a call to `exec()`. In that case, all the effort to duplicate the threads and LWPs would be wasted. So, there are two possible ways of defining `fork()`. In *fork1* semantics, only the calling thread is duplicated. In *forkall* semantics, all threads and LWPs are duplicated. POSIX chose to define `fork()` (and all the variants) to have fork1 semantics. UI threads chose forkall semantics.

Should you use `fork()` and not immediately call `exec()`, you should be cautious about touching any locks that might be held by threads that do not exist in the child process. It would be easy to arrive at a deadlock. Even just calling `printf()` from the child can cause a deadlock. So, if you're doing this stuff, be very, very careful!

Fork Safety and `pthread_atfork()`

POSIX defines a function intended to help with the deadlock-in-the-child problem. The function `pthread_atfork()` will place three functions on three stacks to be called when a thread calls `fork()`. The first function is called just before `fork()` takes place. The second is run in the parent after the fork completes, the third is run in the child. The idea is that the prepare function can lock all necessary locks so that no other thread can get them. Once forked, the locks are then released in the parent and child.

This could be done by hand, writing all the code in-line with the call to `fork()`, but it's nicer to have it separated out. This way different modules can place their own atfork handlers onto the stack so that their functions can be fork-safe. The prepare handlers are called off the top of the stack, Last-in, First-out. This order will be important if there are interactions between the different modules. The after-fork functions are called in FIFO order, though this doesn't make any difference.

In order to be able to do fancy things in the child before exec'ing a new program (or instead of), you have to ensure that all locks that the child will ever want are controlled in an atfork fashion. Any functions that use locks that are not controlled must not be called from the child.

So, for example, `printf()` has a private lock that is not controlled. The Sun library writers could have added an `atfork()` call for this lock, but they didn't. So `printf()` is not fork-safe in Solaris 2.5. You must not call it from a child process in a multithreaded program. If you do, it will deadlock every now and then (try it!). Being a race condition, you may safely assume that such a program will pass all SQA and release engineering tests, only to deadlock the first time your most important customer uses it.

In addition to that little problem, it's also the case that POSIX defines `fork()` in such a way that it isn't even legal to call anything except async-safe functions in the child! (This is presumably a minor error in the updating of the POSIX spec and should soon be fixed.) The long and the short of this matter is that you, the programmer, are fully responsible for this issue and need to work with your vendor.

Practically speaking, the easiest way to handle this case is to have the forking thread wait for all the other threads to arrive at a known, fork-safe location, and then call `fork()`. A trio of functions, our "help functions" library, do exactly this, `wait_for_others()`, `wait_for_forker()`, and `awake_others()`.

The best answer to all of these issues above is "Don't do that!" If the child process calls `exec()` immediately, there are no deadlock issues.

Executing a New Program

The call `exec()` does exactly what it did before—it deletes the entire memory mapping for the calling process and replaces it with one appropriate for the new program. A program with multiple threads that calls `exec()` will have all of those threads (and any LWPs) terminated, and the only thing left will be the new program.

Are Libraries Safe?

There are four categories in which library functions may or may not be safe (see Table 12.2). The requirements for being defined as safe in each of the four categories are similar, but distinct. A function can be in any combination of these categories. If the manual pages for all library functions were complete, they would list the status of each function in all five categories. Currently the only functions listed are signal safety and MT safety.

Table 12.2 *Safety Categories of Library Calls*

Category	Meaning
MT safe	A function that may be called concurrently from different threads.
Signal Safe (Async Safe)	A function that may be called from signal handlers. (It may just block out all signals temporarily.)
Asynchronous Cancellation Safe	A function that may be running when an asynchronous cancellation request arrives. (It may just disable cancellation temporarily.)
Fork Safe	A function that may be called from the child process after a fork. This is actually identical to "Signal Safe."

Threads Debugger Interface

If you are not involved in writing a debugger or some other related tool for threads, then this section is not interesting. You will never use any of this information in an end-user MT program. You may be interested in knowing that it exists, however. This is implementation-specific; there is no POSIX standard for a debugging interface.

Basically, the debugging library (`libthread_db.so`, for Solaris; `libthreaddebug.so` for Digital UNIX, etc.) provides an interface to the internals of the threads library. With it you can do all sorts of things that you can't do otherwise, such as look at the scheduling queues, lists of extant threads, synchronization variable sleep queues, TSD data arrays, and current LWP lists and their internal states. You can also "reach in" and alter these things directly, look at and change the individual thread's stack, etc. The library provides all the power necessary to implement a debugger, a garbage collector, or other kinds of tools.

Again: Do not even *think* of writing a "normal" MT program that depends upon anything in this library. Use the standard API for everything.

Mixing Solaris Pthreads and UI Threads

It is legal to write a program that uses APIs from both libraries. It is certainly not anything you should do voluntarily. Read the manual pages very carefully if you do. There are going to be different semantics for some library calls. For example, SIGALRM is sent to the LWP under UI threads, not like the process in POSIX.

The one place where you may find yourself mixing the two libraries is when you write a Pthreads program and link in a library written in UI threads (say, libc.so). The good news here is that the two libraries actually call the same underlying functions. This means that you can safely link in UI libraries and everything will just work.

Comparisons of Different Implementations

We now touch on an issue that is slightly sensitive. Comparisons of different implementations are not difficult to do, but they are difficult to do 100 percent correctly and without bias. We contacted each of the different vendors and asked them about their current status and their plans. There are enough things that happen quickly enough that we might be out of date already. Consider this list to be something to check out when porting, not as the gospel truth.

Table 12.3 *Comparison of Different Operating Systems (July '97)*

Feature	Solaris 2.5	Linux Threads 0.6	OS/2	NT 4.0	Digital UNIX 4.0D	HP-UX 10.30	IRIX 6.2	AIX 4.1 AS400
Multithreaded Kernel	Yes	Yes	Yes	Yes	Yes	Yes	Yes	Yes
SMP Support	Yes	Yes	Yes	Yes	Yes	Yes	Yes	Yes
User Threads Libraries Bundled?	Yes	Yes	Yes	Yes	Yes	Yes	Yes	Yes

Table 12.3 *Comparison of Different Operating Systems (cont.) (July '97)*

Feature	Solaris 2.5	Linux Threads 0.6	OS/2	NT 4.0	Digital UNIX 4.0D	HP-UX 10.30	IRIX 6.2	AIX 4.1 AS400
Current POSIX Library (draft level)	Yes Full	Yes Full	Option (4)	Free-ware	Yes Full	Yes Full	Yes Full	Yes Full
Architecture	M:M	1:1	1:1	1:1	M:M	M:M	M:M	M:M
Automatic Threading Compilers	FTN C Ada	No	No	No	FTN C Ada	No	FTN C Ada	No
All Libraries MT Legal?	All	Some	All	All	Most	?	?	?
Debugger Interface Public?	Yes	No	?	?	Yes	?	?	?

Architecture refers to the scheduling model (see *Different Models of Kernel Scheduling* on page 62), where M:M is Many-to-Many, M:1 is Many-to-One, and 1:1 is One-to-One.

The major point of this chart is not that one vendor is so much better than any other, but rather that all major vendors are actively working on some sort of threads library, and all the libraries are based on the same paradigm. In spite of the differences we have noted throughout this book, all the libraries are actually very similar, and knowing how to write a program in one gives you just about everything you need to write in another.

Summary

Many library functions are not MT safe and several different techniques are used in dealing with this, some by POSIX, some by individual vendors. Stub functions allow a library that uses locks to operate unchanged in a non-threaded environment. Forking new processes has a set of MT safety issues surrounding it.

13

Design

In which we explore some designs for programs and library functions. Making both programs and individual functions more concurrent is a major issue in the design of these functions. We look at a variety of code examples and the trade-offs between them.

Making Libraries Safe and Hot

Now that we've discussed the grand generalities of what's possible, let's move to the other extreme and take a look at some of the specific programming issues that MT programs come up against and how they can be dealt with. We'll look at the issues of designing and working with libraries—the vendor's libraries, third party libraries, and your own libraries—how they can be written to be both correct and efficient. *By far, the most important design issue is simplicity.* Debugging multi-threaded programs is difficult and the current tools are not that good (because none of us have figured out how to build better tools!), so this is a major issue.

Often there are simple, obvious methods of making functions MT-safe. Sometimes these methods work perfectly, but sometimes they introduce contention between different threads calling those functions. The job of the library writer is to analyze those situations and make things fast.

We can divide functions into a number of categories:

Trivial Library Functions

A great number of functions are trivially safe. Functions like `sin()` have no need to write any shared data and can be used exactly as first implemented thirty years ago.

Another set of functions has very little shared state and can be made thread-safe simply by surrounding the use of global data with a lock. The pseudo random number generator, `rand()` is a very small, fast function that takes about 1µs on an SS10/40. It uses a seed value that it changes on each call. By protecting that seed, the function can be made safe:

```
rand_1()
{static unsigned int seed;
 static pthread_mutex_t m = PTHREAD_MUTEX_INITIALIZER;
 int value;

 pthread_mutex_lock(&m);
 value = _rand(&seed);     /* Calculate new value, update seed */
 pthread_mutex_unlock(&m);
 return(value);
}
```

Code Example 13–1: *Simple MT-Safe Implementation of* `rand()`*, Version 1*

This new version of rand() is safe and now runs about 1µs slower due to the mutex. For most programs, this is fine.

Functions that Maintain State Across Invocations

There are cases where you might wish a function to set values in one invocation and use those same values in another invocation, but don't want those values shared by different threads. When you call strtok(), for example, you first pass it a string to be parsed, and it returns the pointer to the start of the first token in that string. When you call it a second time (with a NULL argument), it returns a pointer to the start of the second token, etc.

It is highly unlikely that you would want thread 1 to get the first token in a string, and thread 2 to get the second, although this is exactly what strtok() will do.

Two solutions propose themselves. One is to write a new function, strtok_r(), which takes an extra argument that the programmer uses to maintain state explicitly. This is a good technique because the programmer can explicitly choose how to use the arguments to best advantage. But at the same time, it puts an additional burden on the programmer who must keep track of those arguments, passing them from function to function as required.

The second solution is to use thread specific data and have strtok() maintain separate state for each thread (this is what Win32 does). The advantages to this solution are consistency (no code changes required) and simplicity at the cost of some efficiency.

We'll use rand() again to illustrate these points. Normally, a function like rand() will be used only occasionally in a program, and there will be very little contention for its critical section (which is very short anyway). However, should your program happen to call rand() a great deal, such as in a Monte Carlo simulation, you may experience extensive contention. By keeping the seed as thread specific data, this limitation can be avoided.

With the rand_2() definition, there is no contention for a critical section (as there is none). However, even rand_2() is two times slower than rand(). One advantage of rand_1() and rand_2() is that they

don't change the interface of rand(), and existing libraries that use
rand() don't need to be changed.[1]

```
int rand_2()
{unsigned int *seedp;
 int value;

 seedp = (int *) pthread_getspecific(rand_key);
 value = _rand(seedp);       /* Calculate new value, update seed */
 return(value);
}
```

Code Example 13–2:   *Implementing* rand() *with TSD, Version 2*

POSIX chose to retain the old, fast, MT-unsafe definition of
rand(), while defining a new, (also) fast, safe version, rand_r(). This
leaves programmers with the following options:

1. For maximum performance, use rand_r() and just deal
   with the confusion of tracking the use of the seed throughout
   the code. (If you only call it from one function, this is no
   problem at all.)

2. For maximum simplicity, implement rand_1() or
   rand_2().

3. For the best of both, combine 1 and 2 and design your
   program with this issue in mind.

Making malloc() More Concurrent

The implementation of malloc() on Solaris 2.5 is quite simple
(Figure 13–1). There's one global lock that protects the entire heap.
When a thread calls either malloc() or free() it must hold that
lock before doing the work. It's a simple, effective design that works fine
in most programs. When you have numerous threads calling
malloc() often, then you can get into a performance problem. These
two functions take some time to execute and you can experience

---

[1]The semantics of rand_2() are different than rand(), inasmuch as pseudo random number
generators *are* deterministic, and their results *are* repeatable when a known seed value is used. Both rand()
and rand_1() would be non-deterministic, as thread scheduling is non-deterministic. This is unlikely ever
to be a problem.

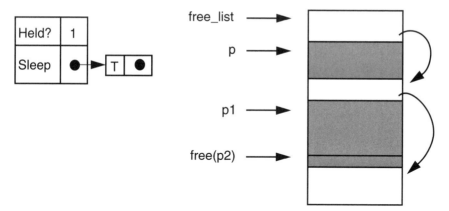

Figure 13–1 *Current Solaris Implementation of* `malloc()`

contention for that one lock. Let's consider some other possible designs. Keep in mind that we are not going to be changing the definition of `malloc()`, nor will we change the API. We are only going to change the implementation underneath.

Using Thread-Specific Data to Make `malloc()` More Concurrent

When used sparingly, a simple mutex works fine. But when called very often, this can suffer from excessive contention. The TSD solution is a possibility, but it introduces some problems of its own.

What if T2 mallocs some storage and T1 frees it? How does T1 arrange to return that memory to the correct free list? (Because `free()` will glue adjacent pieces of freed memory together into a single large piece, the `free()` must be called with the original malloc area, see Figure 13–2.) If T2 exits, who takes care of its malloc area? If an application creates large numbers of threads but seldom uses `malloc()`, it will be creating excessive numbers of malloc areas.

So this is possible, but not very attractive. One of the fellows in our group actually implemented this for a customer with a very specific problem. It worked well, but it was not at all generalizable.

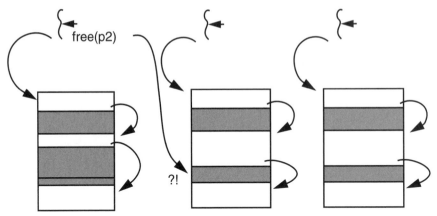

Figure 13–2   *Threads with Individual TSD* `malloc()` *areas.*

Using Other Methods to Make `malloc()` More Concurrent

It is possible to assign a mutex to protect each individual piece of free storage and have threads skip over those areas when locked. Although possible, this technique suffers from excessive complexity. It also suffers from excessively fine-grained locking. (If `malloc()` has to lock a mutex for every single node in the free list, it could easily spend more time doing the locking than looking for the memory. We do exactly this in *One Local Lock* on page 220.)

A different approach to this problem is to build a static array of malloc areas to be shared by all threads (Figure 13–3). Now a thread calling `malloc()` can check for an unlocked malloc area by calling `pthread_mutex_trylock()` on the area's mutex. If held, the thread will simply check the next area. The probability of more than a few malloc areas being locked is vanishingly small for any vaguely normal program. This version of `malloc()` would be safe, fairly fast, and relatively simple.

Storage being freed must still be replaced into its area of origin, but this is a manageable problem. The freeing thread could simply block. It could place the pointer to be freed onto a list for that area, and let the thread holding the lock take care of doing the free on its way out. We could dedicate a special thread to the task of returning freed storage to its proper location.

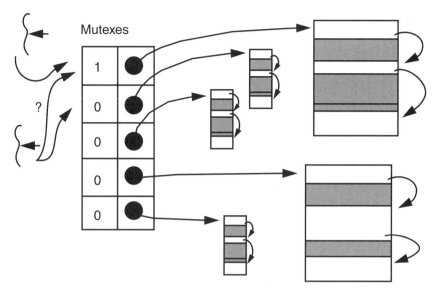

Figure 13–3   *Threads Using an Array of* `malloc()` *Areas.*

These are a few of the most common problems that we have seen. There are two points worthy of note: 1) There are many viable solutions to every problem; 2) no one solution is optimal for all aspects of a problem. Each of the three versions of `malloc()` is fastest in some situation.

As of the writing of this book, several people were working on different variations of this last solution. We will probably see them in later operating system releases by the different vendors.

Manipulating Lists

Now we are going to take a look at some designs for a program that adds, removes, and searches for entries on a singly linked list (Figure 13–4). The program creates a list of people with their salaries. One set of threads is going to search down that list, looking for friends of Bil's, and give those people raises. Another set of threads is going to search down the list looking for people whom Dan detests, and remove those people from the list. There may be some overlap of Bil's friends and Dan's enemies.

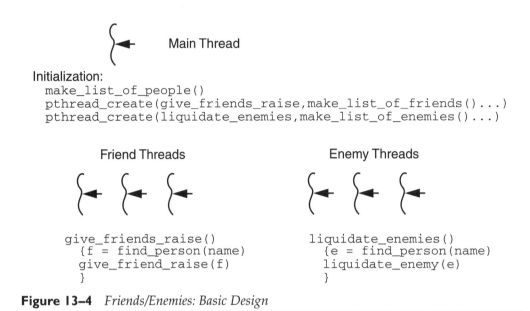

Initialization:
```
make_list_of_people()
pthread_create(give_friends_raise,make_list_of_friends()...)
pthread_create(liquidate_enemies,make_list_of_enemies()...)
```

Friend Threads   **Enemy Threads**

```
give_friends_raise()            liquidate_enemies()
  {f = find_person(name)          {e = find_person(name)
  give_friend_raise(f)            liquidate_enemy(e)
  }                               }
```

Figure 13–4   *Friends/Enemies: Basic Design*

In order to make the program a bit more interesting (and emphasize certain issues), we will associate a delay time with each raise and liquidation. These delays may represent the time to write to disk or to do additional computation. For this purpose we'll make a call to `nanosleep()`. On Solaris, the minimum sleep time is 10ms (it's based on the system clock), which is typical for most OSs. The main question we'll be asking is, "For a given configuration of CPUs, delay times, list length, and number of threads giving raises and performing deletions, which design is best?" For different configurations we'll get different answers.

Basic Design

The complete code for all examples is available on the web (see *Code Examples* on page 314). Here we show the basic outline:

A few notes about the program. The function `find_person(char *name)` is to be used by both the friends and enemies threads; hence it will return a pointer to the *previous* element of the people list (the liquidate function needs access to the previous person in order to remove a person from the list). The appropriate element of the list must remain locked when `find_person()` returns, and which lock is appropriate will change with the different designs. It is

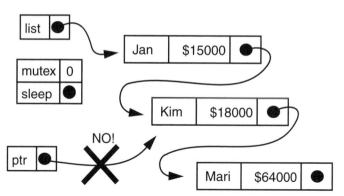

Figure 13–5 *Friends/Enemies: Global Mutex Lock*

possible to search for someone who has been liquidated, so NULL is a possible return value. We'll have to be careful.

Single, Global Mutex

This is by far the simplest design. All that is necessary is to lock the mutex before starting a search and release it after the thread is finished with liquidation or giving raises. This is the extreme case of *course grain locking*. It has very little overhead and has the best performance when there is only one thread or when the delay times are zero. Once the delay times go up and more threads are added, the wall clock performance of this design goes to pot. It will not get any advantage from using multiple CPUs either.

There are a couple of things worth noting. The mutex protects the entire list—every element on it, all of the pointers, and the data inside (name and salary). It is not legal for a thread to hold a pointer to any element of the list if it does not hold the mutex. (It would be possible that some other thread could remove that element from the list, free the storage, and then reallocate that same storage for a completely different purpose, see Figure 13–5.) *Don't do that!*

One other thing that you may notice if you run this code is an odd tendency for one thread to get the mutex and then keep it. Typically one thread will get the lock and execute a dozen or more iterations of its loop before another thread ever runs its loop at all. Often, one thread will run to completion before any other thread even starts! Why?

```
void *give_friends_raise(void *arg)
{person_t *p, *friends = (person_t *) arg;

  while(friends != NULL)
    {pthread_mutex_lock(&people_lock);
     p = find_person(friends->name);
     give_raise(p);
     pthread_mutex_unlock(&people_lock);
     friends = friends->next;
   }
  sem_post(&barrier);
}
```

Code Example 13–3: *give_friends_raise() (list_global_lock.c)*

In Code Example 13–3, we see the central function that runs down a list of friends, looking them up and giving them raises. It locks the mutex, does all its work, then unlocks the mutex. It gets the next friend off the list of friends and starts all over again. There are no more than a few dozen instructions between the time it unlocks the mutex and locks it again! The probability of another thread getting in there fast enough to get the mutex is quite low. Using a FIFO mutex in this code would make it much fairer. And slightly slower.

Global RWLock with Global Mutex to Protect Salaries

Version two of the program uses a Readers/Writer lock to protect the list and a mutex to protect the salaries. This way any number of threads can run down the list, at the same time searching for people to receive raises. Once found, we need to protect the salary data while we update it. We add the Salary_Lock for this purpose. Clearly we could not update the salary if we only held a read lock. When a thread wishes to remove one of Dan's enemies from the list, that thread must hold a writer lock while it searches down the list and removes the offending element (see Figure 13–6).

It's important for us to think very carefully about what each lock is protecting. The RWlock protects the list structures and the pointers. It does not protect the salaries. Surprisingly, the performance of this code is not much better than that of the previous code! Inspecting the code closely, you should realize that very little time is spent actually searching

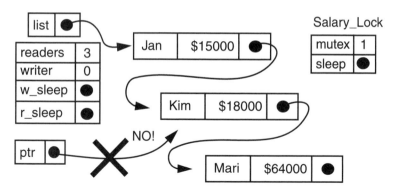

Figure 13–6   *Friends/Enemies: Global RWlock and Salary Lock*

down the list (about 1µs per element). It is the contention for the salary lock when the delay is non-zero that takes all the time.

Once again, no thread may hold a pointer to any portion of the list unless it owns one of the locks.

Code Example 13–4 is the code that updates the salary of Bil's friends. The delay is inside of the critical section; thus while one thread is sleeping here, all the other threads must wait outside. Moving the delay outside would vastly increase the performance of the program. It wouldn't be terribly realistic to do so. As the delay represents a write to disk or some other operation on the salary, it really must be inside the critical section.

```
void give_raise(person_t *p)
{
  if (p != NULL)
    {pthread_mutex_lock(&salary_lock);
     pthread_np_rw_unlock(&people_lock);        /* Unlock here */
     p->next->salary++;
     delay(RAISE_DELAY, 0); /* If the delay is outside the lock? */
     pthread_mutex_unlock(&salary_lock);
    }
  else
    pthread_np_rw_unlock(&people_lock);         /* Unlock here */
}
```

Code Example 13–4:   *give_raise() (list_global_rw.c)*

Note that we release the RWLock as soon as we obtain the salary lock, allowing other threads to begin their searches. Even the liquidator threads

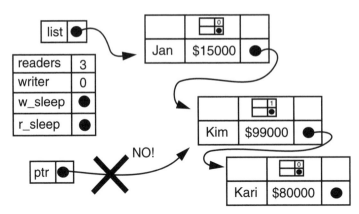

Figure 13–7   *Friends/Enemies: Global RWlock and Local Salary Lock*

are allowed to run while we're updating the salary! To make this work correctly, the function `liquidate_person()` must also lock the salary lock before it frees the storage (see Code Example 13–7 on page 224).

Global RWLock with Local Mutex to Protect Salaries

Version three of the program (Figure 13–7) uses a Readers/Writer lock to protect the list and a local mutex to protect individual salaries. This way any number of threads can run down the list searching for people to give raises to at the same time. Once found, we need to protect the individual salary data while we update it. Now we have overcome the major bottleneck of this program. Many threads may now update different salaries at the same time.

Once again, no thread may hold a pointer to any portion of the list unless it owns one of the locks. If it only holds a local salary lock, it may not do anything except access that one data item. As before, the liquidator must lock the local salary lock before freeing the element (Code Example 13–5 on page 219). It does not need to own that lock to *remove* the element from the list, as removal does not involve accessing the salary. It's when the structure is *freed* that the salary is affected. Once the element is removed from the list, we can release the RWlock.

The addition of the mutex to the structure increases its size. You could reduce memory requirements by allocating an array of global mutexes, each of which would protect a subset of the structures. A simple hash function would assign all structures located at 0 mod(N) to `global_salary_mutex[0]`, those located at 1 mod(N) to `global_salary_mutex[1]`, etc. This technique would also improve runtime due to the reduction in cache misses. (This is left as an exercise for the reader.)

In this code, the only points of contention are:

• Only one liquidator at a time may search.

• Only one thread at a time may give a raise to a given individual.

Something that you might consider at this point is: Why not allow multiple liquidators to search at the same time, then once they've found the object, convert the read lock into a write lock? We could modify the definition of RWlocks to allow this possibility; however it wouldn't work. We would have to ensure that only one thread ever wanted to make the conversion at a time, and as soon as it made that request, every other thread with a read lock would have to eventually release that lock without making a conversion request. In other words, it's possible to do, but it's so limited in functionality as to be nearly worthless.

For pretty much any program of this nature, design #3 will turn out to be the best. However, there are other possibilities.

```
void liquidate_person(person_t *p)
{person_t  *p1;

  if (p)
    {p1 = p->next;
     p->next = p1->next;
     thread_rw_unlock(&people_lock);

     pthread_mutex_lock(&(p1->salary_lock));
     pthread_mutex_unlock(&(p1->salary_lock));
     pthread_mutex_destroy(&(p1->salary_lock));
     free(p1->name);
     free(p1);
     delay(LIQUIDATE_DELAY, 0);
    }
  else
    thread_rw_unlock(&people_lock);
}
```

Code Example 13–5: *Removing an Element from the List*
(list_global_rw2.c)

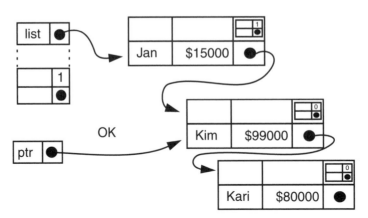

Figure 13–8 *Friends/Enemies with Only One Local Mutex Lock*

One Local Lock

What if we allocated one mutex per element to protect only one element? In Figure 13–8, each mutex protects a pointer and the structure to which the pointer points. (The global mutex protects only the global pointer and first structure.) With this design, multiple threads may search down the list at the same time, either to update a salary or to remove an element. Yes, multiple liquidator threads may search and destroy simultaneously! Unfortunately, as soon as one thread finds the element it is searching for, it will continue to hold the lock while it finishes its work. Other threads will quickly pile up behind it, waiting to acquire that mutex.

This design yields abysmal results for every combination of CPUs, threads, list length, delay times, etc.

It is illegal for a thread to hold a pointer to an element unless it holds the appropriate mutex. In this case, the appropriate mutex is local, so numerous threads may hold pointers to different elements. Note that the mutex in Jan's structure protects the "next" pointer and the following structure (Kim's).

To update Kim's salary, a thread will need to hold the mutex in Jan's structure, not the one in Kim's. To remove Kim from the list, once again the thread must hold the mutex in Jan's structure. To free Kim's structure, the thread must hold Kim's mutex. As soon as it has been removed from the list, Jan's mutex may be released. It will be impossible for any other thread to get a pointer to Kim.

Let's look at the searching routine (used by both liquidators and raisers). The basic loop is simple: look at each element, compare the name strings, return the previous pointer if found. What is interesting about this function is the order in which locks are acquired and released.

```
person_t *find_person(char *name)
{person_t *p = &people, *p1, *p2;

 pthread_mutex_lock(&(p->lock));
 p1 = p->next;
 while(p1 != NULL)
    {if (strcmp(p1->name, name) == 0)
       /* Found! Return previous, Still holding p->lock ! */
       return(p);
    pthread_mutex_lock(&(p1->lock));
    pthread_mutex_unlock(&(p->lock));
    p = p1;
    p1 = p->next;
  }
 pthread_mutex_unlock(&(p->lock));
 return(NULL); /* Couldn't find 'em!  Too bad. */
}
```

Code Example 13–6: *The Searching Code (`list_local_lock.c`)*

First we lock the global lock and compare our name to the first element (Jan). If this isn't it, we lock Jan's lock, release the global lock, and compare again. The locking/unlocking is being done in an overlapping fashion! (It's often called *chain locking*.) This makes it somewhat challenging to ensure that the correct locks are locked and unlocked in the correct order in all the different functions.

Two Local Locks

A superior version of the local lock design may be had by providing two local locks, one to protect the element and one to protect the salary. Now we have the advantage of allowing multiple liquidators to search down the list while not causing bottlenecks. The only points of contention occur when two threads wish to operate on the same element. There's nothing we can do about that.

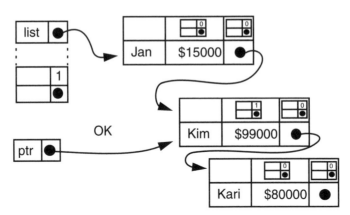

Figure 13–9 *Friends/Enemies: Two Local Locks*

That's the good news. The bad news is that it takes time to lock mutexes. It may well take more time to lock and unlock each mutex than it takes to do the comparison! In this code, it does. This version of the program, shown in Figure 13–9, is significantly slower than the RWlock version. Only if the time to execute a comparison were long, would this design give superior results.

Local RWLock with Local Mutex to Protect Salaries

Just for the sake of completeness, we'll consider one more design (Figure 13–10). By making the local lock be an RWlock, we can allow multiple threads to do comparisons on the same element at the same time. If comparisons took significant amounts of time, this could be a viable design. For our program, which does a simple string compare, this design proves to be the worst yet. It takes up much more space, adds more complexity, and is slower by a very significant amount.

We've now completed the journey from very course-grained locking to very fine-grained locking and come to the obvious conclusion. The best results are usually found in the middle, but the only way to know is to try.

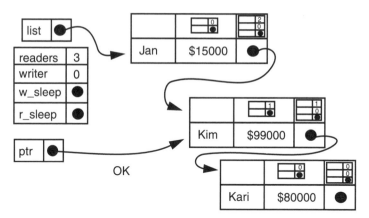

Figure 13–10   *Friends/Enemies: Local Lock and RWLock*

Program Design

There is a small number of high-level design strategies which have been discussed in several books (see *The Authors on the Net* on page 315). These names are not used completely uniformly. They are:

- Master/Slave: One thread does the main work of the program, creating other threads to help in some portion of the work.
- Client/Server (Thread per Request): One thread listens for requests, then creates a new thread to handle each request.
- Client/Server (Thread per Client): One thread listens for new clients to attach, then creates a new thread to handle each client. The thread is dedicated to its client, doing work only for that client.
- Producer/Consumer (aka *Work Queue* or *Workpile*): Some threads create work requests and put them on a queue. Other threads take the work requests off of the queue and execute them.
- Dogpile: Similar to the workpile, but instead of maintaining a queue, all the threads look for work directly.
- Pipeline: Each thread does some work on a task, then passes the partially completed task to the next thread.

In the discussion below, we will elaborate on each of the designs and include some sample code. All of the code will be based on a client/server program that takes in requests from a socket, processes them, and sends replies back out over the same socket file descriptor. The complete code for three versions of the program (Thread per Request, Producer/Consumer, and non-threaded) is on the web site.

Master/Slave

The master/slave design is the most obvious for many kinds of tasks. In its most elemental form, it will be implemented by a library and the programmer will not even be aware of there being multiple threads. A matrix multiply routine (see *Dakota Scientific Software* on page 240) may well spawn a set of threads to do the work, but all the programmer knows is that she called `matrix_multiply()`.

Client/Server (Thread per Request)

This is a master/slave design for client/server programs. The master thread will do the listening. In the fragment of the socket program shown as Code Example 13–7, each time a new request comes in from a client, the main thread spawns off a thread to handle that request. The main thread then returns to its `accept()` loop while the thread works on the request independently, exiting when it's done.

```
while(TRUE)
  {newsockfd = accept(sockfd, &cli_addr, &clilen);
   PTHREAD_CREATE(&tid, &thr_attr, process_request, newsockfd);
  }

void *process_request(void *arg)
{
 read(mysocfd, data, LENGTH);
 result = process_data(data);
 write(mysocfd, result, LENGTH);
 close(mysocfd);
 pthread_exit();
}
```

Code Example 13–7: *Master/Slave Socket Design*

While this design has some positive aspects to it, e.g., simplicity and directness, it also admits to some drawbacks. The cost of thread creation is not going to be significant unless the task itself is very short (< 10ms). Of more significance is that the programmer has no simple control over the number of threads running at any one time. Should there be a sudden spike in the number of requests, there will be an equal spike in the number of threads, causing performance degradation due to the excessive number of threads competing for the same locks, CPUs, virtual memory, and other resources. (Running this program on a fast 32-bit machine will crash the program when it runs out of virtual memory.)

Rewriting the program to limit the number of threads would be somewhat ugly, and there are better ways of handling the problem. This is probably not a good design for any program!

Producer/Consumer

In the producer/consumer model, the programmer can exert full control over the number of threads with very little effort. The threads may be created at startup time and then be left to wait for work to appear on the queue. Should some of the threads never run at all, there will be no great cost—probably immeasurable. Should there be too many incoming requests, they can be placed on the queue and handled when convenient.

```
for (i=0; i<N; i++)
   PTHREAD_CREATE(&tid, &thr_attr, process_request, NULL);
 ...
 while(TRUE)
   {newsockfd = accept(sockfd,  &cli_addr, &clilen);
    add_to_queue(newsockfd);
   }

void *process_request()
{
 ...
 while(TRUE)
  {socfd = get_from_queue();
   read(socfd, data, LENGTH);
   result = process_data(data);
   write(socfd, result, LENGTH);
   close(socfd);
  }
}
```

Code Example 13–8: *Producer/Consumer Socket Design*

An important aspect of the work queue is that you can allow the queue to grow to any length you deem appropriate. If your clients block, waiting for the results of query 1 before issuing query 2, then allowing the length of the queue to grow to the number of clients will assure you that requests will never be lost, and you can maintain peak efficiency.

If clients are able to issue unlimited overlapping requests, then you have no choice. At some point you must begin rejecting requests. However, as long as the average rate of incoming requests is below what your server can handle, then by allowing the queue to grow up to some modest limit, you can effectively buffer burst traffic while retaining peak efficiency. This is the general design of NFS.

Dogpile

The dogpile[2] (pigpile for those in the East) is the name for the same program as above, only that each thread waits to do an accept itself. There is no single producer thread that calls accept() and puts work onto the queue for other threads. All the threads take turns calling accept(), and then doing the work directly. In the steady state situation, there should be no difference in efficiency between the workpile and the dogpile. But where the work queue can neatly handle burst traffic at user level, the dogpile would expect the kernel to queue those requests for it—probably not a good thing.

```
for (i=0; i<N; i++)
    PTHREAD_CREATE(&tid, &thr_attr, process_request, NULL);

void *process_request()
{
  ...
  while(TRUE)
   {pthread_mutex_lock(&m);
    newsockfd = accept(sockfd,  &cli_addr, &clilen);
    pthread_mutex_unlock(&m);
```

Code Example 13–9: *Dogpile Design*

---

[2]This is the name of a favorite game for eight-year-old boys in California. We ran around in circles until somebody yelled "Dogpile on Bil," whereupon all the boys would pile on top of poor Bil. As soon as he had extricated himself, it would be his turn to yell.

```
        read(mysocfd, data, LENGTH);
        result = process_data(data);
        write(mysocfd, result, LENGTH);
        close(mysocfd);

    }
}
```

Code Example 13-9: *Dogpile Design*

Pipeline

The pipeline model is based directly on the same work model that is used in CPUs and on factory floors. Each processing element will do a certain amount of the job, and then pass the partially completed task on to the next element. Here the processing elements are threads of course, and each thread is going to do a portion of the task, then pass the partial results on to the next thread.

```
 PTHREAD_CREATE(&tid, &thr_attr, process_request_a, NULL);
 PTHREAD_CREATE(&tid, &thr_attr, process_request_b, NULL);

void *process_request_a()
{
 ...
 while(TRUE)
  {newsockfd = accept(sockfd, &cli_addr, &clilen)
   read(mysocfd, data, LENGTH);
   result_a = process_data_a(data);
   add_queue_b(result_a);
  }
}

void *process_request_b()
{
 ...
 while(TRUE)
  {result_a = get_from_queue_a();
   result_b = process_data_b(result_a);
   write(mysocfd, result_b, LENGTH);
   close(mysocfd);
  }
}
```

Code Example 13-10: *Pipeline Design*

We can certainly see where this model would be valuable for simulations where what you're simulating is a pipeline. For other situations, it's not so clear. In silicon and on factory floors, specialization is important. One section of a chip can only execute a single task (the instruction fetch unit can only fetch instructions, never decode them), and it takes time for a workman to put down a wrench and pick up a paint brush.

This is not so for threads. It is actually easier, faster, and the programming is simpler for one thread to execute an entire operation than to do a little work, package up the partial result and queue it for another thread. Although a number of programs that use this paradigm have been suggested, it is not clear to us that any of them are superior to using one of the other designs.

Client/Server (Thread per Client)

The final model is also somewhat questionable to us. In this model, each client will have a thread devoted to it, and that thread will remain inactive the vast majority of the time. The advantage of having a thread devoted to an individual client is that the thread can maintain state for that client implicitly by what's on the stack and in thread specific data. While this does save the programmer the effort of encapsulating that data, it's unclear that it's worth it. Nonetheless, a number of database vendors are interested in this model, and they do have some pretty clever folks there.

```
while(TRUE)
  {newsockfd = accept(sockfd, &cli_addr, &clilen);
    PTHREAD_CREATE(&tid, &thr_attr, process_requests, newsockfd);
  }

void *process_requests()
{
  ...
  while(TRUE)
   {read(mysocfd, data, LENGTH);
    if (done(data)) break;
    result = process_data(data);
    write(mysocfd, result, LENGTH);
   }
}
```

Code Example 13–11:   *Thread per Client Design*

We'll consider these last two as interesting, possible designs that need some practical fleshing out.

Summary

Numerous trade-offs exist in the creation of MT-safe and MT-hot libraries. No one locking design works best for all programs. How different threads will interact and how they will be created and exit are open questions. We offer a few insights and some examples. *The most important design issue is simplicity.*

14

Languages

In which the use of threads in various programming languages is considered and a few minor notes about special features and requirements are made. A number of public Pthreads libraries and some commercial products exist and are noted.

C

The basic interface to all of the libraries is ANSI C. Function prototypes are supplied for each of the functions, and both the constants and datatypes are defined in C.

C++

As far as threads are concerned, C++ adds only a few things to the picture. Some limit your programming slightly, some ease your programming burden slightly, and some simply reassure you that they aren't problems.

Thing one is the compiler. Some C++ compilers make assumptions about global data and use it in a non-thread-safe fashion. Such compilers cannot be used to compile MT programs at all. These are generally the older compilers (e.g., Sun's 1992 version of C++). The newer versions of those compilers (e.g., Sun's 1994 version and onwards) do produce thread-safe code. Obviously you cannot mix modules compiled with the older compiler with those from the newer. Ask your compiler vendor.

Thing two is the library. Some public and commercial libraries are not thread-safe; others are. There are no special issues here beyond what we've already covered. If the library is not specifically listed as being thread-safe, you must assume it is not.

Thing three concerns stack-allocated classes and their destructors. Obviously, when you exit from a function normally, the destructors will be run. Less obviously, when the thread exits, the destructors will also be run. This latter is a compiler-dependent issue and it is possible that some compilers don't ensure this, though the ones we're aware of do. So, if you call your thread-exit function (in OS/2, Win32, or POSIX) the destructors should run. If you cancel a thread, the destructors should also run. In Win32 and OS/2, the destructors will not run for terminated threads.

Thing four is C++ exception handling. Basically, everything works just fine as long as you don't use cancellation. Catch and throw blocks are pretty much independent of threads, so there are no issues there. For unhandled exceptions, it is possible for you to install thread-specific versions of `terminate()` and `unexpected()`, which will cause only the one thread to exit. (The default versions of these will exit the entire program.) Of course, if you are writing a robust program, you'd better not have any unhandled exceptions!

Thing five is the function prototype the thread create functions use. They all require a function that takes a single (`void *`) argument. The function may then cast that argument to anything you want. Both member functions and overloaded C++ functions need to know their argument type at compile time. Thus, you cannot pass such functions to the thread create function. No big deal. Just write a wrapper function taking a (`void *`) which then calls the function you actually want. Or use static functions.

Thing six concerns a few nice features of classes that allow you to build nice encapsulations of thread functions. The most important of these is the monitor (*Monitors* on page 113), where you create an instance of a monitor on the stack (which just locks a mutex), knowing that when that function exits, the class destructor will run (unlocking that mutex). The good thing about a monitor class is that you can never forget to unlock a mutex from complex code. Moreover, the generated code will be as fast as calling lock/unlock directly (assuming a sufficiently intelligent compiler!). The one limitation is that a monitor can't be used to do chained lock/unlocks.

Thing seven concerns mixing exception handling and cancellation in POSIX. Can you catch cancellation? No. What if you push a cleanup handler onto the stack and then throw an exception? Unless that exception ends up exiting the thread, the cleanup handler will not get called and your program will be in serious trouble. *Don't do that.* What if you throw an exception from inside a cleanup handler? What if you get cancelled while in `terminate()`? What if you have interaction between a stack-allocated destructor and a cleanup handler? *Don't do that!*

Once again, most of these things are not part of any standard. They're logical, they're the way the compilers we're aware of work, but they are not required. Ask your vendor.

Java

The paradigm of multithreading in Java is the same as in the other thread libraries—a new thread is created to run a function. That thread then runs independently, sharing access to all global data and resources. Synchronization methods are defined to coordinate thread interactions. When the final thread exits, the program also exits.

Overlaid on this is the object-oriented nature of Java. There is a class called "Thread" and an arbitrary number of thread objects can be instantiated from this class. Each thread runs independently sharing access to class-level data.

The major distinctions between Java's model and that of Pthreads, etc., is that threads are a more integral part of the Java virtual machine. The Java VM even has three threads of its own running at all times. Essentially, Java thread classes constitute a base part of the language. Beyond this, the implementation is distinct, being based on classes, and some of the details of the semantics are different.

Scheduling is handled by the Java VM which allows, but does not require, time-slicing. A portable program must, therefore, work correctly with or without it. Moreover, as Java is defined independently of any host OS threading model, Java does not require the existence of multiple LWPs. On some implementations (e.g., the first Solaris implementation), Java threads were unable to take advantage of either multiple processors, or overlapping, blocking I/O. Later releases of Java can do so. Thus Java programs are multithreaded more for the sake of programming clarity and simplicity than for any efficiency reasons.

Java defines two different ways of creating threads—both of which are essentially the same. The programmer subclasses a base thread class, and then specializes a run method. Instantiating a member of that subclass and calling its run method gets a thread up and going. The run method is defined to take zero arguments, so any necessary parameters must be passed to the thread object constructor, and saved there for when the thread starts running.

```
// The definition of the subclass MyThreads
class MyThread extends Thread
{public void run() {work(); } }

MyThread t1 = new MyThread();
...
t1.start(); // start() calls run() ...
```

Code Example 14–1: *Starting a New Thread in Java*

Java has two forms of synchronization, which, with enough effort, map directly onto the POSIX synchronization variables. Java monitors, defined by use of the keyword *synchronized,* encapsulate data and locking into a single form. The programmer calls a method to read or write the data, and the monitor class ensures that a lock is taken and released correctly. The lock itself is part of a specific Java object. By default, this object will be the class instance. Optionally, you may specify a different object to use. This makes simple programs easier to build, but it lacks the fine grain of control that some programmers have come to expect, making some things more difficult to do.[1]

In Java:

```
class Counter
{static int counter = 0;

 public synchronized int count(int i)
 {counter += i;
  return(counter);
 }
}



...
Counter c1 = new Counter();
c = c1.count(10);
```

Code Example 14–2:   *Using a Monitor in Java*

The second form of synchronization is the wait/notify construct which is Java's equivalent of condition variables. Defined only within the context of a monitor, this construct allows the programmer to define arbitrary synchronization methods. For example, counting semaphores (implemented in Code Example 14–3) can be used to create POSIX-style mutex locks.

In summary, Java's high-level thread constructs are designed to allow simple programs to be built easily and safely. In this they succeed. Unfortunately, the limitations of these constructs also make the building of complex programs less efficient and slightly more difficult.

---

[1]In their very fine book, *Java Threads*, one of the first things Scott Oaks and Henry Wong do is to violate the synchronization design by implementing (rather inefficient) mutex locks! Later they build a scheduler. One hopes that the language will address these problems in a later release.

Nonetheless, Java threads are Turing-equivalent to Pthreads, and anything you can do with one model, you can do with the other.

```
class Semaphore
{static int value = 0;

 public synchronized void semphore_wait()
    {while (value == 0) wait();
     value--;
    }

 public synchronized void semphore_post()
    {value++;
     notify();
    }
}
```

Code Example 14–3: *Creating a Semaphore in Java*

Fortran

Along with the automatic threading compilers, it is possible to call threads functions directly from Fortran. This is done by declaring an interface to the C functions from Fortran in the appropriate fashion for the compiler which you are using. One would expect that a program that did this would be very simple. Fortran is not known as a terribly good language for general symbolic computation.

Ada

Ada is really ahead of the other languages in this respect. Ada tasks can be mapped directly onto the underlying threads library by the compiler. This allows normal Ada programs to continue to work exactly as they have before, only now they will take advantage of multiple processors and overlapping I/O without any additional programming effort.

Ada does require the POSIX realtime scheduling for validation. Its synchronization is also rather specialized and limited in a similar fashion to Java.

Pascal

www.sparc.spb.su/0io/baobab/science/using_mt.txt

It is possible to call the threads functions directly from Pascal, merely linking in the library. To do so, you'll need appropriate ".h" files for Pascal. These are included in the Sun Pascal distribution for an interface to UI threads as `thread_p.h` and `synch_p.h`. Some of Sun's Pascal support is being done in Russia, and the link above points to a short page at the University of Saint Petersburg that shows a few of the "Threads Primer" demonstration programs done in Pascal. (This is the only MT Pascal we're aware of.)

Smalltalk

Object Connect +33 558 82 84 72
www.objectconnect.com

This is a threaded version of Smalltalk, which is based on Win32 threads and can make use of all of the functionality of the Win32 Threads API. It is possible to call Smalltalk objects that implement the functionality, or to call the various functions directly via a foreign language interface. Smalltalk blocks can also be called from other programs, and all of the threads functions, synchronization, etc. will work across both. Smalltalk has the capability to build stand-alone EXEs and DLLs callable from other languages, and support for building ActiveX components.

The Smalltalk MT system includes a graphical, interactive, multi-threaded debugger, and a garbage collector that runs in a background thread.

Lisp

http://ci.etl.go.jp/~matsui/eus/manual/manual.html

The Japanese Electrotechnical Laboratory has a project, EusLisp, which implements threads inside of an (almost) Common Lisp language/environment. It allows you to build threads in a POSIX style, run on multiple processors, and use POSIX-like synchronization. It runs on Solaris 2 and is based on the underlying UI threads library.

Eiffel

ISE Inc. (805) 685-1006
`http://www.eiffel.com`

Eiffel is a language designed and marketed by Bertram Meyer and his company in France. It is a strict, object-oriented language with enforced static typing. In its latest release (4.1, March 1997), Eiffel provides a threads library on Win32 and Solaris (others to come), which maps directly onto the native threads libraries. Shared objects are implemented by using proxy objects, which do all of the synchronization for you (at a cost, of course). A different approach to threading will be provided in a later release, in which a language construct (Thread-SCOOP) will do all of the synchronization for you. Eiffel is also a garbage-collected language, and the GC has been extended to work with threads. Because objects cannot be shared directly between different threads, Eiffel can use a per-thread GC.

Commercial Products

There are a number of companies that write thread-oriented libraries for a variety of purposes. You might find some of these useful.

ObjectSpace

`www.objectspace.com`   (800) 625-3281

The ObjectSpace C++ Component Series provides a full set of features ranging from a portable implementation of the C++ Standard Template Library to libraries for systems programming and World Wide Web development. All libraries are portable across popular hardware platforms, operating systems, and compilers, and are safe for use in multithreaded environments. Full source portability for threads and synchronization is available on a wide variety of platforms.

Thread<ToolKit> is one library in their C++ Component Series that specializes in classes for multithreaded development, and it includes a variety of classes useful for creating and synchronizing threads. Synchronization objects include: critical sections, simple mutexes, recursive mutexes, simple/recursive FIFO mutexes, simple/recursive priority mutexes, event semaphores, sentinels, readers/writer locks, barriers, and guard classes.

RogueWave

`www.roguewave.com` (800) 487-3217

The Threads.h++ provides C++ objects for thread functionality and handles the low-level details of multithreading for you, portable across: Win NT, Win 95, Solaris, HP-UX, AIX, Digital Unix, IRIX, and OS/2.

The runnable classes provide: simple synchronous classes that use existing threads to perform their tasks, threaded classes that create their own threads to accomplish their tasks, and runnable servers that accept other runnable objects for execution in each server's own thread or threads. The thread creation paradigm uses functors (essentially an encapsulated object plus method) instead of function plus (`void *`) argument. It also provides for lazy evaluation—the ability to have a function return an IOU for a value whose calculation might take a while to complete.

Synchronization objects include: critical sections, simple mutexes, FIFO mutexes, recursive mutexes, condition variables, semaphores, readers-writer locks, barriers, and guard classes.

Geodesic Systems, LLC

`www.geodesic.com` (800) 360-8388

Great Circle is both a conservative garbage collector that can be linked into existing applications (no changes required), and a "smart" GC that can be integrated into applications (hence changes required). It works with C and C++ programs and libraries, effectively eliminating the vast, vast majority of problems of memory leaks. It also shadows calls to `free()` and prevents premature recycling of memory.

It works with multithreaded programs and runs on numerous platforms, including Solaris, SunOS, HP-UX, and Windows NT/95, with more on the way. Although somewhat difficult to do exact comparisons, the best estimations show a GC'd version of X Windows system running 25% faster than the standard version runs.

Garbage collection is a wonderful thing which vastly simplifies your programming task, letting you concentrate your efforts on writing your program, not trying to follow memory leaks. While we do not want to endorse any particular product here, we do wish to endorse the concept.

Dakota Scientific Software

sales@scisoft.com (800) 641-8851
www.scisoft.com

Although not specifically a multithreading company, Dakota is notable for its extensive use of threads in its products, high-performance numerical libraries that are used in thousands of scientific programs. For this purpose, threads are just one of many means towards the ultimate end of high-performance libraries. Even their single-CPU LAPACK, LINPACK, and BLAS libraries run upwards of an order of magnitude faster than naive implementations. Libraries are available for Fortran, C, and C++.

Dakota also has a series of coproducts called Performance Plus that accelerate other mathematical products including Math.h++ and LAPACK.h++ from Rogue Wave, POOMA from Los Alamos National Laboratory, IDL from Research Systems, Inc., and others. Finally, Dakota does extensive consulting and contract optimization using threads and other techniques.

Adaptive Communication Environment

www.cs.wustl.edu/~schmidt/ACE.html

The Adaptive Communication Environment (ACE) is an object-oriented toolkit that implements fundamental design patterns for communication software. ACE provides a rich set of reusable C++ wrappers and frameworks that perform common communication software tasks across a range of operating system platforms. The communication software tasks provided by ACE include event demultiplexing and event handler dispatching, service initialization, interprocess communication, shared memory management, message routing, dynamic (re)configuration of distributed services, multithreading, and concurrency control.

ACE has been ported to a wide range of OS platforms including Win32 (i.e., Win NT and Win95), most versions of UNIX (e.g., SunOS 4.x and 5.x, SGI IRIX, DG/UX, HP-UX, OSF/1, AIX, Linux, UNIXware, Tandem, FreeBSD, and SCO), VxWorks, MVS OpenEdition, and Tandem. It is currently used in commercial products by dozens of companies. There are C++ and Java versions of ACE available.

RT++ —Higher Order Threads for C++

http://www.risc.uni-linz.ac.at/software/rt++

Wolfgang Schreiner et al., at the Johannes Kepler University in Linz Austria, have written RT++, a software package that provides higher-order threads in the programming language C++. Its features include a type-safe functional thread interface, lazy thread creation, garbage-collected types (lists, arrays, pointer structures) and controlled non-determinism (thread bags). Threads are first-order objects that can be used like any other objects and that are automatically reclaimed when they are not referenced any more. The package has been ported to numerous types of mono-processors and shared memory multiprocessors and can be easily embedded into existing application frameworks.

Centerline

www.centerline.com (415) 943-2114

C++ Expert is a tool that performs comprehensive error checking of C and C++ programs throughout the development cycle: at compile time, link time, and run time. Its run time error detection works by analyzing the program source code and generating error-checking instrumentation based on that analysis. The errors it catches include: incorrect use of typed pointers (resulting from improper casts), using freed pointers, freeing a pointer twice, array bounds checking, and memory leaks. Furthermore, C++ Expert was carefully designed from scratch to be robust in the presence of multithreaded applications.

GNU (via Cygnus)

www.cygnus.com (800) 294-6871

GDB, the GNU debugger, is being extended by Cygnus Support to support the debugging of multithreaded programs.

Pure Atria (Rational)

`www.pureatria.com` (408) 863-9900

Pure Atria (now Rational Software) has its Run-Time memory error checker, Purify, which has been extended to work with multiple threads. It also has a performance monitoring tool, Quantify, which will show performance data for multithreaded programs.

Purify comprehensively identifies memory-related software errors anywhere they occur within a software application, including third-party libraries using the Object Code Insertion technology. Purify automatically pinpoints memory access violations and memory leaks and keeps tracks of all threads during the execution of a program.

Quantify is a performance profiler tool which automatically identifies portions of application code that slows down execution speed. In addition, Quantify measures the execution speed of each thread in the application.

Public Pthreads Implementations

FSU Pthreads

`http://www.informatik.hu-berlin.de/~mueller/pthreads`

As part of the PART project (POSIX/Ada-Runtime Project) Florida State University/Humboldt University Berlin have implemented a library package of pre-emptive threads that is compliant with POSIX 1003.4a Draft 6. The implementation runs under SunOS 4.1.x, Solaris 2.x, Linux, SCO, FreeBSD and DOS.

The current scheduling policies are strict priority scheduling (according to POSIX.4a FIFO scheduling), which pre-empts when signals are caught or round-robin (RR scheduling), which changes context to another thread of the same priority after a time-slice of 20msec. Besides asynchronous delivery of signals, context switches only occur when required by the priority policy, e.g., when resources (mutexes) are locked, etc.

MIT Portable Pthreads

`www.mit.edu:8001/people/proven/pthreads.html`
Christopher Angelo Provenzano heads a project that has written a Pthreads library that is portable across NetBSD, FreeBSD, LInux, SunOS 4.1, Solaris, Outrides, OSF/1, IRIX and HP-UX. It implements the full POSIX standard in a Many-to-One model.

PCThreads

`www.aa.net/~mtp/PCthreads.html`
Michael T. Peterson has written a Pthreads library for Linux. It is a Many-to-One model with a series of extensions in several of the system libraries to allow the library calls to run in a non-blocking mode. The various blocking system calls are wrapped by "jacket" routines for the threads library. This wrapping allows several threads to make blocking calls, which are turned into their non-blocking equivalents, allowing yet another thread to continue running. It is included in the current Linux release. It is also available for FTP from the address above.

LinuxThreads

`http://pauillac.inria.fr/~xleroy/linuxthreads`
Xavier Leroy at INRIA (Paris, France), with input from Pavel Krauz, Richard Henderson and others, has developed a Pthreads library that implements the One-to-One model, allowing it to take advantage of multiple processors. It is based on the new Linux system call, `clone()`.[2] It runs on Linux 2.0 and up, on Intel, Alpha, SPARC, m68k, and MIPS machines. One limitation is its non-standard implementation of signal handling.

---

[2]This is actually an interesting variation on how to create threads. It's sort of a `fork()` call for threads. (See Linux documentation for more detail.)

Pthread Debugger Project: SmartGDB

`http://hegel.ittc.ukans.edu/projects/smartgdb`

A team at the University of Kansas has built a debugger atop GDB. It is designed to allow the user to tailor it to his application environment. It supports MIT Pthreads on Linux and allows extension to other thread packages. A tcl/tk interpreter makes scripting possible.

Some of the unique aspects of this debugger include:

- Checking for data races.
- Monitoring the number of threads accessing a certain critical section.
- Checking for deadlocks.
- Forcing the program to follow a specific context switching sequence to reproduce aberrant behavior.
- Declaring thread-specific breakpoints.

Summary

We looked at the use of threads in various programming languages, comparing them to how Pthreads works. Once again, the primary conclusion is that threads work pretty much as expected and hoped for, with some few limitations. We also pointed out a number of commercial products that might be useful.

15

Tools

In which we consider the kinds of new tools that a reader would want when writing a threaded program. An overview of the Solaris tool set is given, as representative of what should be looked for.

Programming with threads adds new challenges to the development tools that you use. "Normal" toolsets, in most cases, will not work well with threaded programs, because they were designed with single-threaded programs in mind. All of the vendors have some set of products to be used with multithreaded programs—debuggers, code analyzers, and performance analysis programs.

This chapter focuses on some of the current tools that Sun Microsystems provides for the development of multithreaded programs. Tool offerings from DEC, SGI, etc. are fairly similar.

Static Lock Analyzer

LockLint is a lint type program for locks. It verifies consistent use of mutexes and RWlocks in multithreaded ANSI C programs. LockLint performs a static analysis of the program and looks for inconsistent or incorrect use of these locking techniques. In looking for inconsistent use of locks, it detects the most common causes of data races and deadlocks. LockLint can generate many different types of reports:

- Locking side effects of functions (i.e., when a function locks a mutex but doesn't unlock it).
- Variables that were not consistently protected by a lock or that violate assertions made about which locks are supposed to protect them.
- Cycles and inconsistent lock order acquisitions.
- Which locks were consistently used to protect which variables. This information can assist in judging the appropriateness of the chosen granularity of locks.

LockLint is a static analyzer. You compile your program with the -Zll flag. This analyzes the program and builds a file of results (e.g., ll_exam.ll). You then use the LockLint analyzer to examine that file.

Using a Thread-Aware, Graphical Debugger

All of the different vendors have some version of a graphical debugger, all of which have the same basic functionality. We'll look at a few screen shots from Sun's Visual Workshop Debugger. Most of the UNIX debuggers are based on the original UNIX debugger, dbx, and allow

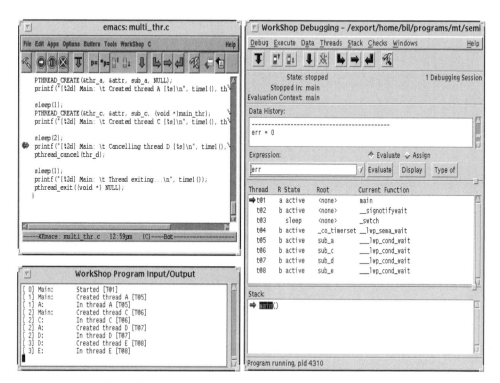

Figure 15–1 *Sun's Debugger (Program Stopped in* `main()`*)*

you to use the old command-line interfaces also. To say the least, the value of a graphical debugger for multithreaded programs is enormous.

Figure 15–1 uses the debugger to take a look at the code in *An Example: Create and Join* on page 54. We started by loading the program into the debugger and then setting a breakpoint in `main()`. Then we started the program, and let it hit the breakpoint.

When *any* thread hits a breakpoint, *all* threads will stop. (This is a good thing, because you *want* things to stop while you try to figure them out.) Notice that the Sun Pthreads implementation creates several threads for its own use: `t@2`, `t@3`, and `t@4`. The first is the sigwaiter thread, which captures all asynchronous signals. The second is the reaper thread, which cleans up after other threads. The third is a special tools agent, created only for certain of the SunSoft tools (e.g., the newest debugger, but not the previous debugger). They are managed by the library and have no effect on your programing.

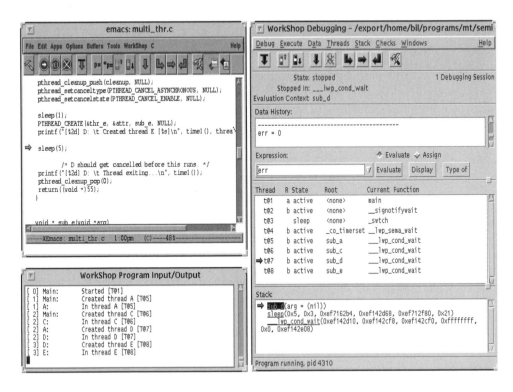

Figure 15–2 *Sun's Debugger (Program Stopped at Breakpoint)*

Also notice that the main thread is always t@1. This is a Solaris arti-fact. IRIX starts numbering threads at 65535, AIX at 1, HP-UX, and Dig-ital UNIX all have their own, similar, systems. You can see from the thread pane that t@1 is stopped at a breakpoint in main(). The stack pane will show the entire call stack for the selected thread.

In Figure 15–2, we select t@7 from the process inspector. Both the source code window and the stack inspector will display the state of that thread. We select our function, sub_d(), in the process inspector, to see where in our code the thread is. (As there is no source code available for system functions, the code window will show nothing for __lwp_cond_wait()). Not surprisingly (considering the program), t@7 is in the middle of sleep().

Also note the b next to the thread ID. That informs us that the thread is bound on an LWP. The letter a indicates that those threads are locally scheduled and active (have an LWP). Thus, the main thread is unbound, but active, while `t@3` is unbound and not active, and all the others are bound (hence active).

It is possible to single step an individual thread, to continue one thread, or to continue all threads. No other options exist. Some caution must be exercised, as the first two options can get you into trouble. If you step into a call to `pthread_mutex_lock()`, and that mutex is locked, the program will hang and the debugger will wait for it, ignoring any desperate calls from you. In that case, you must kill the program (not the debugger!) from another window. If you kill the debugger, the program will continue to exist, and may even spin, eating up CPU cycles. *Don't do that.*

Debug Mutexes

Even in the best designed programs, it is common to have problems getting critical sections to work exactly the way you want. When you do run into problems, it can be extremely time consuming to find the information you need in order to fix them. The POSIX definition of mutexes does not allow you to find out which thread owns them, nor is it a simple matter even to get an inventory of all the mutexes in your program. POSIX does allow mutexes to detect self-deadlock situations, but this is an optional portion of the spec which many vendors don't implement.

Part of the reason for this dearth of information is that it's only useful during the debugging phase of the programming—you would never use this information in a shipping program. It would slow the program down and it wouldn't be useful. What is really needed is a mutex that will give out this information during debugging, but not burden you with it later. If your vendor supplies such a mutex, great! If not, there's a debug mutex in our extensions library that may prove to be a useful debugging tool.

The dmutex module implements a mutex that

- records its owner.
- records all the threads sleeping on it.
- detects self-deadlock and non-owner unlock.
- is placed on a list so you can see all mutexes with a single command.
- records the number of times it has been locked and the number of failed wakeups.

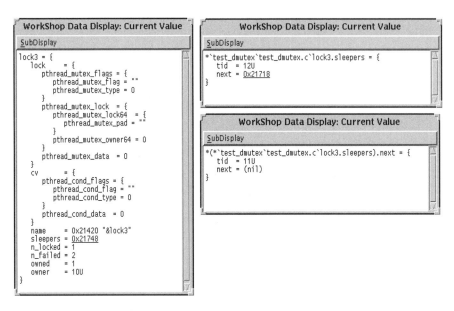

Figure 15–3   *Using the Data Display to Examine a dmutex*

To use this module, it is sufficient to do a global replace of "_mutex_" with "_dmutex_" in your code. In order to be placed on the list of mutexes used by `print_mutexes()`, you have to dynamically initialize all your mutexes.

You can tell the debugger to run the `print_dmutexes()` function:

```
(debugger) call print_dmutexes()

&lock3 T@12 Locked:   6.  Failed:   6.  Sleepers: ( T@11 )
&lock2 ---- Locked:   0.  Failed:   0.  Sleepers: ( )
&lock1 T@5 Locked:    6.  Failed:  10.  Sleepers: ( T@6 T@7 T@8 T@9 )
```

Code Example 15–1:   *Using the Debugger to Look at All `dmutexes`*

From the debugger you can display a dmutex in the data inspector and see something like Figure 15–3, which will tell you everything about the dmutex in question. In this example, dmutex &lock3 was locked once, is currently owned by t@10, has had two threads try to lock it and fail. Both of those threads (t@11 and t@12) are still waiting.

Once you have your program debugged, optimized, and working properly, you should go back to normal mutexes.

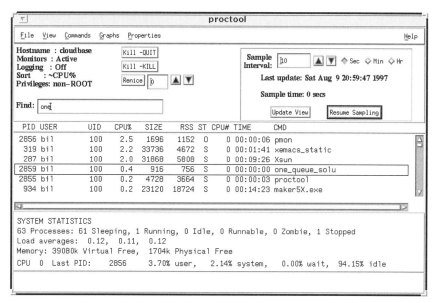

Figure 15–4 *Proctool, Main Display Window*

Proctool

For Solaris 2 systems, there is a very nice system status display tool (Figure 15–4), which is freely available via FTP (see *Freeware Tools* on page 315). It will show you all of the system statistics on your program, including the details for each individual LWP. This tool can be useful when you want to know how your threads are behaving with respect to system calls.

In the main display window you see the complete status line for each process (you get to select what to display). Selecting one of those, you can look at detailed information about that process. In Figure 15–5, you see the detailed statistics for each LWP. (This is one of the places where it's nice to have bound threads, because you get to see what each individual thread is doing.)

TNFview

Many of the new, multithreaded kernels have internal instrumentation in both the kernel and standard libraries. In Solaris, this instrumentation takes

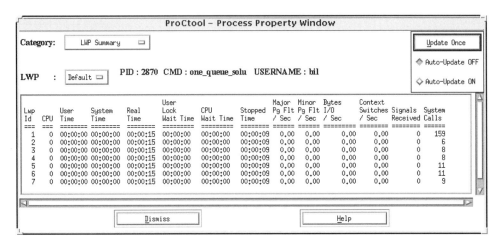

Figure 15–5   *Proctool, LWP Display Window*

the form of a *TNF* (Trace Normal Form) probe. The basic idea for all these types of instrumentation is that probes are included in various important routines. These probes write information about their position in the code and, optionally, details of the current program state (i.e., some variable values) into a file, along with the exact time of the call. The probes are normally turned off but can be enabled when timing data is desired.

In Figure 15–7, we see calls to TNF_PROBE_*N*() (*N* is the number of data values that the probe will write out) in the Pthread library code, in the UNIX kernel, and even calls that we included in our own code. When we run the program with tracing enabled, the probes will write their information out into a file.[1] The timing information is based on the high-resolution clock, which is part of all new (post-1992) Sun hardware. That clock can be read directly (no system call required) with a resolution of 10µs.

Once that data is collected, all that's left is to make sense of it. While you could simply read the file itself, that would probably prove to be rather difficult—there's just too much data to read from a printout. A better method is to use a special viewer, TNFview (also available via FTP), which condenses that data into graphical form and produces a series of histograms and plots.

---

[1]Actually, it's a bit more complicated than we show, as there is an intermediate, binary format between the probe and the human-readable file. Kernel probes write out to an internal buffer instead of a file, so that must be merged into the final output.

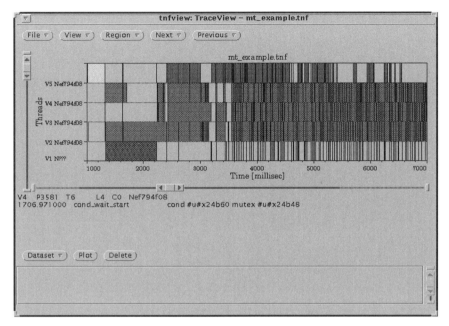

Figure 15–6 *Main Data Display Window for TNF*

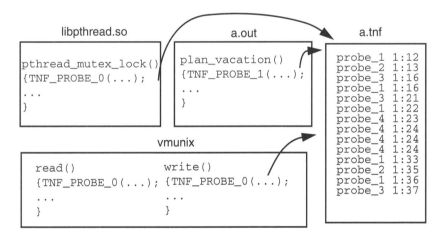

Figure 15–7 *Data Collection for TNF*

In Figure 15–6, the one thing to keep in mind is that the beginning of a colored section is the time the event occurred. The color that extends beyond it is just there for looks and has no particular meaning attached.

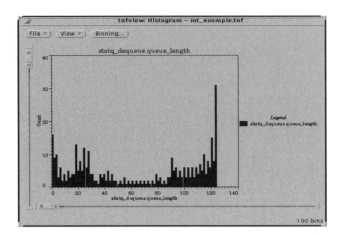

Figure 15–8   *Histogram Display Window for TNF*

Summary

Using the Solaris toolset as an example, a brief overview of what you can expect from MT tools was given, along with a few hints about what to look for and what to look out for.

16

Performance

In which we make things faster, look at general performance issues, political performance issues, and thread specific performance issues. We conclude with a discussion of the actual performance of multithreaded NFS.

Optimization: Objectives and Objections

Performance is an incredibly wide topic that means different things to different people. It is often referred to broadly and vaguely as an obvious requirement for all programs, without ever defining exactly what it is. We are not aware of any truly good and comprehensive texts on the subject.[1] In one short chapter, about all we can do is point out the things you probably already know.

Before you begin optimizing your program, you must answer the fundamental question: "What do you really want?" We're not being silly. This is not an easy question. Major factors surrounding performance tuning include:

- Time to Market
- Available Human Resources and Programming Costs
- Portability
- User Perception
- Competition
- Targeted Machine Configuration
- Algorithm
- CPU Time, I/O Time, Contention, Etc.

In general your customers' only objective is going to be "Do my work for the least cost." They really do not (well, should not) care about any of the details. They have their job to do and that's the sole value of your software to them. Many of us engineering types have a tendency to skip over all this touchy-feely stuff and jump straight into the code. Let us resist for a moment and consider these details that affect our paychecks so much. We may not like this, but it really is vitally important.

Time to Market

Most of the optimization issues are ultimately marketing issues. These marketing aspects are important and have to be hashed out with

---

[1]There are a number of books discussing kernel tuning, many discussing algorithmic issues for general programs, and numerous texts and papers do detailed analyses of theoretical limits. These are all fundamental and important places to start, but they are all weak on many important aspects of actual implementation.

management. It's no use having a program that runs twice as fast if your company's out of business. We'll get to the techniques in a moment, but we wish to emphasize this point. The amount of optimization to do on a program is a marketing issue.

Related to this is correctness. Correctness is more important than either performance or time to market. Minor bugs and occasional crashes can be traded off against time to market, but fundamental correctness is essential. Unfortunately, this is a major battle between engineering and marketing all the time.

Available Human Resources and Programming Costs

If you can speed your program up by 50 percent, but it takes 60 programmers two years to do it, is it worth it? Maybe yes, maybe no. It's up to you and you should be thinking in these terms when you begin the optimization efforts.

Portability

Some of the techniques we're going to discuss will require customizing to a particular platform, or even to a particular configuration. Is such specialization worthwhile to you? Maybe yes, maybe no. Sunsoft does a PSR (*Platform Specific Release*) of Solaris for each different machine (one for the SS1, another for the SS2, a third for the SS10, etc.). Ninety-nine percent of the code will be shared, but things like byte copy will be optimized for the exact CPU, memory bus, and cache configuration.

It is highly unlikely you would ever go as far in your own code. The normal thing is to optimize for a specific configuration (typically the highest performance one), and admit that the others will be a bit suboptimal. Would you want to write and maintain upwards of 20 PSRs just for Sun machines? And another 20 for SGI, DEC, etc.?

User Perception

Yes, you might be able to optimize an editor to process keystrokes twice as fast. The user wouldn't care, because the user can't tell the difference between 1ms and 2ms response time anyway. Don't waste your time on useless optimization.

Easier said than done, of course. Especially as the world is rife with inappropriate benchmarks upon which people do base their buying decisions. Sorry.

Competition

Being 10 percent faster means nothing to the user. It looks great on the data sheets, but that's about it.[2] Your program is not a commodity, don't sell it as if it were. Of course, if your program runs 50 percent slower than the competition, you may need to speed it up significantly. Make sure you get the time and support you need.

Targeted Machine Configuration

You have to select your primary target machine and you have to declare some configurations inadequate. If you can't get your desired performance on a x286, then don't sell on a x286.[3] Next year's machines will be twice as fast anyway.

Sometimes, "throwing money at the problem" is the right answer.

Algorithm

There are three vitally important aspects of performance optimization: algorithm, algorithm, and algorithm. Seriously. Forget all of this other stuff until you have settled on the very best possible algorithm. We can show you programs that will run faster on a uniprocessor VAX 780 than on a 64-way, 500 MHz, Alpha Server, simply due to algorithm choice.

You *can* multithread bubblesort, and it *will* run twice as fast, but....

---

[2]Yes, performance numbers on data sheets are important sometimes because people do make decisions based upon a one percent difference in a published benchmark (dumb, but real). Nonetheless, given a choice between releasing five percent slower than the competition today and five percent faster next year, we'd opt for today.

[3]At one of Bil's first software division meetings (back when everyone fit into the cafeteria!), there was a big debate concerning the poor performance of SunOS on a 4 MB machine. Some of management wanted to restrict all developers to 4 MB machines so we would be more motivated to control code inflation. The final resolution was to make 8 MB the minimum shippable configuration.

CPU Time, I/O Time, Contention, Etc.

That should be enough moralizing on the practicalities of dealing with the real world. Now let's get serious—you're an ISV and you really want to get the best performance you can (for some "reasonable" programming cost). First let's look at the overall system design and define our true objectives.

The primary components are the CPU, the cache, the main memory bus, main memory, the I/O bus, and the peripherals (disks, tapes, possibly displays, networks, etc.), all of which can be viewed generically as resources. There is a tendency to view the CPU as unique, and we often speak of maximizing CPU usage before considering any other subsystems. However, that's not really what we want We really want our program to run in minimal wall clock time. Let's consider these subsystems.

CPU

Some programs are completely CPU-bound. They don't make great demands upon the peripherals and have a small enough working set to be largely cache-resident. A huge number of programs are partially CPU-bound. To optimize such programs, our primary technique will be to reduce the number of instructions executed, and our primary method of doing so will be by choosing the best algorithms.

Our secondary method will be to examine our code very carefully to see if there are places where loops can be made tighter. Sometimes we will even examine assembly code to verify the tightness of the complied code. In all cases, we will first analyze our program, then focus our efforts on those sections that consume the most time.

Clever usage of registers, optimal instruction scheduling, and the like we will leave to the compiler. Only in the rarest of circumstances will we ever "bum" code (write assembly code). *Byte copy* can be written in a single line of C code. On Sun machines, the actual library call occupies roughly 500 lines of carefully hand-optimized assembly code. It is specialized for each of the different byte alignments, and a different version is written for each PSR. The programmer counts the instructions, spreads data across numerous registers to maximize pipelining and multiple instruction issues, etc. It runs upwards of ten times as fast as the one line of C.

The chances of you doing anything similar is quite small. It takes a lot of effort, and it is valuable for only a few very tight, very intensively used loops. The hassle of maintaining "bummed" code is also quite significant. Don't do this at home!

Memory Latency

The speed at which the main memory system can fill cache requests is a major factor on the CPU side of performance. It is not at all unusual for memory latency to occupy 50% of total CPU time. Memory latency is difficult to identify as separate from CPU time because there are no standard tools for measuring the amount of time it takes. As far as the OS is concerned, the entire CPU/cache system is a single entity and is lumped into a single number—CPU time.

No measurements of cache activity are recorded, so the only means of distinguishing cache from CPU are (a) counting instructions, (b) comparing target code to known code, and (c) using simulators. Simulators are not generally available.[4] We'll focus on (a) and (b). Once we determine the cache behavior of our program, we may be able to reorganize data access to improve performance. (See *Reducing Cache Misses* on page 293.)

Memory Bandwidth

No single CPU can come vaguely close to saturating a main memory bus. At the insane rate of one memory access per cycle, a 200 MHz Ultra could demand nearly 100 MB/sec—one-twelfth of the UPA bus' bandwidth. Of course the CPU wouldn't have any time to do anything. Realistic programs demand data rates closer to 50 MB/sec, and 95% or more of that is serviced by the cache. Main memory bus rates of 5 MB/sec per CPU are normal for actual programs. A UPA bus can sustain data rates of over 1GB/sec.

It is true that a maximally configured ES10000 with 64 CPUs can easily saturate the 100 MHz UPA cross-bar switch. We don't have any clever techniques for minimizing it.

---

[4]They're too complex to use easily, so there's no reasonable way for vendors to market them. If you are willing to go through a lot of pain and spend big bucks for one, tell your vendor. Vendors will do anything for money.

I/O Latency

Making a disk request takes a long time, around 20ms. During this time, a thread will typically go to sleep, letting others run. Depending upon the details of the access pattern, there are a couple of things we can do to either reduce the number of requests or to pipeline them. When the working set is just a bit larger than main memory, we can simply buy more memory.

When the working set is really enormous, we can duplicate the techniques that we'll use for optimizing memory access (see *Reducing Cache Misses* on page 293). Disk accesses are easier to deal with than cache misses because the OS does collect statistics on them and because the CPU is able to run other threads while waiting.

Other types of I/O must simply be endured. There really is no way to optimize for asynchronous network requests.

Contention

Sometimes one CPU will hold a lock that another CPU needs. This is normal and unavoidable, but it may be possible to reduce the frequency. In some programs, contention can be a major factor in reducing the amount of parallelism achieved. Contention is only an issue for multithreaded (or multi-process) programs, and primarily only on MP machines. Although threaded programs on uniprocessors do experience contention, the most important cause of the contention is the speed of other components of the system (e.g., you're holding a lock, waiting for the disk to spin). Reducing contention is always a good thing, and is often worth a lot of extra work.

Throughput vs. Latency

Given these resources, we next must refine our definition of performance—do we want to minimize latency for individual subsystems, such as having an NFS server respond to individual requests as fast as possible, or do we want to maximize the number of requests per second that the server can handle? This is a serious consideration and we cannot blithely answer "both."

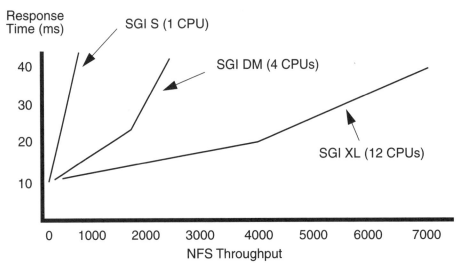

Figure 16–1   *NFS Throughput vs. Latency on Some SGI Machines*

Consider Figure 16–1.[5] We get to select the point on the graph where we wish to operate. For some programs (e.g., numerical calculations), this latency vs. throughput issue is non-existent; for others (e.g., NFS), it is paramount. The answer to the question is almost always, "Maximize throughput with 'reasonable' latency." For NFS this means that everyone designs their servers to give maximum throughput at 40ms average latency.[6]

The question now becomes "For my individual application, which of these subsystems is the limiting factor, and how much can I accelerate that before another subsystem becomes saturated?"

Limits on Speedup

A naive view of multiprocessing says that we should expect a 2-CPU machine to do twice as much work as a 1-CPU machine. Empirically, this is not at all the case. Indeed, it is not unusual to hear reports of people who see very little improvement at all. The truth is that it all depends upon what you are doing. We can cite examples of programs

---

[5]Program data and graphs from Hennessy & Patterson, *Computer Architecture, 2nd Edition*

[6]40ms is also the limit chosen for the maximum allowable latency for the SPEC Laddis benchmark.

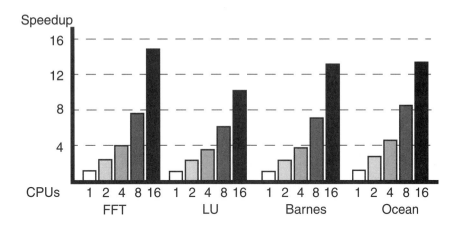

Figure 16–2 *Parallel Speedup on Several Numerical Programs*

that get near-linear speedup, a few that show super-linear speedups, a large majority that show some speed up, and even a few that slow down.

One basic fact should be acknowledged up front: There is always a limit. For every program or system load that you can imagine, there is an optional number of CPUs to run it on. Adding more CPUs to the machine will slow it down.

You could, if you wanted, build a one-million-CPU SMP machine. It just wouldn't be very efficient. And while we can invent programs that would make good use of all million CPUs (e.g., analyze all 20 move chess games), they would be highly contrived. Most "normal" programs can make use of only a small number of CPUs (typically 2–20).

Let's start by looking at some data from some simple programs (Figure 16–2). These are numerically intensive programs that run entirely in memory. Because there is no I/O involved, and because the amount of shared data is often quite limited, all of these programs show a superb scaling up to 16 CPUs.

Fast Fourier Transforms are performed by a set of matrix manipulations. It is characterized by largely independent operations with significant inter-thread communication in only one section. The next three programs all have largely constant amounts of inter-thread communications. *LU factorization* is dense matrix factorization, and also performed

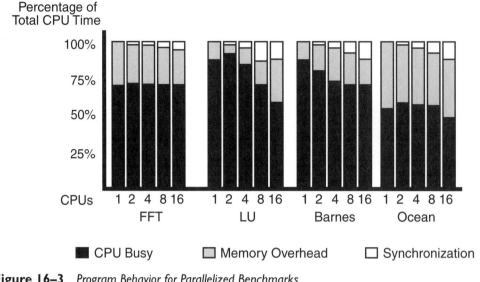

Figure 16–3 *Program Behavior for Parallelized Benchmarks*

by a set of matrix manipulations. *Barnes-Hut* is an N-body simulation for solving a problem in galaxy evolution. *Ocean* simulates the effects of certain currents on large-scale flow in the ocean.

Notice that all of these program do show a fall off in performance for each additional CPU. At some point, that fall off will drop below zero and begin to slow the total throughput. Why? Well, let's take a look at where these programs are spending their time. As you can see from Figure 16–3, the amount of time the CPUs actually spend working on the problem drops as the number of CPUs increases, the requirement for synchronization taking up more and more of the time. Extrapolating out to just 128 CPUs, we can infer that performance would be dismal indeed.

Superlinear Speedup

In a very small number of programs, such as Ocean on two and four CPUs (Figure 16–2), it is possible to see speedups slightly better than linear. This is a result of having more cache and possibly reducing overhead because of fewer context switches. It's nice if you get it, but don't expect it.

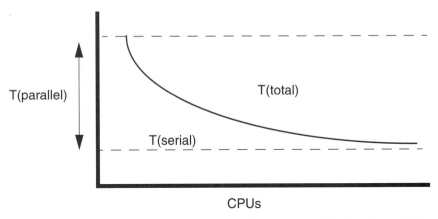

Figure 16–4   *Amdahl's Law: Time(total) = Time(serial) + Time(parallel) / Number_of_CPUs*

Timing Threaded and Non-Threaded Programs

In our measurements, we compare the runtime of identical code that creates different numbers of threads, appropriate to the available CPUs. This isn't really fair, because we're including the synchronization overhead (and possibly a less efficient algorithm) for the one CPU case, which doesn't need that synchronization.

Unfortunately, for any real program, it's far too complex to implement, optimize, and maintain two different programs (the PSR argument again). Most ISVs ship a single binary and simply run suboptimally on uniprocessors. Library writers will ship a single library module, running the stub code when the threads library is not linked in. You may console yourself (and your marketing department) by noting that you can probably find more performance improvement in the techniques mentioned above than you can in writing a uniprocessor-only version.

Amdahl's Law

Amdahl's law (Figure 16–4) states: "If a program has one section which is parallelizable, and another section that must run serially, then the program execution time will asymptotically approach the time for the serial section as more CPUs are added."

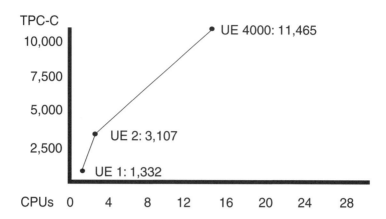

Figure 16–5 *TPC-C Performance of a Sun UE6000*

Although obviously true, this fact is of no interest to many programs. Most programs with which we have worked (client/server, and I/O intensive) see other limitations long before they ever hit this one. Even numerically intensive programs often come up against limited memory bandwidth sooner than they hit Amdahl's limit. Very large numeric programs with little synchronization will approach it. So, don't hold Amdahl's law up as the expected goal. It might not be possible.

Client/Server programs often show a lot of contention for shared data and make great demands upon the I/O subsystem. Consider the TCP-C numbers in Figure 16–5. Irrespective of how representative you think TPC-C is of actual database activity (there's lots of debate here), it is very definitely a benchmark into which vendors put enormous effort into optimizing. So it is notable that on a benchmark as important as this, the limit of system size is down around 20 CPUs.

So, what does this mean for you? That there are limitations. The primary limiting factor might be synchronization overhead, it may be main memory access, it might be the I/O subsystem. As you design and write your system, you should analyze the nature of your program and put your optimization efforts towards these limits. And you should be testing your programs along the way.

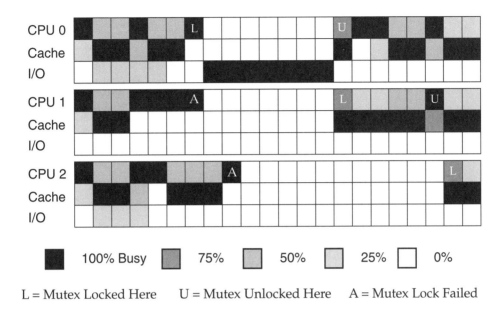

Figure 16–6 *Performance Bottlenecks and Capacities of Programs*

Performance Bottlenecks

Wherever your program spends its time, that's the bottleneck. We can expect that the bottleneck for a typical program will vary from subsystem to subsystem quite often during the life of the program. "Bottleneck" is a somewhat pejorative term that isn't really fair. After all, whichever subsystem is the bottleneck is the one that's doing your work! There is also a general tendency to want to "balance out" the work across the different subsystems, keeping them all busy all the time. Once again, that's a bit inaccurate. Balancing the work is only useful if it helps your program run faster.

In Figure 16–6 we show a representation of where a program is spending its time and where the bottleneck is with respect to CPU, cache latency, and I/O latency. Each block represents how busy that subsystem is during some period of time (say, 10µs).

Black indicates a subsystem used at full capacity, white indicates zero usage. A black CPU is never stalled for anything; the other subsystems are waiting for it to make requests. A black cache indicates that the CPU is stalled, waiting for data at least some of the time, ditto for I/O. Depending upon system design, it may or may not actually be possible for CPU and cache to be busy simultaneously. (We show a system where there is overlap.) The solid white sections for CPU 1 and 2 indicate that they are suffering contention, waiting for CPU 0 to release a lock.

Typically, we expect CPU and cache to take turns being the bottleneck, alternating very rapidly. When I/O is the bottleneck, it will be so for extended periods of time (the latency on a disk read runs on the order of 20ms).

By definition, there must be a line of solid black from one end of our graph to the other. In some sense, the more solid black in the CPU section, the more work is getting done. A typical sub-goal will be to maximize the amount of time all the CPUs actually work. (The primary goal is to make the program run fast. Normally you expect that making more CPUs do more work will have that effect.) Eliminating contention is a major factor in doing so.

Benchmarks and Repeatable Testing

Before you get into the details of optimizing your code, you need to be very clear on what your starting point is, and what your objective is. Your overall objective is to make the entire system run faster. Perhaps you have a specific target (you need 13.5% improvement to beat the competition); perhaps you just want to spend six months and get as much improvement as you can. Your starting point will be a specific release of your program, a specific machine to run it on, and a very well-defined set of input data. You absolutely must have an unambiguous, repeatable test case for which you know the statistics.

Things you may have to control for include other activity on the test machine, unanticipated network traffic, file layout on your disk(!), etc.

Once you have all of that, you will generally find that most of your time is used by a few small loops. Once you're convinced that these loops really are the right ones, you'll separate them out into their own little testbeds and verify that you can produce the same behavior there. Finally, you will apply your efforts to these testbeds, investigating them in great detail and experimenting with the different techniques below.

When you feel confident that you've done your best with them, you'll compare the before and after statistics in the testbeds, then integrate the changes and repeat the tests in the original system. It is vitally important that you repeat the test in both original version and in the new version. Far, far too many times people have discovered that "something changed," that the original program now completes the test faster than before, and that the extensive optimizations they performed didn't actually make any improvement at all.

Doing this stuff well is not at all obvious and doing it wrong is all too common.

General Performance Optimizations

By far, the most important optimizations will not be specific to threaded programs, but rather the general optimizations you do for non-thread programs. We'll mention these optimizations, but leave the specifics to you. First, you choose the best algorithm. Second, you select the correct compiler optimization. Third, you buy enough RAM to avoid excessive paging. Fourth, you minimize I/O. Fifth, you minimize cache misses. Sixth, you do any other loop optimizations that the compiler was unable to do. Finally you can do the thread specific optimizations.

Best Algorithm

That's your problem.

Compiler Optimization

This is not necessarily obvious and is highly dependent upon the individual compiler.

You need to select the individual machine to compile for. For example, Sun supports SS1s and SS2 (both SPARC version 7 machines, which trap to the kernel to handle the integer multiply instruction), SS10s, SS20, SS1000s, and SC2000s (all SPARC version 8 machines, which have hardware integer multiply); and Ultras (SPARC version 9 machines, which have 64-bit registers and 64-bit operations). Optimizing for an Ultra might produce lousy code for an SS1. Optimizing for an SS1 will produce OK code for an SS10 or Ultra. (This is a marketing decision, of course.)

You need to choose the optimization level for your program. You may choose different levels for different modules! Sun compilers, for example provide five levels of optimization. Level -xO2 is the normal good optimization level, producing fairly tight code, highly reliable and highly correct. Levels 3, 4, and 5 produce extremely fast code (it may be larger) which is much faster than -xO2 in some cases, and possibly *slower* in others. They are much more likely to fail (i.e., not compile at all).

Thus, expect to compile and test your program at -xO2 (default). Compile and profile it at -xO2. Separate out the high time functions and recompile them at higher levels. If they work and are faster, great. If not, too bad.

Buy Enough RAM

Test the program with different amounts of memory and select the best price/performance level.

Minimize I/O

Organize your data so that when you do read a disk block, you make maximum use of it, and you don't have to read it again. One obvious thing is to use the mmap() calls to map files into the address space instead of calling read(). This eliminates an extra kernel memory copy and allows you to give access pattern hints to the OS.

Minimize Cache Misses

Organize your data so that when you do load a cache line, you make maximum use of it, and you don't have to load it again (see *Reducing Cache Misses* on page 293).

Any Other Loop Optimizations

There are all sorts of things you might be able to do to assist the compiler in performing optimizations that it can't do by itself for some reason: inlining functions, loop unrolling, loop interchange, loop fusion, etc. Generally these things are done by the optimizer. We will look at the assembly code for very tight loops just to verify our expectations. Your vendor documentation will help here.

Thread-Specific Performance Optimizations

Now that we have wildly emphasized the importance of doing all the normal performance work first, let's take a look at the stuff that's specific to multithreaded programs. There are just a couple of performance areas specific to MT: reducing contention, minimizing overhead, and creating the right number of threads.

Reducing Contention

Clearly we do not want to have lots of CPUs waiting around idle because they can't get a mutex they need. Equally obviously, we cannot neglect proper locking to avoid this contention. Your options for dealing with this situation are limited by what you're doing.

In some circumstances, you will be able to divide your global data into smaller groups, with more locks. Then a thread that needs to use item 1 will not block other threads that need item 2. This will only work if the two items are not used together all the time. This is fine-grained locking. There is a trade-off between grain size and overhead.

Other times you'll be able to substitute readers/writer locks for mutexes.

In those rare cases where you have tiny critical sections that are used very, very often, spin locks are a possible solution. Be aware that if you're in this situation, you're already very close to the performance limit of your algorithm. Don't expect spin locks to solve all your problems.

Minimizing MT Overhead

There are a few different threads functions that you might call often enough to make a significant impact upon performance. The first case is the fine-grained vs. course-grained locking trade-off. In cases where different data items are used together, making the locking finer-grained will increase the overhead due to locking, slowing the total performance even though contention may be reduced. In the Friends/Enemies program (*Manipulating Lists* on page 213), it is possible for us to lock every single list node individually. This will increase the parallelism of the program over the global mutex design, but total runtime will be many times worse.

What is the right granularity? It will be obvious in most cases, but sometimes the only solution is to experiment. The debug mutex (see *Debug Mutexes* on page 111) provides statistics that will help you refine the granularity.

The other case of overhead concerns cancellation and signal handling. If you have a tight loop that is pushing and popping cancellation handlers regularly, or where you are enabling/disabling cancellation or changing signal masks, you may be suffering enormous overhead. If we remove the delays (the simulated work) in *A Cancellation Example* on page 142, then that code will spend more time manipulating the cancellation handlers than doing the work. So, *don't do this.*

The probable solution to this problem is to remove these calls from inner loops. Perhaps you can move them completely out of the loop, running the entire loop with cancellation or signal handling turned off. If time constraints prohibit this complete removal, you may be able to check for cancellation or signals only once every thousand iterations. These problems you can generally find by inspection of long-running functions.

Reducing Paging

In most cases, overlapping I/O and computation can be accomplished without threads. Most operating systems have some sort of asynchronous I/O that allows you to issue an I/O request, then go back to what you were doing without waiting for it to complete. When it does complete, a signal will be sent to your process and you will then ask the operating system which request it was that completed, and deal with it as you please.

This asynchronous I/O can be awkward to deal with, but it will do the job. Using threads instead of asynchronous I/O is much easier to program and equally fast (Figure 16–7). The one place where async I/O will not work is with page faults. When a non-threaded program takes a page fault, it waits. Threaded programs can finesse this, because there is no problem with thread 4 continuing to run while thread 1 is waiting for a page fault. The finesse yields a nice performance improvement for many programs, even on uniprocessor machines.

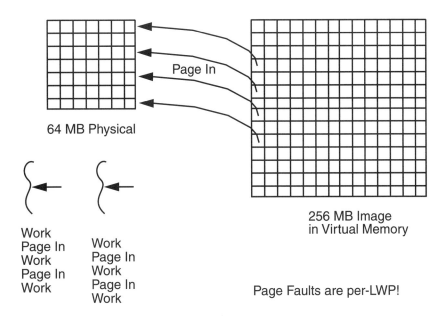

64 MB Physical

256 MB Image
in Virtual Memory

Work
Page In
Work
Page In
Work

Work
Page In
Work
Page In
Work

Page In

Page Faults are per-LWP!

Figure 16–7 *Using Threads to Optimize Paging*

Communications Bandwidth

Sometimes the amount of data that needs to be exchanged between threads for a program is very low compared to the total computing time. For example, a chess position can be encoded into a dozen or so bytes, while the time to compute the best move might be hours. Such a problem, which also requires only a tiny amount of synchronization, can be productively spread across thousands of very distant processors that don't even share memory.[7] Distributed parallel systems such as PVM are well suited to such problems.

When the data/computation ratio is higher, or when more synchronization is required, distributing across a network is not feasible, as the communications costs would exceed the CPU time to execute the entire computation locally. Most image processing programs fit into this

---

[7]In one of the big computer chess tournaments back in the late 80s, one of the contestants managed to convince several thousand of us to run a networked chess program over the weekend.

category. Dithering a 1,000 x 1,000 image might take one second on one CPU and require very little synchronization. Executing this program on 1,000 CPUs would only take 1ms of computation time, yet moving that 1meg image out and back across a network would take far longer. Executing it on a 10 CPU shared-memory multiprocessor would make far more sense, taking more like 100ms total.

Right Number of Threads

You want to have enough threads to keep all of the CPUs busy all of the time (if possible), but not so many that the CPUs are doing unnecessary context switching. Determining exactly the right number is ultimately an empirical experiment. We give rough estimates in *How Many LWPs?* on page 74.

Short-Lived Threads

Thread creation and synchronization time is quite low (about 80μs on an 167 MHz Ultra 1), making it reasonable to dispatch relatively small tasks to different threads. How small can that task be? Obviously it must be significantly larger than the thread overhead.

Something like a 10 x 10 matrix multiply (requiring about 2000 FP Ops @ 100 MFLOPS = 20μs) would be much too small to thread. By contrast, a 100 x 100 matrix multiply (2M FP Ops @ 100 MFLOPS = 20ms) can be threaded very effectively. If you were writing a matrix routine, your code would check the size of the matrices and run the threaded code for larger multiplies, and run the simple multiply in the calling thread for smaller multiplies. The exact dividing point will be about 100μs. You can determine this empirically, and it is not terribly important to hit exactly.

One ISV we worked with was doing an EDA simulation, containing millions of 10μs tasks. To say the least, threading this code did not produce favorable results (it ran much slower!). They later figured out a way of grouping the microtasks into larger tasks and threading those.

The opposite case is something like NFS, which contains hundreds of 40ms tasks. Threading NFS works quite well.

The Lessons of NFS

One practical problem in evaluating the performance of threaded programs is the lack of available data. There are simply no good analyses of real threaded programs that we can look at. (There are analyses of strictly computational parallel programs, but not of mixed usage programs; client/server, etc.) Nobody's done it yet! Probably the best data we have comes from NFS, which we shall now look at.

The standard metric for evaluating NFS performance is the SPEC LADDIS benchmark, which uses a predefined mix of file operations intended to reflect realistic usage (lots of small file information requests, some file reads, and a few file writes). As the NFS performance goes up, LADDIS spreads the file operations over a larger number of files on more disks to eliminate trivial, single-disk bottlenecks.

An NFS server is very demanding on all subsystems and as the hardware in one area improves, NFS performance will edge up until it hits a bottleneck in another. Figure 16–8 shows configurations and performance results for a variety of different systems. Notably, all of these systems are configured below their maximum size. Adding disks, controllers, or CPUs will not improve the performance. They do not use the maximum throughput of either I/O or memory busses.

In all of these maximum performance configurations, the bottleneck is contention and memory latency. One CPU will be working on some portion of a file system and will have locked inodes, allocation tables, etc. that another CPU requires. Once these locks are released, the other CPUs may have to context switch to the appropriate thread. It will certainly have to take a lot of cache-misses in order to load those newly changed tables. Additional CPUs will not improve the situation, but higher performance CPUs will. This is because one CPU can now do more work, hence the data in cache will be used more, reducing both the number of misses and the amount of contention.

NFS is not a "typical" client/server application in one particular aspect: NFS is started as a typical user-level process, but all that process does is to make a single call into the kernel. For the rest of its lifetime, NFS remains in the kernel, spawning threads there as it deems necessary. Thus, NFS does not have to do any context switching for I/O as

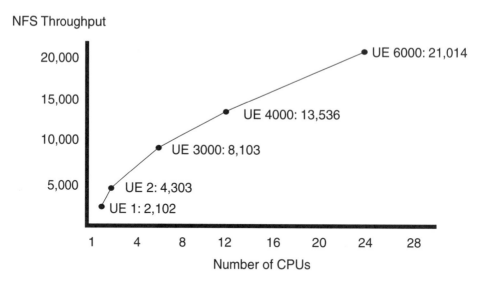

NFS Throughput

Figure 16-8   *NFS Throughput on a Series of Sun UE Machines. (The performance improvement is somewhat exaggerated, as a 2-way UE6000 will outperform a 2-way UE 2.)*

normal user-level programs must do, and it can avoid the extra step of copying data from kernel buffer to user space.[8]

NFS could have been written as a user-level program, but the context switching would have killed performance. It was never tried.[9]

A 24-way ES6000 can sustain ~21,000 NFS operations/second (about 900 ops/CPU) with a latency of about 40ms. A one-way machine gets about 2,000 ops. This implies a requirement of 500µs on the CPU per NFS op and thus 80 outstanding requests (waiting for the disks) at any one time. The limiting factor is CPU power plus locking contention. There is plenty of room for more or faster disks, and more network cards, but they wouldn't help.

---

[8]Most programs would not benefit from the "optimization" of executing entirely in the kernel. Outside of the horrible complexity of trying to build and maintain a patched kernel using constantly changing internal kernel interfaces, very few programs spend so much time in system calls and so little time in their own code. NFS spends about 45% of its time in the transport layer, 45% in the filesystem, and 10% in actual NFS code. Even DBMSs which are known for their enormous I/O demands pale in comparison to NFS. The distinction is that DBMSs are going to use much of the data they load, as opposed to just pushing it across the network like NFS.

[9]There is one example of precisely this being done, but it was never optimized to any degree, so we can't validly compare the (abysmal) results.

Actual data transfers are accomplished via DMA from/to disks and the network. The data is brought into the CPU only to perform checksums; it is never written by the CPU. Checksums have horrible data locality—they load lots of data, but use that data only once, and only for a single addition. This means that the CPU will spend an inordinate amount of time stalled, waiting for cache loads, but that it will do virtually no writes. (Some folks are building checksumming hardware for exactly this purpose.)

Normal programs spend more time using the data once loaded into cache, do more writes, and generally spend less time stalled on cache misses.

NFS is constructed as a producer/consumer program. The master/slave design was rejected as being inappropriate because of the nature of interrupt handling. When a network card gets a packet, it issues an interrupt to one of the CPUs (interrupts are distributed in a round-robin fashion on Sun's UE series). That CPU then runs its interrupt handler thread.

For an NFS request, the interrupt handler thread acts as the producer, building an NFS request structure and putting that onto a list. It is important for the interrupt handler thread to complete very quickly (as other interrupts will be blocked while it's running); thus it is not possible for that thread to do any appreciable amount of work (such as processing the request or creating a new thread). The consumers pull requests off the queue (exactly like our P/C example) and process them as appropriate. Sometimes the required information will be in memory, but usually a disk request will be required. This means that most requests will require a context switch.

Many of the original algorithms used in single-threaded NFS proved to be inappropriate for a threaded program. They worked correctly, but suffered from excessive contention when appropriate locking was added. A major amount of the work on multithreaded NFS was spent on writing new algorithms that would be less contentious.

The results? An implementation that scales extremely well on upwards of 24 CPUs.

Summary

Performance tuning is a very complex issue which has numerous trade-offs to be considered. Once a performance objective and level of effort has been established, you can start looking at the computer science issues. Even then the major issues will not be threading issues. Only after you've done a great deal of normal optimization work, will you turn your eyes towards threads. We give a cursory overview of the areas you need to consider, and wish you the best of luck.

17

Hardware

In which we look at the various designs for SMP machines (cache architectures, interconnect topologies, atomic instructions, invalidation techniques) and consider how those designs affect our programming decisions. Some optimization possibilities are looked at.

Types of Multiprocessors

In dealing with MT as we have described it here, we are also making some assumptions about the hardware we are going to be using. Everything we discussed is based on our using shared-memory, symmetric multiprocessor (SMP) machines. There are several other types of multiprocessor machines such as distributed shared-memory multiprocessors (Cray T3D, etc.) and massively parallel multiprocessors (CM-1, etc.), but these require very different programming techniques.

Shared-Memory, Symmetric Multiprocessors

The fundamental design of this machine requires that all processors see all of main memory in an identical fashion. Even though a memory bank might be physically closer to one CPU than another, there is no programming-level distinction in how that memory is accessed. (Hardware designers can do all sorts of clever things to optimize memory access behind our backs, as long as we are never aware of them.)

The other distinguishing aspect of this machine is that all CPUs have full access to all resources (kernel, disks, networks, interrupts, etc.) and are treated as peers by the operating system. Any CPU can run kernel code at any time (respecting locked regions, of course) to do anything. Any CPU can write out to any disk, network device, etc., at any time. Hardware interrupts may be delivered to any CPU, though this is a weaker requirement and is not always followed.[1]

All of the multiprocessors in the PC, workstation, and server realms are shared-memory symmetric multiprocessors: the two-way Compaq machines, all of the Sun, SGI, HP, DEC, HAL, and IBM RISC machines. (IBM also builds the SP-2, a large, distributed memory machine—basically a cluster of PowerServers.) Obviously all manufacturers have their own internal designs and optimizations, but for our purposes, they have essentially the same architecture.

---

[1]In practice, interrupts are generally distributed to CPUs in a round-robin fashion.

The CPU

All of the CPUs have the same basic design. There's the CPU proper (registers, instruction set, fetch, decode, execution units, etc.), and there's the interface to the memory system. There are two components of the memory interface which are of particular interest to us. First there's an *internal cache* (*I$*—typically 20–32kb), then an *external cache* (*E$*—typically 0.5–16 mb),[2] and finally there's a *store buffer*. The I$ holds all of the most recently accessed words and provides single-cycle access for the CPU. Should the I$ in CPU 0 contain a word that CPU 1 changes, there has to be some way for CPU 0 to beware of this change. E$ access is about 5 cycles, with the same coherency issue. Problem #1.

The store buffer is a small, specialized cache that holds words the CPU is writing out to memory. The idea is that instead of requiring the CPU to stall while a write is going on (it takes 30–100 cycles), the word will be placed into the store buffer, which will then arrange to write the word out to main memory when it sees fit. This way the CPU can run at full speed, not worrying about exactly when a word arrives in main memory.

Of course the store buffer must be closely coupled with the I$ and memory fetch unit to ensure that the CPU has a coherent view of memory. It wouldn't do for CPU 0 to write `x1234545F` into location `x00000010`, then load `x00000010` and not see `x1234545F`. Hardware architects take care of that, so we don't have to bother. The other issue with using a store buffer is that of determining when writes arrive in main memory. CPU 0 might write out dozens of words, placing them in the store buffer, while CPU 1, which then accesses those words, wouldn't see the changes, because the store buffer hasn't written them out yet. Problem #2.

Just to further complicate the hardware picture, it is possible for the hardware designers to give the store buffer more latitude in its choice of which words to write out when. *Total Store Order* refers to a design that requires the store buffer to write words to main memory in the same order as the instruction stream. It can be more efficient for the store buffer to write words out in a different order (perhaps it can write a series of contiguous words out together; perhaps it can write a word to memory bank 1, then memory bank 2). There are a variety of schemes for this out-

---

[2]The distinction between unified caches and divided caches (one section for instructions, a different section for data) is not particularly interesting for what we're doing.

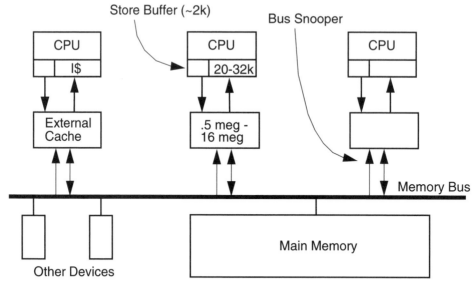

Figure 17–1 *SMP System Architecture*

of-order writing (*Partial Store Order, Weak Order*, etc.). The importance to us is that we must not rely on write order! Problem #3.

One more complication is that CPUs might do out-of-order execution too. If a CPU has to wait for a cache fill before executing instruction #1, it is allowed to look at instruction #2. If there is no dependency on #1, then the CPU may proceed to execute #2 first. This is a wonderful thing for hardware architects, as it gives them enormous leeway in their designs, allowing the CPU to run at maximum possible speeds. It also complicates CPU design, ensuring full employment for hardware designers. For us software types, it means that we cannot rely on order of execution.[3] Also problem #3.

The System

Figure 17–1 shows a typical SMP system.

Each CPU has its own on-chip I$ and store buffer. It also has a much larger, off-chip E$. All external communication is done over a single

---

[3]There are some fancy algorithms such as Decker's algorithm, which avoid using mutexes by depending upon the write order of CPUs. These techniques will not work on modern SMP machines.

memory bus. Part of the memory bus protocol for all these machines is that each CPU will do *bus snooping*. Every memory transaction will be observed by every bus snooper and every time CPU 0 writes a word out to main memory, every other bus snooper will see it and invalidate[4] that entry in its own caches (both E$ and I$). The next time CPU 1 wants to use that word, it will look in its own cache, see that the entry has been marked invalid, and go out to main memory to get the correct value.

What if CPU 1 also wants to write out the same word? What if CPU 1's store buffer is waiting to write it out? No answer. It would never happen, because that would mean that two different threads were manipulating the same data at the same time without a mutex and that's not proper. Problem #1 solved.

What if a global variable is in a register so the CPU doesn't see the invalidated word in cache? This also won't happen because the compiler is not allowed to keep non-local data in registers across function calls (e.g., `pthread_mutex_lock()`!).

Problems #2 and #3 are solved with the same mechanism—*store barriers*. A store barrier is a machine instruction which says "flush the store buffer." The CPU will then stall until the store buffer has been written out to main memory. On a SPARC machine, this is the instruction `stbar`.

Now then, when should we flush the store buffer? Whenever a CPU has changed some data that it wants other CPUs to see. This would be shared data, of course, and shared data may be used by other CPUs only after the first CPU has released the lock protecting it. And that's when `stbar` is called—when a mutex is being released. This is done by all the synchronization variable functions, so you will never call it yourself.

Thus, the short answer to all of the problems above is "Protect shared data with a mutex."

Bus Architectures

The design of the main memory bus does not have much effect on how we write MT programs specifically, but it does have enormous influence over how fast our programs run, and for high performance programs we must pay it respect. Depending upon the specific program, anywhere from 25% to 90% of the runtime will be devoted to waiting for the

---

[4]There are other schemes for dealing with this problem, such as cache broadcast, which simply sends out the updated value immediately, but this won't change our programming decisions.

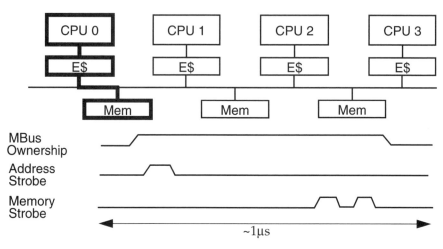

Figure 17–2 *Direct-Switched Memory Bus*

memory bus. (You can find programs which run entirely in cache and have zero percent bus waits, but they are the exceptions.)

There are two primary bus designs in use in SMP machines. There is the simple, *direct-switched bus* such as the MBus which was used in Sun's early SMP machines and the SPARCstation 10s and 20s. Then there is the more expensive, more complex, *packet-switched bus* (aka *split-transaction bus*) such as is used in all of the server machines from all the manufacturers (Sun's SPARCservers, Sun's Ultra series, SGI's Challenge series, HP's PA-RISC, IBM's POWERservers, DEC's Alpha servers, HAL's Mercury series, Cray's S6400 series, etc.). In addition to these, there are also *crossbar* switches that allow several CPUs to access several different memory banks simultaneously (Sun's Ultra servers, and SGI's Origin servers).

Direct-Switched Busses

In a direct-switched bus (Figure 17–2), memory access is very simple. When CPU 0 wants to read a word from main memory, it asserts bus ownership, makes the request, and waits until the data is loaded. The sequence is:

1. CPU 0 takes a cache miss. E$ must now go out to main memory to load an entire cache line (typically 8 words).

2. CPU 0 asserts bus ownership (perhaps waiting for a current owner to release).

3. CPU 0 loads the desired address onto the bus address lines, then strobes out that address on the address strobe line.

4. Memory sees the strobe, looks at the address, finds the proper memory bank, and then starts looking for the data. DRAM is fairly slow and takes roughly a microsecond[5] to find the desired data.

5. Once found, memory puts the first set of words onto the bus' data lines and strobes it into the E$. It then loads the next set of words, strobes that out, and continues until the entire cache-line request has been satisfied.

The total bus transaction latency, from initial request to final transfer, is on the order of one microsecond for all machines. It simply takes DRAM that long to find the data. Once found, DRAM can deliver the data quite rapidly, upwards of 60ns per access, but the initial lookup is quite slow.

On a direct-switched bus, the total memory bandwidth is quite small, not because of limited bus speeds, but because each transaction occupies the bus for so long, most of the time just waiting. Obviously, this is not an optimal situation. Sun's MBus was designed to accommodate up to four CPUs. In practice, it was found that four CPUs generated too much bus traffic in most programs and the vast majority of MBus machines were shipped with just two CPUs.

Packet-Switched Busses

In a packet-switched bus (Figure 17–3), the transaction is split between the CPU's request and the memory's reply. The objective of this design is to overcome the enormous periods of dead time that the direct-switched busses suffer. In this design, the CPU will release bus ownership while memory is busy looking up the address, hence freeing it for use by other CPUs.

---

[5]Depending on when you're reading this book!

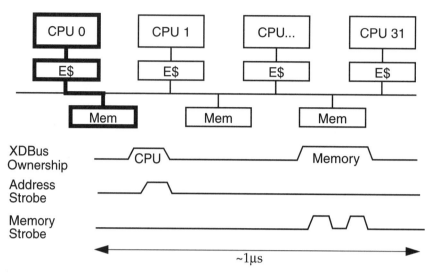

Figure 17–3 *Packet-Switched Memory Bus*

The sequence is:

1. CPU 0 takes a cache miss. E$ must now go out to main memory to load an entire cache line (typically 8 words).

2. CPU 0 asserts bus ownership (perhaps waiting for a current owner to release).

3. It loads the desired address onto the bus address lines, then strobes out that address on an address strobe line.

4. Memory sees the strobe, looks at the address, finds the proper memory bank, and then starts looking for the data.

5. At this point, CPU 0 releases bus ownership.

6. Once found, memory reasserts bus ownership.

7. Memory then strobes the data into CPU 0's E$.

Total latency for a packet-switched bus is no shorter than for a direct-switched bus, but because the bus is now free for use by other CPUs, the total throughput is much, much higher. Sun's UE10000 can run productively with upwards of 64 CPUs on a single bus.

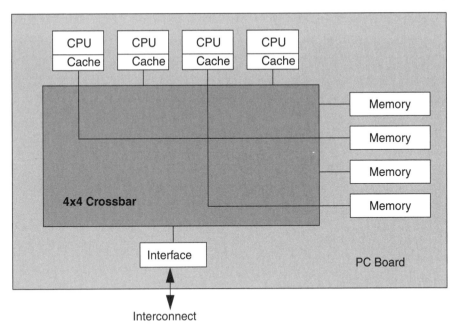

Figure 17–4 *A Cluster Using a Crossbar Switch*

Crossbar Switches

A crossbar is a routing switch that allows any one element on one axis to communicate directly with any one element on the other axis. This does not impact the ability of other elements on the first axis to communicate with other elements on the second. Contention occurs only when two elements on one axis want to communicate with the same element on the second. Crossbar switches are much faster than busses. And more expensive.

The practical limit on cross bar switches right now (1997) seems to be about 4x4 (Figure 17–4), the size of both the Sun and SGI designs. To build machines larger than 4 CPUs, some additional interconnect is required. On the larger Sun Ultra machines, a centerplane bus is used that can accommodate up to 16 quad CPU boards. On the larger SGI machines, an entirely different approach is used.

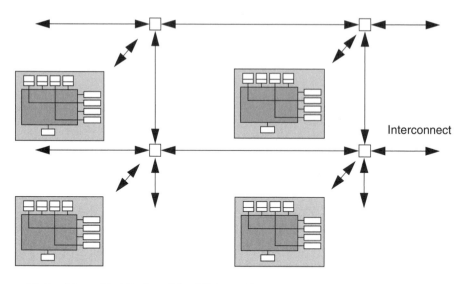

Figure 17–5   *Hierarchical Design of the SGI Origin Series*

Hierarchical Interconnects

The practical (and legal[6]) limit to bus length is approximately 16 boards. Beyond that, you have horrendous problems with signal propagation. The "obvious" solution to this limit is to build a hierarchical machine with clusters of busses communicating with other clusters of busses, ad infinitum. In its simplest form, this is no big deal. Want some more CPUs? Just add a new cluster! Sure, you'll see longer communication latencies as you access more distant clusters, but that's just the way things are.

There is one aspect of SMP design that makes a mess of this simple model—cache memory. We need to use caches to avoid saturating the interconnect, but at the same time caches need to be kept coherent and *that's* tricky. If the cache for CPU 169 contains an entry for address x31415926, and CPU 0 writes into that address, how is cache 169 going to get invalidated? Propagating every invalidate across the entire interconnect would quickly saturate it. The object now becomes finding a method to propagate invalidations only to those caches that need them.

Built along the designs of Stanford's DASH project, the SGI Origin (Figure 17–5) uses a small crossbar for its clusters, and an expandable,

---

[6]186,000 miles/second. It's not just a good idea, it's the law!

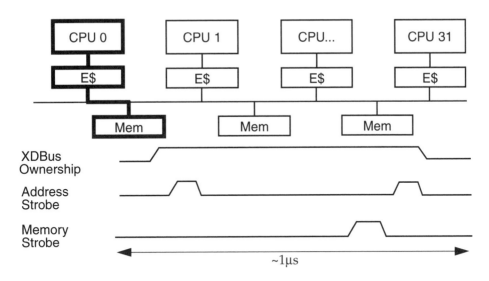

Figure 17–6 *Packet-Switched Memory Bus Running* `ldstub`

hierarchical lattice instead of a bus. Embedded in each cluster is an invalidation directory, which keeps track of which other clusters have cached copies of its local memory. When main memory is written to, the directory knows to which clusters to send invalidations. The result is that the basic machine can be expanded well past the 16 board limit of bus-based machines, at a cost of about 150ns extra latency for each hop across the lattice. The Origin is spec'd to expand out to 4096 CPUs. Now the only problem is writing programs that can use 4096 CPUs....

Packet-Switched Busses and `ldstub`

There is one place we care about the bus design very directly (see Figure 17–6). Remember `ldstub`, the mutex instruction? Well, the definition of `ldstub` says that it must perform its work atomically. For a packet-switched bus, this means that it must retain bus ownership throughout the entire operation, first fetching the byte in question, then writing all ones out to it. In other words, using `ldstub` completely defeats the packet-switched nature of a packet-switched bus!

There is no way around the fundamental problem, as ldstub must be atomic. It *must* occupy the bus for the duration. What we can do is simply not call it too often. In particular, this means modifying our definition of spin locks. Whereas our first definition of spin locks resulted in our calling ldstub on every iteration of the loop (thus flooding the bus), our better definition will avoid calling ldstub unless we're fairly sure it will succeed. What we'll do is spin in a loop, looking at the value of the ownership byte. As long as it's owned, we'll just keep spinning, looking at the value in cache, not generating any bus traffic at all.

When the lock is released, the owner CPU will write out zero, which our bus snooper will see, invalidating our copy of the byte. On our next iteration we'll get a cache miss, reload from main memory, and see the new value. We'll call trylock (hence ldstub) and if we're lucky, it will succeed and we'll get lock ownership. On the off chance that some other CPU sneaks in there at exactly the right nanosecond, our ldstub will fail, and we'll go back to spinning. Generally, you should expect spin locks to be provided by your vendor.

```
/* Implementation dependent. This is valid only for Solaris 2.5 */
void spin_lock(mutex_t *m)
{int i;

  for (i = 0; i < SPIN_COUNT; i++)
    {if (m->lock.owner64 == 0)                   /* Check w/o ldstub */
            if (pthread_mutex_trylock(m) != EBUSY)
                    return;                       /* Got it! */
        /* Didn't get it, continue the loop */
    }

  pthread_mutex_lock(m);                          /* Give up and block */
}
```

Code Example 17–1: *Spin Locks Done Better*

The Thundering Herds

This is as far as we're going to go with spin locks. This covers 99.9% of all programs that need spin locks. For that final 0.1%, where there is enormous contention for a single spin lock, even this scheme will suffer. If there are 10 CPUs all spinning on this lock, then the moment it's released, all ten of them will take cache misses, flooding the bus first with cache load requests, then ldstub requests. This is known as the *thundering herds* problem and is discussed in more detail by Hennessy & Patterson. Suffice it to say, if you're suffering from this problem, you have real problems. The best thing you can do is to find another algorithm with less contention.

LoadLocked/StoreConditional and Compare and Swap

We mentioned that there are other types of atomic instructions that are a bit more versatile. On SPARC v9, there is the *Compare and Swap if Equal* instruction. On the Alpha, there is a different approach to the same issue, using two instructions, known as *Load Locked* and *Store Conditional*.

The Alpha instructions require a tiny bit more hardware, but reward the designer with an atomic instruction that *doesn't* lock the memory bus. (Especially nice for spin locks!) Along side of the bus snooper hardware is one more register. When a `LoadLocked` instruction is issued, the data is fetched directly from main memory, and that address is recorded in the register. Should some other CPU write to that address, the register notices it. Later the program will issue a `StoreConditional` instruction. This instruction looks at the register before doing the store. If the register says the address is unchanged, then the store proceeds. If the address has been written to already, then the store doesn't take place. After `StoreConditional` is finished, the programmer must check to see if the store took place. If so, then all is well. If not, then go back and repeat.

Building a mutex with these instructions is simple. Of more interest are the other types of synchronization we can do, such as atomic increment/decrement, and atomic list insertion. In effect we will be implicitly locking the word in question, updating it, and releasing the implicit lock. The important distinction is that we can now execute these operations with no possibility of the lock owner going to sleep.

In Code Example 17–2, we assume that memory location `address_1` will not change between the time we read it and the time we execute the `StoreConditional`. If it does change, we simply loop back and try it again. This operation is equivalent to acquiring a lock, incrementing the word, and releasing the lock, with the exception that it is impossible to go to sleep while holding the lock. We cannot mix use of these instructions and normal mutex locks.

```
try_again:LoadLocked address_1 -> register_1
         add register_1, 1 -> register_2
         StoreConditional register_2 -> address_1
         Compare register_2, 0
         branch_not_equal try_again
```

Code Example 17–2:   *Atomic Increment Using `LoadLocked` and
                          `StoreConditional`*

The advantage to these instructions is that they run roughly twice as fast as mutex-protected code and there is no danger of being context switched in the middle of execution. The disadvantage is that the operations you can perform are very simple and may not be sufficient to our purposes. Inserting an element onto the front of a list is simple, but inserting elsewhere in the list is impossible. (Yes, we can correctly change the next pointer of `item_n`, but `item_n` might have been removed from the list while we were reading the next pointer!) For more general usage, we need mutex locks.

The tricky part is that you can use these instructions to automatically increment or decrement a variable, but you can't make any decisions based on "current" value, because the variable's value may change before you make your decision. In normal code, you would make a decision based on the value of a variable while in a critical section, so that the variable couldn't change.

You will sometimes see the use of these instructions referred to as *lock-free synchronization*.

Lock-Free Semaphores and Reference Counting

Semaphores need to know if a decrement attempt succeeded or not. If successful, there is nothing else for the semaphore to do. It's done (this will be our "fast path"—the most common case). Should the semaphore value already be zero, then a bit of careful programming will allow the thread to go to sleep, confident that the next `sem_post()` will wake it up. This means that `sem_wait()` can execute in a single instruction (we don't even have to block out signals, because no lock is being held)! Calls to `sem_post()` will be somewhat more complex (they have to look for sleepers), but still *very* fast.

Reference counting is one of the few other things that you can use such atomic instructions for, because the only decision you make in reference counting occurs when the count hits zero. Once zero, the reference count cannot be changed (there are no pointers left to the item to copy), hence you can rely on this value.

Memory Systems

The memory system in modern SMP machines is designed to be ignored. You shouldn't have to spend any time thinking about it, it should just work. And it succeeds in this, to a degree. As long as you are writing a program that is reasonably well behaved and that doesn't have overwhelming needs for absolute maximum performance, then you can skip over this section. Probably 95% of all programs fit into this category. As for the other five percent....

In 1980, memory speeds were about the same as CPU speeds, and a machine could access main memory in a single cycle. Since then, DRAM speeds have improved by an order of magnitude and CPU speeds by almost four. Direct main memory access now costs between 30 and 100 CPU cycles. It is not at all unusual for a CPU to spend over half its time stalled, waiting for memory. To the degree that you can reduce the number of main memory accesses (i.e., cache misses), you will be handsomely paid in program performance. (NB: There is nothing unique to MP machines or MT programs here.)

Reducing Cache Misses

So, how to reduce cache misses? There are a couple of generalities that we can point to, but not much more. Happily these generalities do cover a lot of programs.

1. Write your program so that you never have to load a cache line more times than is absolutely necessary.
2. Organize your data so that when you do load a cache line, you are able to make use of all of the data.
3. Keep data used regularly by different threads out of the same cache line.

Depending upon your particular program, it may or may not be reasonable to apply the above. For well-behaved programs that reuse the data in cache many times, a great deal can be done just covering these three rules. We can show a factor of ten difference between a naive matrix multiply and the most highly optimized implementation, all due to better cache management. For programs with very poor data locality, such as NFS or databases, which spend a lot of time bringing in new data and looking at it only once, it is almost impossible to do anything at all.

Cache Blocking

For something like matrix manipulation or image processing, a naive algorithm might load and reload a cache line numerous times. The same operation can be performed much faster in a more clever algorithm that does *cache blocking*—arranging to load a subset of the data and use it many times before loading a new block.

A naive multiply algorithm would multiply all of row 1 by column 1. Then row 1 by column 2, column 3, etc. Next row 2 would be multiplied with each column, etc. For a 1,024x1,024 matrix, each row would be loaded only once, but the columns would be reloaded 1,024 times! Assuming 64-bit floats and 64-byte cache lines, that adds up to a total of 128k cache loads.

A cache-blocked program would multiply rows 1–64 with columns 1–64, then columns 65–128, then 129–192, etc. Each of those sets will fit completely in a two meg E$, so the total number of cache loads will be reduced to a mere 16k column load plus 1k row loads.

That's the basics of cache blocking. There's plenty more that can be done. For example, you can optimize I$ blocking on top of the E$ blocking. You can take into account the writing scheme (does the CPU write back via the cache, write through the cache, or write around it?). You can recall that E$ is physically mapped, hence it requires a TLB translation. (The *translation lookaside buffer* performs high-speed virtual-to-physical mappings.) Of course TLBs are very small. The Sun TLB for the large SC2000 server holds a translation for only 0.5 meg, so if you can avoid referencing data in cache beyond the current contents of the TLB, you can avoid extraneous TLB misses. Then you may also wish to consider which data is coming from which memory bank....

We really don't expect you to deal with these fine-grained optimizations. We don't. They involve a lot of careful estimation and painstaking verification, and they have to be tailored to individual machines. But this kind of thing is possible, it does yield impressive improvements for some programs, and the truly high performance obsessive types do it. (Dakota

Scientific's numerical libraries take all of these parameters into account and get impressive results. See *Dakota Scientific Software* on page 240.)

Data Reorganization

What if you had a large number of records about people—names, ages, salaries, addresses, favorite programming languages, etc.? To calculate the average salary for these folks, you would have to bring in the cache block with the first person's salary in it (along with seven other words), add that to the total, then bring in the next person's salary, etc. Each cache miss would bring in exactly one piece of useful data, and every salary would require a cache miss.

If you organized the data differently, placing all of the salaries into one array, all of the names in another, etc., then you would be able to make much better use of each cache load. Instead of one salary being loaded with each miss, you'd get eight, significantly reducing cache wait times.

This is not something you'd do for a casual program. When you have this kind of program design and data usage, and you are desperate for optimal performance, that's when you do this kind of thing. (See *Portability* on page 257.)

False Sharing

A cache memory is divided up into cache lines (typically eight words) which are loaded and tracked as a unit. If one word in the line is required, all eight are loaded. If one word is written out by another CPU, the entire line is invalidated. Cache lines are based on the idea that if one word is accessed, it's very likely that the next word will be also. Normally this works quite well and yields excellent performance. Sometimes it can work against you.

If eight integers happened to be located contiguously at a line boundary, and if eight different threads on eight different CPUs happened to use those (unshared) integers extensively, then we could run into a problem. CPU 0 would write a[0]. This would of course cause the a[0] cache line to be invalidated on all the other CPUs. CPU 1 now wishes to read a[1]. Even though it actually has a valid copy of a[1] in cache, the line has been marked invalid, so CPU 1 must reload that cache line. And when CPU 1 writes a[1], CPU 0 will invalidate its cache line. Etc., etc.

```
int a[128];

void *foo((void *) index)
{
 while (MANY_INTERATIONS)
  a[index]++;
}

...
for (i=0; i<8 ;i++)
   PTHREAD_CREATE(NULL, NULL, foo, (void *) i * SEPARATION);
...
```

Code Example 17–3: *False Sharing*

This is what is called *false sharing*. On an 8-way, 244 MHz UE4000, the program above runs in 100 seconds when the integers are adjacent (SEPARATION == 1), and in 10 seconds when the integers are distant (SEPARATION == 16). It is an unlikely problem (it can happen, however), one that you wouldn't even look for unless you did some careful performance tuning and noticed extensive CPU stalls. Without specialized memory tools, the only way you could find this out is by counting instructions and dividing by CPU speed. If there is a large discrepancy, you can infer memory system stalls. (See *Memory Latency* on page 260.)

Summary

There are numerous machine designs, most of which will not affect our programming decisions. There are a lot of issues concerning memory coherency, all of which are solved by using proper locking. For very high performance programs, clever, semi-portable cache blocking schemes and data organization can have enormous impact.

18

Examples

In which several complete programs are presented. The details and issues surrounding the way they use threads are discussed and references to other programs on the net are made.

This chapter contains several examples that use the POSIX threads library. The examples use threads to demonstrate different concepts from previous chapters. All the example code has been compiled and run on Solaris 2.5, IRIX 6.2 Digital UNIX 4.0D, and HP-UX 10.30.

Please use this code in whatever manner you choose; many of the concepts demonstrated in the examples can be reworked to be used in your applications. Of course, there are some bugs in the code somewhere.... All the source code used in this book is available on the web (see *Code Examples* on page 314).

Threads and Windows

This example uses threads in conjunction with X11 and Motif®. As most of us program only in high-level window toolkits (such as CDE Motif), it doesn't make much difference if X11 is MT safe or not. The toolkits are not, so we must write our programs with that in mind.

In a "normal" windowing application, when a button is pressed, some task is executed and then control in the program is returned to the window. This is fine if the time required to execute the task is minimal. If the time required for the task is not minimal, then the window *freezes* or the clock icon is displayed while the task is executing. This behavior, in most cases, is not desirable, because the graphical interface should always be active for the user to select other actions.

This example demonstrates how we can get around the *freezing* problem. A simple window is created and filled with push-button widgets. When a button is pushed, the program simulates some processing (i.e., `sleep(6)`) that would normally cause the interface to freeze. In this example the work is performed in separate threads. This way, when a button is pressed, a thread is created to do the work, and the window can return to its event processing for the user.

When you run this example, you will see that when a button is pressed, it changes colors and is deactivated while the work is being done. However, you can press as many buttons as you like, one right after the other without waiting for the first to complete.

This program is exactly what was described in *Are Libraries Safe?* on page 194. The main thread opens a pipe and creates a callback for it (`WorkComplete()`). It then enters the event-loop and waits for input. When you push a button, the callback `ButtonPushed()` runs,

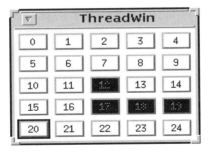

Figure 18–1   *Threaded Window Example*

deactivates the button, changes its colors, and (optionally) creates a new thread (T2) to run the work function (DoWork()).

The main thread then returns to the event loop. You press another button and the cycle repeats. In the meantime (back at the ranch), the new thread has started up and begun running. With our second push, a third thread (T3) has started up, just like T2. After a few seconds, T2 completes its work and writes to the pipe.

The main thread reads from that pipe, runs the pipe callback, WorkComplete(). That function sets the button back to the original colors and reactivates the button. Now only T3 is running. Soon it shall complete and repeat the actions of T2. In this fashion, the event loop is always active and the Motif and X11 calls are made only from the main thread.

This example uses a command-line argument that can enable or disable the threads in the process, so you can see how the program behaves with and without threads (see Figure 18–1).

```
> ThreadWin MT
```

The X11 programming libraries will not be thread safe until release 6 (X11R6). Code Example 18–1 was originally written for use on X11R6; however, it may run just fine on nonsafe X11 libraries. If you run this program and it fails, it's likely you are not running a thread-safe X11 library.

```
/*
Simple window program that inverts the colour of each button for
 6 seconds.

  In the non-spawning version, it hangs for 6 seconds with the GUI
  inactive (tho events are queued).  In the MT version, it spawns off a
  new thread to do that long "calculation," hence the GUI remains active.
  Upon completion, the thread writes to a pipe.  The X notifier reads
  from that pipe and inverts the colour back to the original colour.
*/
/*
cc -o ThreadWin ThreadWin.c -L. -R. -g -lpthread -lthread
   -lthread_extensions -lposix4 -I/usr/dt/include
   -I/usr/openwin/include -L/usr/openwin/lib -L/usr/dt/lib
   -R/usr/openwin/lib -R/usr/dt/lib -lXm -lXt -lX11 -lm

*/

#define _POSIX_C_SOURCE 199506L
#include <stdio.h>
#include <unistd.h>
#include <stdlib.h>
#include <math.h>
#include <X11/Intrinsic.h>
#include <X11/X.h>
#include <X11/StringDefs.h>
#include <Xm/Xm.h>
#include <Xm/RowColumn.h>
#include <Xm/PushB.h>
#include <pthread.h>
#include "thread_extensions.h"

#define READ 0
#define WRITE 1


/* function prototypes */
int ButtonPushed(Widget, XtPointer);
void *DoWork(void *);
XtAppContext _XtDefaultAppContext();
XtInputCallbackProc WorkComplete();
static int message[2];
pthread_attr_t attr;
```

Code Example 18–1: *Using a Pipe to Communicate with X11,*
(ThreadWin.c)

```
void *killer(void *arg)
{
  sleep(30);/* Don't run forever, these are demos! */
  exit(NULL);
}


main(int argc, char **argv)
{Widget      toplevel, base, button[200];
 Arg         wargs[10];
 int         i, MT=0, N_BUTTONS=25;
 char        but_label[5];
 XEvent      event, fake;
 Display     *disp;
 Window      win;
 XtAppContextapp;
 pthread_t   tid;

 /* check arguments */
 if (argc > 2)
   printf("Usage: %s [MT]\n", argv[0]), exit(0);

 if (argc == 2 && strcmp(argv[1], "MT") == 0) MT = 1;

 if (pipe(message) < 0)
   {fprintf(stderr, "Can't open pipe\n");
    exit(1);
  }
 PTHREAD_ATTR_INIT(&attr);
 pthread_attr_setdetachstate(&attr, PTHREAD_CREATE_DETACHED);
 pthread_attr_setscope(&attr, PTHREAD_SCOPE_SYSTEM);
 PTHREAD_CREATE(&tid, &attr, killer, NULL);

 /* setup our main window */
 toplevel=XtInitialize(argv[0], "ThreadWin", NULL, 0, &argc, argv);

 /* set some arguments for our Row/Column Widget */
 XtSetArg(wargs[0], XmNorientation, XmHORIZONTAL);
 XtSetArg(wargs[1], XmNentryAlignment, XmALIGNMENT_CENTER);
 XtSetArg(wargs[2], XmNisAligned, True);
 XtSetArg(wargs[3], XmNnumColumns,
          (int)floor(sqrt((double)N_BUTTONS)));
 XtSetArg(wargs[4], XmNpacking, XmPACK_COLUMN);
```

Code Example 18-1:   *(cont.) Using a Pipe to Communicate with X11,*
(ThreadWin.c)

```
     /* create the Row/Column Widget */
     base=XtCreateManagedWidget("base", xmRowColumnWidgetClass,
                 toplevel, wargs, 5);


     /* create the button widgets with the button number as it label */
     for (i=0;i<N_BUTTONS;i++)
       {sprintf(but_label, " %d ", i);
        XtSetArg(wargs[0], XmNlabelString,
            XmStringCreate(but_label, XmSTRING_DEFAULT_CHARSET));
        button[i] = XmCreatePushButton(base, "button", wargs, 1);

        /* tell the button to call ButtonPushed() when pushed */
        XtAddCallback(button[i], XmNactivateCallback,
            (XtCallbackProc) ButtonPushed, (void *)MT);
      }

     /* manage the buttons and go into the X event loop */
     XtManageChildren(button, N_BUTTONS);
     XtRealizeWidget(toplevel);
     app = _XtDefaultAppContext();
     XtAppAddInput(app, message[READ], (void *)XtInputReadMask,
               (XtInputCallbackProc)WorkComplete, NULL);
     XtMainLoop();
}

XtInputCallbackProc WorkComplete()
{Pixel fg, bg;
 Arg warg[2];
 Widget w;

 if (read(message[READ], &w, sizeof(w)) != sizeof(w))
   {fprintf(stderr, "Read error\n");
    exit(1);
 }

 /* get the buttons foreground and background colors */
 XtSetArg(warg[0], XmNforeground, &fg);
 XtSetArg(warg[1], XmNbackground, &bg);
 XtGetValues(w, warg, 2);

 /* swap the buttons foreground and background colors */
 XtSetArg(warg[0], XmNforeground, bg);
 XtSetArg(warg[1], XmNbackground, fg);
```

Code Example 18–1:   *(cont.) Using a Pipe to Communicate with X11,*
                          (ThreadWin.c)

```
 XtSetValues(w, warg, 2);

 XtSetSensitive(w, True);
 return((XtInputCallbackProc)0);
}


/*
    Button callback routine -- Called when a button is pushed
*/

int ButtonPushed(Widget w, XtPointer MT)
{int        mt = (int) MT;
 Pixel      fg, bg;
 Arg        warg[2];
 pthread_t  tid;

 XtSetSensitive(w, False);

 /* get the buttons foreground and background colors */
 XtSetArg(warg[0], XmNforeground, &fg);
 XtSetArg(warg[1], XmNbackground, &bg);
 XtGetValues(w, warg, 2);

 /* swap the buttons foreground and background colors */
 XtSetArg(warg[0], XmNforeground, bg);
 XtSetArg(warg[1], XmNbackground, fg);
 XtSetValues(w, warg, 2);

 if (MT)
   PTHREAD_CREATE(&tid, &attr, DoWork, (void *)w);
 else
   DoWork((void *)w);


 return(0);
}


void *DoWork(void *arg)
{Widget w = (Widget) arg;
 pthread_t tid = pthread_self();
 char *name = thread_name(tid);

 printf("Thread %s: Start Processing...\n", name);
```

Code Example 18–1:   *(cont.) Using a Pipe to Communicate with X11,*
*(*ThreadWin.c*)*

```
    sleep(6);
    printf("Thread %s: Processing done...\n", name);

    if (write(message[WRITE], &w, sizeof(w)) != sizeof(w))
      {fprintf(stderr, "Write error\n");
        exit(1);
    }
  return((void *)0);
}
```

Code Example 18–1:   *(cont.) Using a Pipe to Communicate with X11, (ThreadWin.c)*

Socket Server (Master/Slave Version)

The socket server example (Code Example 18–2) uses threads to implement a "standard" socket port server. The example shows how you can use pthread_create() calls in the place of fork() calls in existing programs.

A standard socket server listens on a socket port and, when a message arrives, forks a process to service the request. Since a fork() system call is used in a nonthreaded program, any communication between the parent and child must be done through some sort of interprocess communication, something our program avoids.

The server program first sets up all the needed socket information. The server then enters a loop, waiting to service a socket port. When a message is sent to the socket port, the server creates a new thread to handle the requests on this file descriptor.

The newly created listener thread then receives requests on this file descriptor in the function producer() until the string "End" comes across. For each request, the listener thread creates a new thread to handle it. That worker thread processes the request in process_request(), which sleeps for a bit (simulating disk I/O), and then sends a reply back across the file descriptor.

The client side of the example (not shown) sends 10,000 requests to the server for each file descriptor you request on the command line (default 1). It waits for each reply and exits when the server returns "End". This client code can also be run from different machines by multiple users.

The code is a little bit artificial because we wrote it to look as much as possible like our producer/consumer example. We also added some instrumentation to it, so it will count the number of threads created and running. One notable artifice is that we accept 10,000 requests from each socket, rather than one request from each of 10,000 sockets as you might expect. Our design gives the program a two-level structure, with the main thread waiting for new socket requests (in the accept() call). The main thread creates a new thread to handle each new socket, and that new thread then waits for the 10,000 requests, spawning 10,000 additional threads, one per request.

```
/*
A simple server program.  It sets up a TCP port for the client
  program to connect to.

  This version creates lots and lots of threads without bound.
  Maybe even too many threads (when the delay is long).  Scope
  is PROCESS local to emphasize how bad it can get.


cc -o server_ms server_ms.c -L. -R. -g -lpthread -lthread
   -lthread_extensions -lposix4 -lnsl -lsocket
*/

#define _POSIX_C_SOURCE 199506L

#include <stdio.h>
#include <stdlib.h>
#include <unistd.h>
#include <sys/types.h>
#include <sys/socket.h>
#include <netinet/in.h>
#include <string.h>
#include <sys/uio.h>
#include <unistd.h>
#include <pthread.h>
#include <semaphore.h>
#include <time.h>
#include "thread_extensions.h"


struct request_struct
{int                     socket_fd;
 char                    *buf;
 pthread_t               tid;
```

Code Example 18–2: *Thread per Request Socket Server from*
server_ms.c

```
  struct request_struct *next;
};
typedef struct request_struct request_t;

pthread_attr_t        attr;
int                   TCP_PORT = 6500;
int                   SLEEP = 10;
int                   SPIN = 0;
int                   SPAWN = 1;



void count_threads(int i)                 /* Note the encapsulation
{static int count=0, old_count=0, max_count = 0;
 static pthread_mutex_t count_lock = PTHREAD_MUTEX_INITIALIZER;

 pthread_mutex_lock(&count_lock);
 count += i;
 if (i == 0) printf("Max thread count: %d\n", max_count);
 if (abs(count - old_count) > 9)
   {printf("%d threads running\n", count);
    old_count = count;}
 if (count > max_count)
   max_count = count;
 pthread_mutex_unlock(&count_lock);
}


void count_requests(int i)                /* Note the encapsulation
{static int count=0, old_count=0, max_count = 0;
 static pthread_mutex_t count_lock = PTHREAD_MUTEX_INITIALIZER;

 pthread_mutex_lock(&count_lock);
 count += i;
 if (i == 0) printf("Max thread count: %d\n", max_count);
 if (abs(count - old_count) > 999)
   {printf("Processed %d requests.\n", count);
    old_count = count;}
 if (count > max_count)
   max_count = count;
 pthread_mutex_unlock(&count_lock);
}
```

Code Example 18–2:   *(cont.) Thread per Request Socket Server from*
                        `server_ms.c`

```
void *process_request(void *arg)
{char          obuf[100];
 request_t     *request = (request_t *) arg;
 pthread_t     tid = pthread_self();

 DEBUG(printf("[%s] received: \"%s\"\n", thread_name(tid),
                                      request->buf));
 delay(SLEEP, SPIN);

 /* Typical msg: "Server[T@9] "DATA SEGMENT 693 [T@4]"" */
 sprintf(obuf, "Server[%s] %s", thread_name(tid), request->buf);
 write(request->socket_fd, obuf, 50);
 free(request->buf);
 free(request);
}


void *process_request_thr(void *arg)/* Just a wrapper function */
{
  process_request(arg);
  count_threads(-1);
  pthread_exit(NULL);
}


request_t *get_request(int socket_fd)
{request_t     *request;
 char          ibuf[100];

 read(socket_fd, ibuf, 50);
 if (strcmp(ibuf, "End") == 0) return(NULL);

 request = (request_t *) malloc(sizeof(request_t));
 request->socket_fd = socket_fd;
 request->buf = (char *) malloc(strlen(ibuf)+1);
 strcpy(request->buf, ibuf);
 count_requests(1);
 return(request);
}
```

Code Example 18–2:   *(cont.) Thread per Request Socket Server from*
server_ms.c

```
void producer(int socket_fd)
{request_t *request;
  pthread_t tid;

 while (1)
    {request = get_request(socket_fd);
     if (request == NULL) return;
     if (SPAWN == 0)
       process_request(request);              /* Don't create new thread
     else
       {PTHREAD_CREATE(&tid, &attr, process_request_thr,
                        (void *)request);
        count_threads(1);}
   }
}


void *accept_requests(void *arg)/* Expect 10,000 msgs per socket */
{int socket_fd = (int) arg;
 char ibuf[100], obuf[100];
 int i, j;
 pthread_t tid = pthread_self();
 char *name = thread_name(tid);

 printf("[%s] Accepting on socket: %d\n", name, socket_fd);

 producer(socket_fd);
 write(socket_fd, "End", 4);
 close(socket_fd);
 count_threads(-1);
 printf("[%s] Done Processing. ", thread_name(tid));
 count_threads(0);
 pthread_exit(NULL);
}


void *killer(void *arg)
{
  sleep(30);
  exit(NULL);
}
```

Code Example 18–2:   *(cont.) Thread per Request Socket Server from*
                          `server_ms.c`

```
main(int argc, char **argv)
{int         i, sockfd, newsockfd, clilen;
 struct      sockaddr_in cli_addr, serv_addr;
 pthread_t   tid;

 if (argc >= 2) TCP_PORT = atoi(argv[1]);
 if (argc >= 3) SLEEP = atoi(argv[2]);
 if (argc >= 4) SPIN = atoi(argv[3]);
 if (argc >= 4) SPAWN = atoi(argv[4]);
 printf("TCP_PORT = %d SLEEP (ms) = %d SPIN (us) = %d SPAWN = %d\n",
   TCP_PORT, SLEEP, SPIN, SPAWN);

 if((sockfd = socket(AF_INET, SOCK_STREAM, 0)) < 0)
   fprintf(stderr,"server: can't open stream socket\n"), exit(0);
 memset((char *) &serv_addr, 0, sizeof(serv_addr));
 serv_addr.sin_family = AF_INET;
 serv_addr.sin_addr.s_addr = htonl(INADDR_ANY);
 serv_addr.sin_port = htons(TCP_PORT);

 if(bind(sockfd, (struct sockaddr *)
         &serv_addr,sizeof(serv_addr)) < 0)
   fprintf(stderr,"server: can't bind local address\n"), exit(0);

 PTHREAD_ATTR_INIT(&attr);
 pthread_attr_setdetachstate(&attr, PTHREAD_CREATE_DETACHED);
/* pthread_attr_setscope(&attr, PTHREAD_SCOPE_SYSTEM); Why?-Try!*/
 PTHREAD_CREATE(&tid, &attr, killer, NULL);

 listen(sockfd, 5);

 while (1)
   {clilen = sizeof(cli_addr);
    newsockfd = accept(sockfd,
                   (struct sockaddr *)&cli_addr,&clilen);
    if(newsockfd < 0)
      fprintf(stderr,"server: accept error\n"), exit(0);

    /* A new socket!  Expect 10,000 msgs */
    PTHREAD_CREATE(&tid, &attr, accept_requests,
                (void *)newsockfd);
    count_threads(1);
  }
}
```

Code Example 18–2: *(cont.) Thread per Request Socket Server from*
`server_ms.c`

Socket Server (Producer/Consumer Version)

Run the master/slave code on a fast enough machine and you will discover that it creates so many threads that it runs out of memory! This is not a good thing. One solution is to keep careful track of how many threads you have created and how many have exited. A better solution would be to redesign the program to be a producer/consumer model. This way you will be able to control the number of threads with no problem and you will be able to use the list of outstanding requests as a buffer for when the number of requests exceeds the ability of the program to handle them.

Of course, if the rate of incoming requests exceeds the ability to reply for too long, then you will eventually have to simply reject the requests. You could have the producer thread send explicit rejections to the client programs, or it could simply refuse to call `accept()` until there is room on the list. In this case, the kernel will queue up a few requests, then simply refuse to acknowledge any more requests.

Most of the code for the producer/consumer version is identical to that in Code Example 18–2. The relevant changes are shown in Code Example 18–3. You will notice that most of the code is stolen directly from Code Example 6–7 on page 92. Both the `producer()` and `consumer()` functions are identical. Really all we're doing is redirecting the producer above, from creating new threads for each request, to placing those requests onto a queue and letting the consumers worry about them.

```
void producer(int socket_fd)
{request_t *request;

  while (1)
    {request = get_request(socket_fd);
     if (request == NULL) return;
     SEM_WAIT(&requests_slots);
     add_request(request);
     sem_post(&requests_length);   }
}
```

Code Example 18–3: *From* `server_pc.c`

```
void *accept_requests(void *arg)
{int        socket_fd = (int) arg;
 char       ibuf[100], obuf[100];
 int        i, j;
 pthread_t  tid = pthread_self();
 char       *name = thread_name(tid);

 printf("[%s] Accepting on socket: %d\n", name, socket_fd);

 producer(socket_fd);
 write(socket_fd, "End", 4);
 close(socket_fd);
 count_threads(-1);
 printf("[%s] Done Processing.    ", name));
 count_threads(0);
 pthread_exit(NULL);
}

main()
{
...

 for (i=0; i<N_THREADS; i++)
    PTHREAD_CREATE(&tid, &attr, consumer, NULL);

PTHREAD_CREATE(&tid, &attr, stopper, NULL);

 while (1)
   {newsockfd=accept(sockfd,(struct sockaddr *)&cli_addr, &clilen);
    if(newsockfd < 0)
       fprintf(stderr,"server: accept error\n"), exit(0);
    PTHREAD_CREATE(&tid, &attr, accept_requests,(void *)newsockfd);

   }
}
```

Code Example 18–3: *From* `server_pc.c`

Now a little problem we've glossed over…. You may have noticed that our program has no way to tell if it has sent out all of the pending replies before the "end" request comes across. It is possible that the client program takes care of this, though ours doesn't. Obviously, this must be done to have a properly running program. Lots of techniques are possible, none of which are uniquely outstanding. We leave it as an exercise for the reader.

Other Programs on the Web

There are a small series of other programs on the web page that may be of some interest. Each of them has points of interest, but none of them is sufficiently interesting for us to print in its entirety. You may well find the programs helpful in clarifying details about how to write code for specific situations, and for how to use the APIs. Several are variations of the programs in previous chapters, and several are simple test programs which illustrate how some of the fancier extension functions work, such as FIFO mutexes, recursive mutexes, mutexes with timeouts, an "atfork" alternative. The program ipc.c is the producer/consumer program running in shared memory across two processes.

Summary

Several POSIX programs were shown, each with a certain point to elucidate. As with all of the example programs, translation to Win32 or OS/2 is (supposed to be) straightforward and left as an exercise for the reader.

Appendix A

Internet

Threads Newsgroup

For discussion, questions and answers, and just general debate about threading issues, there is a newsgroup on the Internet (started by Bil). The issues discussed are not confined to any one vendor, implementation, standard, or specification.

`comp.programming.threads`   There are two FAQs for the newsgroup, the first high-level and general (maintained by Brian), the other very low-level and specific (maintained by Bil):

`http://www.serpentine.com/~bos/threads-faq`

`http://www.LambdaCS.com`

Code Examples

All the code examples in this book are available via the Web:

```
http://www.LambdaCS.com
```

Vendor's Threads Pages

The SunSoft web page (designed by Marianne, maintained by Dan) includes an FAQ on UI threads, performance data, case studies, and demonstration programs. It also has a lot of pointers to other pages on it.

```
http://www.sun.com/sunsoft/Products/Developerproducts/sig/threads/
      index.html
```

The IBM threads page includes a short exposition on POSIX threads programming and IBM's implementation:

```
http://developer.austin.ibm.com/sdp/library/ref/about4.1/df4threa.html
```

On DEC's documentation pages, they include a "Guide to DECthreads."

```
http://redhawk.nis.newscorp.com:8000/unix40docs/Digital_UNIX_Bookshelf.html
```

Threads Research

There is a bibliography of several hundred papers related to threading (created and maintained by Torsten). The papers are largely theoretical, exploring the outer limits of threading and concurrency:

```
http://liinwww.ira.uka.de/bibliography/Os/threads.html
```

The SPILT Package for UI/POSIX Compatibility

In order to make it easier to move UI threads code over to POSIX, the folks at OPCOM (Sun Canada) have written a package that maps the missing parts of UI into POSIX. Readers/writer locks, for example, are included in the SPILT package.

```
http://www.sun.com/sunsoft/Products/Developerproducts/sig/threads/
      index.html
```

Freeware Tools

Two useful tools are available as unsupported from Sun. TNFview (by Bonnie's group) allows you to look at the exact timing of different events in a program. Proctool (Morgan's brainchild) gives you a view of the high-level operations of processes and LWPs on Solaris.

```
http://opcom.sun.ca/toolpages/tnftool.html
```

```
ftp://sunsite.unc.edu/pub/sun-info/mde/proctool
```

Other Pointers

You can see the "Single UNIX® Specification" at:

```
http://www.rdg.opengroup.org/unix/online.html
```

To see all the details on performance measurements, the SPEC homepage is:

```
http://www.specbench.org
```

For about $140, you can get the actual POSIX threads spec (IEEE 1003.1) from IEEE. It is a *specification*, more intended for implementors than programmers, so it is very likely *not* what you want. But, if you do...

```
http://www.ieee.org
```

```
customer.service@ieee.org
```

The Authors on the Net

If you would like to contact the authors directly, you can send mail to **Daniel.Berg@Sun.COM** and **Bil@LambdaCS.COM**. We would like to hear from you about what you liked or disliked about the book, and what we may be able to improve.

Daniel is currently a Systems Engineer at Sun, Houston, focusing on Java issues.

Bil recently left Sun, and is currently running his own company, Lambda Computer Science, teaching, and consulting on multithreaded programming.

Appendix B

Books

Threads Books

The following are the other books in publication to date. Some of the examples, explanations, figures, etc. in them will be better than those in this text. Some of them will simply explain things better for you. We have read each of them carefully and have our own preferences. All of them are sufficient for their purposes.

Kleiman, Shah, and Smaalders, *Programming with Threads*, Upper Saddle River, NJ: SunSoft Press, Feb 1996 (534 pp, source on the Web). Covers POSIX threads, concentrating on the Solaris implementation. It has a small, but adequate introduction, then concentrates on more advanced programming issues. The examples are good because they are realistic and show you what to expect. They are bad because they are very realistic and obscure the main points in the text.

Len Dorfman and Marc J Neuberger, *Effective Multithreading with OS/2*, New York: McGraw Hill, Nov 1995 (280 pp, source on diskette). Gives a brief introduction, then focuses the rest of the discussion on the API and examples. It covers the OS/2 API.

Charles J Northrup, *Programming with UNIX Threads*, New York: John Wiley & Sons, Inc., Mar 1996 (400 pp, source via FTP). Covers the UI threads library, focusing on the UNIXware implementation. The presentation is oriented around the API and contains numerous examples.

Thuan Q. Pham and Pankaj K. Garg, *Multithreaded Programming with Windows NT*, Upper Saddle River, NJ: Prentice Hall, Jan 1996 (220 pp, source on diskette). Focusing on the NT library, this book gives some comparison with other libraries. While it describes concepts and designs well, it lacks many of the practical details and glosses over problems.

Bradford Nichols, Dick Buttlar, and Jacqueline Proulx Farrell, *Pthreads Programming*, Sebastapol, CA: O'Reilly & Associates, Inc., Nov 1996 (268 pp, source via FTP). Concentrates on the Digital implementation of POSIX. It gives a good explanation of the concepts, but is a little too condensed to do them justice. Includes a major section comparing the final standard to draft 4, DCE.

Scott J. Norton and Mark D. Dipasquale, *ThreadTime*, Upper Saddle River, NJ: HP Professional Books, Dec 1996 (530 pp, source on diskette). Describes POSIX threads with concentration on the HP-UX implementation. Includes an excellent introduction, computer science descriptions, and standards discussion.

Dave Butenhof, *Programming with POSIX Threads*, Reading, MA: Addison Wesley, May 1997 (380 pp, source on the Web). Concentrates more on architecture than any specific implementation of POSIX threads. A lucid exposition of concepts and discussion of standards from one of the guys on the committee.

Jim Beveridge and Robert Wiener, *Multithreading Applications in Win32*, Reading, MA: Addison-Wesley, Jan 1997 (368 pp, source on diskette). Describes Win32 threads (NT and Win95). Includes some comparison to POSIX. Excellent discussion of the practical aspects of programming Win32. Many insightful comments on both the good parts and the more problematic parts.

Shashi Prasad, *Multithreading Programming Techniques*, New York: McGraw-Hill, Jan 1997 (410 pp, source on diskette and the Web). Describes and contrasts the multithreading libraries of POSIX, UI, Mach, Win32, and OS/2. Each library has its own chapters and its own code examples. This means that the introduction and presentation of concepts is lighter, but the examples are ported across the different platforms, making this a good reference for porting.

Bil Lewis and Daniel J. Berg, *Threads Primer*, Upper Saddle River, NJ: SunSoft Press, Oct 1995 (320 pp, source on the Web). This is the first edition of the primer which covers UI threads. It lacks the depth of many of the other books, but gives more extensive explanation of the fundamentals. Japanese translation available.

Doug Lea, *Concurrent Programming in Java*, Reading, MA: Addison Wesley, 1997 (240 pp, source on the Web). Describes how to write multithreaded programs in Java, using design patterns. Well written from a computer science point-of-view, though perhaps overwhelming for the hacker-oriented. Familiarity with design patterns is a necessity.

Scott Oaks and Henry Wong, *Java Threads*, Sebastapol, CA: O'Reilly, 1997 (252 pp, source on the Web). Describes how to write multithreaded programs in Java in a more conventional, programmer-oriented style. Explanations are clear, though often simplistic. The programs illustrate the points well, yet tend to gloss over problem areas in Java.

Using Multi-C: A Portable Multithreaded C Programming Library. Upper Saddle River, NJ: Prentice Hall PTR, 1994. This book describes the API and use of the MIX Multi-C library, which is a proprietary library providing similar kinds of functionality to POSIX threads.

Related Books

Jeffrey Richter, *Advanced Windows NT: The Developer's Guide to the Win32 Application Programming Interface*. Microsoft Press, 1994. This book contains about 200 pages that cover the NT threads API and its usage. It covers the API well, contains a good amount of code, but has very little on the concepts.

Robert A. Iannucci, Editor, *Multithreaded Computer Architecture: A Summary of the State of the Art.* New York: Kluwer Academic Publishers, 1994. This book is a collection of papers dealing with hardware design considerations for building specialized machines that can support multithreaded programs.

Derrel R. Blain, Kurt R. Delimon, and Jeff English, *Real-World Programming for OS/2 2.1*. Sams Publishing/Prentice Hall PTR, 1993. This book contains about 50 pages that cover the OS/2 threads API and its usage. It covers the API well, contains one nice example, but is very short.

Solaris Multithreaded Programming Guide, Upper Saddle River, NJ: SunSoft Press, 1995. This is the documentation that comes with Solaris 2.4 and contains the UI API. It is also available as part of the Solaris AnswerBook® and on the Web (see *Vendor's Threads Pages* on page 314).

John L. Hennessy and David A. Patterson, *Computer Architecture, a Quantitative Approach (2nd edition)*, Morgan Kaufman, Inc., 1996 (800 pp). This is the definitive text on computer design—CPU, Memory System, and Multiprocessors. Not about threads per se, but everything underneath. *Superb* research and exposition!

Daniel E Lenoski and Wolf-Dietrich Weber, *Scalable Shared-Memory Multiprocessing*, Morgan Kaufman, Inc., 1995 (340 pp). This takes up in great detail what Hennessy and Patterson describe in mere passing detail. It describes the state of SMP research as it led to the Stanford DASH machine, and now the SGI Origin series and HAL Mercury. *Superb* research and exposition!

Appendix C

Timings

The choice of which synchronization variable to use depends partially on its execution speed. This is particularly applicable when choosing between using a mutex lock and a readers/writer lock. The design of programs calling Pthreads functions in tight loops will also depend upon these numbers for optimizations. For the most part, however, all of these times are short enough that they may be ignored.

Because of the dependence of these tests upon several unusual instructions (`ldstub` and `stbar` on SPARC), machines with different cache or bus designs will exhibit nonuniform scaling (meaning that a context switch may be twice as fast on a 20 MHz processor as it is on a 10 MHz processor, but locking a mutex might take the same amount of time).

Execution times on other platforms may also differ significantly, but probably in roughly the same ratios (e.g., creating a thread will be a couple of orders of magnitude faster than creating a process). The one obvious exception to this is the semaphore, which should be almost as fast as mutexes on machines with the more complex atomic instructions. The major conclusions you should draw from these numbers are:

- Mutexes are faster than RWlocks.
- Changing the signal mask is moderately fast.
- Testing for, and disabling cancellation is very fast.
- Processes are more expensive than threads.
- TSD is fast (but global references are faster).
- `pthread_once()` is fast, but testing first is faster. (Static initialization is best!)

The programs we ran to get the numbers shown in Table C.1 are available on the Web under the names listed.

Table C.1   *Timings of Various Thread-Related Functions on Two SPARC Machines*

Function	110 MHz, SS4		167 MHz, Ultra 1	
	μs	Ratio	μs	Ratio
Mutex Lock/Unlock	1.8	1	0.7	1
Mutex Trylock	1.3	0.7	0.3	0.4
Reader Lock/Unlock	4.5	2.5	2.3	3.3
Writer Lock/Unlock	4.5	2.5	2.6	3.7
Semaphore Post/Wait	4.3	2.4	3.7	5.2
Context Switch (Unbound Threads)	89	1	21	1
Context Switch (Bound Threads)	42	0.5	18	0.9
Context Switch (Processes)	54	0.6	20	1
Change Signal Mask	18.1		4.1	
Cancellation Disable/Enable	0.6		0.6	
Test for Deferred Cancellation	0.25		0.15	
Create an Unbound Thread	330	1	80	1
Create a Bound Thread	720	2.2	170	2.1

Table C.1   *(cont.) Timings of Various Thread-Related Functions on Two SPARC Machines*

Function	110 MHz, SS4		167 MHz, Ultra 1	
	μs	Ratio	μs	Ratio
Create a Process	45,000	136	9,500	120
Reference a Global Variable	0.02	1	0.006	1
Reference Thread-Specific Data	0.59	15	0.45	75
if (!done) pthread_once()	0.07	1	0.03	1
pthread_once()	0.9	13	0.9	30

The tests are respectively:

Mutex Lock/Unlock   `time_lock.c`

Acquire, then release, a mutex with no contention. (It's the same operation, whether in the same process or across processes.)

Mutex Trylock   `time_trylock.c`

Call `pthread_mutex_trylock()` on a held lock.

Reader Lock/Unlock   `time_reader.c`

Acquire, then release, a readers/writer lock as a reader with no contention.

Writer Lock/Unlock   `time_writer.c`

Acquire, then release, a readers/writer lock as a writer with no contention.

Semaphore Post/Wait   `time_sema.c`

Increment an unnamed semaphore, then decrement it. (It's the same operation, whether in the same process or across processes.) On machines with LoadLocked instructions, this operation should take about the same time as a simple mutex lock/unlock.

Local Context Switch (unbound)   `time_cs_unbound.c`

Call `sched_yield()` once from each of two unbound threads. (This number is much higher than expected, much slower than seen on an SS10.)

Local Context Switch (bound)   `time_cs_bound.c`

Call `sched_yield()` once from each of two bound threads.

Process Context Switch   `time_cs_process.c`

Call `sched_yield()` once from each of two processes.

Change Signal Mask   `time_sigmask.c`

Call `pthread_sigmask()` twice.

Cancellation Disable/Enable   `time_cancel_enable.c`

Call `pthread_setcancelstate(DISABLE)` then `ENABLE`.

Test for Deferred Cancellation   `time_testcancel.c`

Call `pthread_testcancel()` once.

Reference a Global Variable   `time_global.c`

Load a single word into a register.

Reference Thread-Specific Data   `time_getspecific.c`

Call `pthread_getspecific()`. (A call to `pthread_set-specific()` takes the same amount of time.)

if (!done) pthread_once()   `time_once.c`

Test a global variable, find out that it's zero, and then do nothing.

pthread_once()   `time_once.c`

Call `pthread_once()` on an initialized variable, and then do nothing.

Appendix D

Mistakes

For a year, Bil was the person who got to answer customers' questions on threads. This is a list of the most common mistakes that he saw people making.

Failure to Check Return Values for Errors

Many of the thread library functions can legitimately return error codes instead of succeeding.

Using errno without Checking the Return Value

This isn't a threads programming bug per-se, but it's very common anyway. It is legal for errno to contain any old crazy value until a system call returns an error code.

Good Programmer	Bad Programmer!

```
err = system_call();            system_call()
if (err)                        if (errno)
    printf("Bug: %d", errno);       printf("Bug: %d", errno);
```

Code Example D–1:   *Checking* errno

Not Joining on Nondetached Threads

If you are not going to join a thread, you must create it as a detached thread. (See *That's Not a Bug, That's a Feature!* on page 51.)

Failure to Verify that Library Calls Are MT Safe

This really ought to be done for you by lint. Until it is, you have to do it yourself. Third-party libraries are a common problem. If they don't say "MT Safe" on them, they probably aren't.

Falling off the Bottom of main()

This is another silly bug, but one that we've gotten lots of calls about. If you don't intend to exit your program after main() is done, then you've got to call pthread_exit() so that only the main thread exits, not the entire program.

Forgetting to Include the POSIX_C_SOURCE *Flag*

This negligence is sort of nasty, as you won't notice a thing until you try to check `errno` or get weird synchronization errors from `getc()`. Compile *all* libraries with the flag. You'll be much happier two years from now when you suddenly decide that you need that library in an MT program.

As an option, you can also include the line below in your files as we do.

```
#define _POSIX_C_SOURCE=199506L
```

Using Spin Locks

You practically never need these things! If you really want to use 'em, prove that they are working for you first. (See *Spin Locks* on page 114.)

Depending upon Scheduling Order

Write your MT programs to depend upon synchronization. While trying to improve the start-up time of Openwindows, Bart was disappointed to see no improvement on the new, high-speed SS10. Investigating the code more closely, he found this line:

```
sleep(5);
/* Enough time for the manager to start. */
```

Don't do that.

Using `errno` for Threads Library Functions

All of the functions in the POSIX threads library return error codes directly and do not set `errno`. You cannot use `errno`, or `perror()`, unless the manual page for the function in question specifically states that it will be set (this goes for all library calls, not just threads). The error codes returned from threads functions are listed in `errno.h`, so `strerror()` will return an appropriate error string. In POSIX, semaphores are not part of the threads library, and they do use `errno`.

Figure D–1

One particularly sneaky aspect of this situation is that it may appear that `errno` is being set in some cases. This has fooled more than one programmer (e.g., the authors). A call to `pthread_create()` may legally fail, returning the error value `EAGAIN`—not enough resources. To find out that there weren't enough resources, `pthread_create()` had to make a system call. That system call returned an error and set `errno` to `EAGAIN`. It was the system call that set `errno`, not `pthread_create()` itself.

Not Recognizing Shared Data

It is not unusual for a programmer to fail to protect some piece of data because it wasn't obvious that it needed protection. This is especially true for complex structures such as lists, where you might protect part of the data without realizing that you've left another part unprotected. Consider the structure shown in Figure D–1, in which the programmer has carefully provided a lock for each element of a list.

What does the mutex protect? The programmer intended it to protect the entire node, which is perfectly acceptable. However, he also expected one thread to be able to do a search down the list at the same time that another thread was changing the order of the nodes. ("As long as I hold the mutex for node 1, I can reposition it in the list without disturbing the rest of the list. And the other threads can do searches, just as long as they don't try to change node 1." He thought.)

Nope. To be able to change the order of the list, the programmer would have to obtain both the lock for the current node and the lock for the previous node. To be able to search the list at the same time, the programmer would have to obtain, then release, each lock as the thread moved down the list. This would work, but it would be very expensive (see: *Manipulating Lists* on page 213).

Assuming Bit, Byte or Word Stores are Atomic

Maybe they are, and maybe they aren't. Any shared data that you change has to be protected by a mutex. That's all there is to it.

Not Blocking Signals When Using `sigwait()`

If you use `sigwait()` to deal with signals as we have suggested, it's important to avoid having that signal delivered asynchronously to a different thread by surprise. Any signal you are sigwaiting for, you must prevent from calling a signal handler (see *Per-Thread Alarms* on page 164).

Passing Pointers to Data on the Stack to Another Thread

If you pass an object pointer to a thread (when you're creating it, or by using a shared variable), the lifetime of the object which the pointer references must be at least as long as the receiving thread needs it. Although it is physically possible to ensure this with stack-allocated data, it isn't worth the hassle (see Code Example D–2).

```
       Good Programmer                      Bad Programmer!

foo()                                foo()
{my_struct *s;                       {my_struct s;
...                                  ...
s = (my_struct *) malloc(...);       ...
s->data = get_data();                s.data = get_data();
pthread_create(... s, ...);          pthread_create(... &s, ...);
pthread_exit();                      pthread_exit();
}                                    }
```

Code Example D–2: *Passing Data on the Stack*

Appendix E

APIs

This appendix contains a very brief description of the POSIX threads API (POSIX 1003.1c). We refer you to your vendor documentation for more detail.

Function Descriptions

In the sample entry below, the interface name comes first. If the interface is one of the optional portions of POSIX, the constant that tells you if it is supported is shown across from it. Next are the interface and argument list (sometimes there'll be two functions shown, should they be very closely related). A short paragraph describing the basic operation follows (it may well leave out some details). Should there be a choice of constants, the default will be shown in bold (not all such functions have defaults). Next comes a reference to the most applicable portion of the text. Then the errors that the function is allowed to return (if listed as "Errors" as below), or the setting of errno (if listed as "errno"). Errors that the function is required to detect are in bold; the others need not be detected. Finally, any comments that seem appropriate are given.

---

pthread_mutexattr_setprotocol   _POSIX_THREAD_PRIO_PROTECT

    int pthread_mutexattr_setprotocol(pthread_mutexattr_t *attr, int
        protocol);

    int pthread_mutexattr_getprotocol (const pthread_mutexattr_t *attr,
        int *protocol);

This sets (gets) the protocol for priority mutexes of *attr* (in) to *protocol*, which must be one of **PTHREAD_PRIO_NONE**, PTHREAD_PRIO_INHERIT, or PTHREAD_PRIO_PROTECT.

References: *Priority Inheritance Mutexes* on page 108.

Errors:

EINVAL	*attr* or *protocol* is invalid.
ENOSYS	Priority mutexes are not supported.
ENOTSUP	The value of *protocol* is unsupported.
EPERM	No privilege to perform the operation.

Comment: Threads using these must be realtime.

Pthread Functions

`pthread_t tid;`

> This is the thread ID datatype. It is an opaque structure of implementation-dependent size.

`pthread_create`

```
int pthread_create(pthread_t *thread, const pthread_attr_t *attr,
    void * (*start_routine)(void *), void *arg);
```

> This creates a new thread, with attributes specified by *attr* If *attr* is NULL, then the default thread attributes are used. Upon successful completion, it stores the ID of the created thread into *thread*. The thread is created by executing *start_routine* with *arg* as its sole argument. The signal mask is inherited from the creating thread and the set of signals pending for the new thread is empty.

> ***References:***   Chapter 4, *Lifecycle*.

> ***Errors:***
> | | |
> |---|---|
> | **EAGAIN** | Not enough resources. |
> | **EINVAL** | The value specified by *attr* is invalid. |
> | **EPERM** | No permission to create this thread. |

`pthread_equal`

```
int pthread_equal(pthread_t t1, pthread_t t2);
```

> This compares the thread IDs *t1* and *t2* and returns a non-zero value if they are equal; otherwise, it returns zero.

> ***References:***   *POSIX Thread IDs* on page 177.

`pthread_exit`

```
void pthread_exit(void *status);
```

> This terminates the calling thread, returning *status*. Any cancellation cleanup handlers are popped and then executed. Next, any TSD destructor functions will be called in an unspecified order. An implicit call to `pthread_exit()` is made when a thread (other than the main thread) returns from its start routine. The function's return value serves as the thread's exit status. When the last thread in a process exits, `exit(0)` will be called.

> **References:**   Chapter 4, *Lifecycle*.

`pthread_join`

```
int pthread_join(pthread_t thread, void **status);
```

> This blocks the calling thread until *thread* terminates. If *status* is not null, the status from `pthread_exit()` will be placed there.

> **References:**   Chapter 4, *Lifecycle*.

> **Errors:**
>
> | | |
> |---|---|
> | **ESRCH** | *thread* does not exist (already exited?). |
> | **EINVAL** | *thread* is not joinable. |
> | EDEADLK | A deadlock was detected. |

`pthread_detach`

```
int pthread_detach();
```

> This turns the current thread into a detached thread.

> **References:**   *Cancellation in pthread_join() on page 152.*

> **Errors:**
>
> | | |
> |---|---|
> | ESRCH | *thread* does not exist (already exited?). |
> | EINVAL | *thread* is not joinable. |

> **Comment:**   Write programs that *don't* use this.

pthread_once_t once_control = PTHREAD_ONCE_INIT;

> This is the once datatype. It is an opaque structure of implementation-dependent size. It must be statically initialized with PTHREAD_ONCE_INIT.

pthread_once

    int pthread_once(pthread_once_t *once_control*, void
       (**init_routine*)(void));

> The first call to pthread_once() by any thread in a process with a given *once_control* will call the *init_routine()* with no arguments. Subsequent calls of pthread_once() with the same *once_control* will not call the *init_routine()*. On return from pthread_once(), it is guaranteed that *init_routine()* has completed.

References: *Initializing Your Data: pthread_once() on page* 179.

Errors:
    EINVAL   Either *once_control* or *init_routine* is invalid.

Comment: Do load-time initialization if at all possible.

pthread_self

    pthread_t pthread_self(void);

> This returns the thread ID of the calling thread.

References: *POSIX Thread IDs on page* 177.

sched_yield

    void sched_yield(void);

> This causes a thread to yield its execution in favor of another thread with the same priority.

References: *Process Contention Scope on page* 66.

Errors:
    ENOSYS   This function is not supported.

pthread_atfork

```
void pthread_atfork(void (*prepare) (void), void (*parent) (void),
    void (*child) (void));
```

> This pushes fork handlers onto a stack. When `fork()` is called, `prepare()` will be run before the actual fork occurs. In the child process, the function `child()` will be run after `fork()` returns, and `parent()` will be run in the parent process.

> **References:**   *Fork Safety and pthread_atfork() on page 202.*

> **Errors:**
> **ENOMEM**   No memory.

Pthread Attributes Objects

pthread_attr_t attr;

> This is the pthread attributes object type. It must be initialized dynamically.

pthread_attr_init

```
int pthread_attr_init(pthread_attr_t *attr);
```

> This initializes *attr* with the default values for all of the individual attributes. It may malloc extra memory.

Table E.1   *Default Settings for Thread Attributes Objects*

Attribute	Default Setting	Our Preference
Scope	Unspecified by POSIX	System Scope
Detach State	Joinable	Detached
Stack Address	Unspecified by POSIX	Implementation Default
Stack Size	Unspecified by POSIX	Implementation Default
Sched Policy	Unspecified by POSIX	Implementation Default
Sched Parameter	Unspecified by POSIX	Implementation Default
Inherit	Unspecified by POSIX	Explicit

References: *Thread Attribute Objects* on page 171.

Errors:

ENOMEM   Insufficient memory.

EINVAL   The value of *attr* is not valid.

---

pthread_attr_destroy

```
int pthread_attr_destroy(pthread_attr_t *attr);
```

This destroys the attributes object, making it unusable in any form. The memory the programmer allocated for the attributes object is not freed, but any memory pthread_attr_init() allocated will be.

References: *Thread Attribute Objects* on page 171.

Errors:

EINVAL   The value of *attr* is not valid.

---

pthread_attr_getdetachstate

```
int pthread_attr_getdetachstate(const pthread_attr_t *attr, int
    *detachstate);
```

```
int pthread_attr_setdetachstate(pthread_attr_t *attr, int
    detachstate);
```

This sets (gets) the detachstate attribute of *attr* (in) to *detachstate*. The value of *detachstate* is PTHREAD_CREATE_DETACHED or **PTHREAD_CREATE_JOINABLE**.

References: *Thread Attribute Objects* on page 171.

Errors:

EINVAL   *attr* or *detachstate* is not valid.

pthread_attr_getstackaddr   _POSIX_THREAD_ATTR_STACKADDR

> int pthread_attr_getstackaddr(const pthread_attr_t *attr, void
>   **stackaddr);

> int pthread_attr_setstackaddr(pthread_attr_t *attr, void
>   *stackaddr);

This sets (gets) the stack address of *attr* (in) to *stackaddr*.

References: *Thread Attribute Objects* on page 171.

Errors:

EINVAL	*attr* is not valid.
ENOSYS	This function is not supported.

Comment: It is quite unusual to allocate the stack yourself.

---

pthread_attr_getstacksize   _POSIX_THREAD_ATTR_STACKSIZE

> int pthread_attr_getstacksize(const pthread_attr_t *attr, size_t
>   *stacksize);

> int pthread_attr_setstacksize(pthread_attr_t *attr, size_t
>   stacksize);

This sets (gets) the stack size (in bytes) of *attr* (in) to *stacksize*.

References: *Thread Attribute Objects* on page 171.

Errors:

EINVAL	*stacksize* is less than PTHREAD_STACK_MIN or exceeds system limit.
EINVAL	*attr* or *stacksize* is not valid.
ENOSYS	This function is not supported.

POSIX Realtime Scheduling

pthread_getschedparam

int pthread_getschedparam(pthread_t *thread*, int **policy*, struct
    sched_param **param*);

int pthread_setschedparam(pthread_t *thread*, int *policy*, const
    struct sched_param **param*);

> This function sets (gets) the scheduling policy and parameters for
> *thread* (in) to *policy* and *param*, respectively. For the policies
> SCHED_FIFO, SCHED_RR, and SCHED_OTHER, the only
> required member of the sched_param structure is the priority,
> sched_priority.

References: *Realtime LWPs* on page 75.

Errors:

ESRCH	*thread* does not refer to a existing thread.
EINVAL	Either *policy* or one of the scheduling parameters is invalid.
ENOTSUP	The implementation does not support *policy*.
ENOSYS	These functions are not supported.

pthread_attr_getinheritsched_POSIX_THREAD_PRIORITY_SCHEDULNG

int pthread_attr_getinheritsched(const pthread_attr_t **attr*, int
    *inheritsched);

int pthread_attr_setinheritsched(pthread_attr_t **attr*, int
    inheritsched);

> This sets (gets) the inheritsched attribute of *attr* (in) to *inherit-
> sched*. The   value   of   *inheritsched*   is   either
> PTHREAD_INHERIT_SCHED (scheduling to be inherited from
> the creating thread) or PTHREAD_EXPLICIT_SCHED (sched-
> uling to be set from this attributes object).

References: *Realtime LWPs* on page 75.

Errors:

EINVAL	*attr* is not valid.
ENOTSUP	*inheritsched* is not supported.
ENOSYS	This function is not supported.

Comment: Normally use PTHREAD_EXPLICIT_SCHED.

---

pthread_attr_getschedparam   _POSIX_THREAD_PRIORITY_SCHEDULING

```
int pthread_attr_getschedparam(const pthread_attr_t *attr,
    struct sched_param *param);

int pthread_attr_setschedparam(pthread_attr_t *attr, const
    struct sched_param *param);
```

This sets (gets) the scheduling parameter attribute of *attr* (in) to *param*. For the SCHED_OTHER, SCHED_FIFO, and SCHED_RR policies, the only required member of the *param* structure is sched_priority.

References: *Realtime LWPs* on page 75.

Errors:

EINVAL	The value of *attr* or *param* is not valid.
ENOTSUP	The value of *param* is unsupported.
ENOSYS	This function is not supported.

---

pthread_attr_setschedpolicy _POSIX_THREAD_PRIORITY_SCHEDULING

```
int pthread_attr_setschedpolicy(pthread_attr_t *attr, int policy);

int pthread_attr_getschedpolicy(const pthread_attr_t *attr, int
    *policy);
```

This sets (gets) the scheduling policy of *attr* (in) to *policy*. The value of *policy* is either SCHED_FIFO, SCHED_RR, or SCHED_OTHER.

References: *Realtime LWPs* on page 75.

Errors:

EINVAL	The value of *attr* is not valid or *policy* is NULL.
ENOTSUP	The value of *policy* is unsupported.
ENOSYS	This function is not supported.

pthread_attr_getscope   _POSIX_THREAD_PRIORITY_SCHEDULING

```
int pthread_attr_getscope(const pthread_attr_t *attr, int
    *contentionscope);
```

```
int pthread_attr_setscope(pthread_attr_t *attr, int
    contentionscope);
```

> This sets (gets) the contention scope of *attr* (in) to *contention-scope*. The value of *contentionscope* is either PTHREAD_SCOPE_SYSTEM or PTHREAD_SCOPE_PROCESS.

> **References:**   *Thread Scheduling* on page 64.

> **Errors:**
> | | |
> |---|---|
> | ENOTSUP | The value of *contentionscope* is unsupported. |
> | EINVAL | *attr* or *contentionscope* is not valid. |
> | **ENOSYS** | This function is not supported. |

---

sched_get_priority_max

```
int sched_get_priority_max(int policy);
```

```
int sched_get_priority_min(int policy);
```

> This returns the maximum (minimum) allowable priority value for *policy.*

> **References:**   *Specifying Scope, Policy, Priority, and Inheritance* on page 77.

> **Errors:**
> | | |
> |---|---|
> | **ENOSYS** | This function is not supported. |
> | **EINVAL** | policy is invalid. |

> **Comment:**   Values are completely implementation-defined. You will need to calculate something like (max + min)/2.

Mutexes

`pthread_mutex_t mutex [= PTHREAD_MUTEX_INITIALIZER];`

> This is the mutex type. Initialization of statically allocated mutexes to default values can be done with this macro; otherwise they must be initialized dynamically.

`pthread_mutex_init`

```
int pthread_mutex_init(pthread_mutex_t *mutex, const
    pthread_mutexattr_t *attr);
```

> This initializes *mutex* with *attr*. If *attr* is NULL, then the default values are used.

> **References:**   *Mutexes* on page 84.

> **Errors:**

> | | |
> |---|---|
> | EINVAL | The value specified by *attr* is invalid. |
> | EBUSY | Attempt to initialize a locked *mutex*. |
> | **ENOMEM** | Insufficient memory. |
> | **EAGAIN** | Insufficient resources. |
> | **EPERM** | No privilege (non-root requesting realtime?) |

`pthread_mutex_destroy`

```
int pthread_mutex_destroy(pthread_mutex_t *mutex);
```

> This destroys the mutex, making it unusable in any form. The memory the programmer allocated for the mutex is not freed, but any memory `pthread_mutex_init()` allocated will be.

> **References:**   *Mutexes* on page 84.

> **Errors:**

> | | |
> |---|---|
> | EINVAL | *mutex* is invalid. |
> | EBUSY | Attempt to destroy a locked *mutex*. |

pthread_mutex_lock

```
int pthread_mutex_lock(pthread_mutex_t *mutex);
```

> This locks the mutex. If the mutex is already locked, the calling thread blocks until the mutex is unlocked. If a signal is delivered to a thread waiting for a mutex, upon return from the signal handler the thread resumes waiting for the mutex as if it had not been interrupted.

> **References:**   *Mutexes* on page 84.

> **Errors:**
>
> | | |
> |---|---|
> | **EINVAL** | *mutex* is invalid. |
> | EINVAL | Attempt to destroy a locked *mutex*. |
> | EDEADLOCK | Caller already owns *mutex*. |
> | EFAULT | *mutex* points to an illegal address. |

pthread_mutex_trylock

```
int pthread_mutex_trylock(pthread_mutex_t *mutex);
```

> This is identical to `pthread_mutex_lock()`, except that if the mutex is currently locked, the call returns immediately with EBUSY.

> **References:**   *Mutexes* on page 84.

> **Errors:**
>
> | | |
> |---|---|
> | **EINVAL** | The caller's priority is higher than the ceiling of this realtime mutex. |
> | EINVAL | *mutex* is invalid. |
> | EDEADLOCK | Caller already owns *mutex*. |
> | EFAULT | *mutex* points to an illegal address. |
> | **EBUSY** | *mutex* is already locked. |

pthread_mutex_unlock

```
int pthread_mutex_unlock(pthread_mutex_t *mutex);
```

This unlocks *mutex* and wakes up the first thread sleeping on it.

References: *Mutexes* on page 84.

Errors:

EINVAL	*mutex* is invalid.
EPERM	The caller is not the owner.

pthread_mutex_getprioceiling

```
int pthread_mutex_getprioceiling (const pthread_mutex_t *mutex,
    int *prioceiling);
```

```
int pthread_mutex_setprioceiling(pthread_mutex_t *mutex, int
    prioceiling, int *old_ceiling);
```

The set function locks *mutex*, changes its priority ceiling to *prioceiling* and releases the *mutex*. The previous value of the priority ceiling is returned in *old_ceiling*. The get function simply gets the current priority ceiling.

References: *Priority Inheritance Mutexes* on page 108.

Errors:

ENOTSUP	prioceiling mutexes are not supported.
EINVAL	*prioceiling* is out of range.
EPERM	No privilege.
ENOSYS	prioceiling mutexes are not supported.
EFAULT	*mutex* points to an illegal address.

Mutex Attributes Objects

---

pthread_mutexattr_t attr;

This is the mutex attributes object type. It must be initialized dynamically.

---

pthread_mutexattr_init

int pthread_mutexattr_init(pthread_mutexattr_t *attr);

This initializes a mutex attributes object with the default values **PTHREAD_PRIO_NONE** and **PTHREAD_PROCESS_PRIVATE**.

References: *Mutex Attribute Objects* on page 175.

Errors:
ENOMEM   Insufficient memory to initialize the object.

---

pthread_mutexattr_destroy

int pthread_mutexattr_destroy(pthread_mutexattr_t *attr);

This destroys the attributes object, making it unusable in any form. The memory the programmer allocated for the object is not freed, but any memory pthread_mutexattr_init() allocated will be.

References: *Mutex Attribute Objects* on page 175.

Errors:
EINVAL   *attr* is invalid.

pthread_mutexattr_getprioceiling   _POSIX_THREAD_PRIO_PROTECT

```
int pthread_mutexattr_getprioceiling (const
    pthread_mutexattr_t *attr, int *prioceiling);
```

```
int pthread_mutexattr_setprioceiling (pthread_mutexattr_t *attr,
    int prioceiling);
```

> This sets (gets) the prioceiling attribute of *attr* (in) to *prioceiling*, which must be within the maximum range of priorities defined by SCHED_FIFO.

References: *Priority Inheritance Mutexes* on page 108.

Errors:

EINVAL	*attr* or *prioceiling* is invalid.
ENOSYS	Priority mutexes are not supported.
EPERM	No privilege to perform the operation.

---

pthread_mutexattr_setprotocol   _POSIX_THREAD_PRIO_PROTECT

```
int pthread_mutexattr_setprotocol(pthread_mutexattr_t *attr, int
    protocol);
```

```
int pthread_mutexattr_getprotocol (const pthread_mutexattr_t
    *attr, int *protocol);
```

> This sets (gets) the protocol for priority mutexes of *attr* (in) to *protocol*, which must be one of **PTHREAD_PRIO_NONE**, PTHREAD_PRIO_INHERIT, or PTHREAD_PRIO_PROTECT.

References: *Priority Inheritance Mutexes* on page 108.

Errors:

EINVAL	*attr* or *protocol* is invalid.
ENOSYS	Priority mutexes are not supported.
ENOTSUP	The value of *protocol* is unsupported.
EPERM	No privilege to perform the operation.

---

pthread_mutexattr_getpshared   _POSIX_THREAD_PROCESS_SHARED

   int pthread_mutexattr_getpshared (const pthread_mutexattr_t
       *attr, int *pshared);

   int pthread_mutexattr_setpshared(pthread_mutexattr_t *attr, int
       pshared);

   This sets (gets) the shared attribute of *attr* (in) to *pshared*, which is either PTHREAD_PROCESS_SHARED (any mutex initialized with this attribute may be used from different processes), **PTHREAD_PROCESS_PRIVATE** (only threads in the same process can use it).

   References: *Cross-Process Synchronization Variables* on
           page 120.

   Errors:
       EINVAL   Either *attr* or *pshared* is invalid.
       ENOSYS   Shared memory mutexes not supported.

   Comment: Obviously a shared mutex must be in shared memory!

Condition Variables

---

pthread_cond_t cond [= PTHREAD_COND_INITIALIZER];

   This is the condition variable type. Initialization of statically allocated condition variables to default values can be with this macro, otherwise they must be initialized dynamically.

---

pthread_cond_init

   int pthread_cond_init(pthread_cond_t *cond, const
       pthread_condattr_t *attr);

   This initializes *cond* with *attr*. If *attr* is NULL, then the default values are used (PTHREAD_PROCESS_PRIVATE).

References: *Condition Variables* on page 94.

Errors:

EINVAL	*attr* is invalid.
EFAULT	*cond* or *attr* points to an illegal address.
ENOMEM	Insufficient memory.
EAGAIN	Insufficient resources.

---

pthread_cond_destroy

```
int pthread_cond_destroy(pthread_cond_t *cond);
```

This destroys the condition variable, making it unusable in any form. The memory the programmer allocated for the object is not freed, but any memory pthread_cond_init() allocated will be.

References: *Condition Variables* on page 94.

Errors:

EINVAL	*cond* isn't a condition variable.
EBUSY	There are waiters for the condition variable.

---

pthread_cond_wait

```
int pthread_cond_wait(pthread_cond_t *cond, pthread_mutex_t *mutex);
```

This atomically releases *mutex* and causes the calling thread to block on *cond*. Upon successful return, the *mutex* will be reacquired. Spurious wakeups may occur. This function is also a cancellation point. When cancelled, the mutex will be reacquired before calling the first cancellation cleanup handler.

References: *Condition Variables* on page 94.

Errors:

EINVAL	*cond* or *mutex* not valid, or not owner.
EPERM	*mutex* not owned by the calling thread.

pthread_cond_timedwait

```
int pthread_cond_timedwait(pthread_cond_t *cond,
    pthread_mutex_t *mutex, const struct timespec *abstime);
```

This is the same as pthread_cond_wait(), except that ETIMEDOUT is returned if the absolute time specified by *abstime* passes before the condition *cond* is signaled or broadcast. Even after a time-out occurs, the mutex will be reacquired.

References: *Condition Variables* on page 94.

Errors:

EPERM	*mutex* not owned by the calling thread.
EINVAL	*cond, abstime,* or *mutex* invalid.
ETIMEDOUT	The time specified by *abstime* has passed.

pthread_cond_signal

```
int pthread_cond_signal(pthread_cond_t *cond);
```

This unblocks the first thread (if any) blocked on a condition variable. When that thread returns from pthread_cond_wait(), it will own the associated mutex.

References: *Condition Variables* on page 94.

Errors:

EINVAL	*cond* is invalid.

pthread_cond_broadcast

```
int pthread_cond_broadcast(pthread_cond_t *cond);
```

This unblocks all threads blocked on a condition variable. You do not know the order in which they awake. Each thread returning from pthread_cond_wait(), will own the associated mutex.

References: *Condition Variables* on page 94.

Errors:
> EINVAL   *cond* is invalid.

Condition Variable Attributes Objects

---

pthread_condattr_t attr;

> This is the condition variable attributes object type. It must be initialized dynamically.

---

pthread_condattr_init

  int pthread_condattr_init(pthread_condattr_t *attr);

> This initializes *attr* with the default value **PTHREAD_PROCESS_PRIVATE**.

> ***References:***   *Condition Variable Attribute Objects* on page 176.

> ***Errors:***
> > **ENOMEM**   Insufficient memory.
> > **EAGAIN**   Insufficient resources.

---

pthread_condattr_destroy

  pthread_condattr_destroy(pthread_condattr_t *attr);

> This destroys the condition variable attributes object, making it unusable in any form. The memory the programmer allocated for the object is not freed, but any memory pthread_condattr_init() allocated will be.

> ***References:***   *Condition Variable Attribute Objects* on page 176.

> ***Errors:***
> > EINVAL   *attr* is invalid.

pthread_condattr_setpshared   _POSIX_THREAD_PROCESS_SHARED

    int pthread_condattr_setpshared(pthread_condattr_t *attr, int
        pshared);

    int pthread_condattr_getpshared (const pthread_condattr_t *attr,
        int *pshared);

> This sets (gets) the value of *pshared*. If *pshared* is PTHREAD_PROCESS_SHARED then any condition variable initialized with this attribute may be used from different processes. If it is **PTHREAD_PROCESS_PRIVATE**, then only threads in the same process can use it.

> ***References:*** *Cross-Process Synchronization Variables* on page 120.

> ***Errors:***
> | | |
> |---|---|
> | ENOSYS | Shared condition variables not supported. |
> | EINVAL | Either *attr* or *pshared* of is not legal. |

> ***Comment:*** Obviously a shared mutex must be in shared memory!

Cancellation Functions

pthread_cancel

    int pthread_cancel(pthread_t thread);

> This function requests that *thread* be cancelled. The target thread's cancellability state and type determines when the cancellation takes effect. When the cancellation is acted on, the cancellation cleanup handlers for *thread* are called. Next, the thread-specific data destructor functions are called for *thread*. When the last destructor function returns, *thread* is terminated.

> ***References:*** Chapter 9, *Cancellation*.

> ***Errors:***
> | | |
> |---|---|
> | ESRCH | *thread* does not exist (exited already?). |

pthread_cleanup_push

```
void pthread_cleanup_push(void (*routine)(void *), void *arg);
```

This pushes the handler routine and argument onto the calling thread's cancellation cleanup stack.

References: *Cancellation Cleanup Handlers* on page 139.

pthread_cleanup_pop

```
void pthread_cleanup_pop(int execute);
```

This removes the routine at the top of the calling thread's cancellation cleanup stack and invokes it if *execute* is non-zero.

References: *Cancellation Cleanup Handlers* on page 139.

pthread_setcanceltype

pthread_setcancelstate

```
int pthread_setcanceltype(int type, int *oldtype);
int pthread_setcancelstate(int state, int *oldstate);
```

This function both sets the calling thread's cancellability type/state to *type/state* and returns the previous value in *oldtype/oldstate*. Legal values for *type* are **PTHREAD_CANCEL_DEFERRED** and PTHREAD_CANCEL_ASYNCHRONOUS. Legal values for *state* are **PTHREAD_CANCEL_ENABLED** and PTHREAD_CANCEL_DISABLED.

References: *What Cancellation Is* on page 138.

Errors:

EINVAL   The specified *type/state* is not valid.

pthread_testcancel

```
void pthread_testcancel(void);
```

> This is a cancellation point. If the cancel state is disabled, it just returns. If there are no outstanding cancellation requests, then it will also return. Otherwise it will not return and the thread will be cancelled.

> ***References:*** *What Cancellation Is* on page 138.

Thread-Specific Data Functions

pthread_setspecific

```
int pthread_setspecific(pthread_key_t key, const void *value);
```

> This sets the TSD value of *key* to *value*.

> ***References:*** Chapter 8, *TSD*.

> ***Errors:***
> | | |
> |---|---|
> | **ENOMEM** | Insufficient memory. |
> | EINVAL | The *key* value is invalid. |

pthread_getspecific

```
void *pthread_getspecific(pthread_key_t);
```

> This returns the TSD value associated with *key* in the calling thread. If *key* is not valid, the results are undefined. *Don't do this.*

> ***References:*** Chapter 8, *TSD*.

`pthread_key_create`

```
int pthread_key_create(pthread_key_t *key, void (*destructor(void
    *)));
```

> This function initializes a thread-specific data key. The initial value for TSD items is `NULL`. An optional *destructor* function may be associated with each *key*. At thread exit time, the *destructor* will be called with the TSD value as its sole argument (if non-null).

> **References:**   Chapter 8, *TSD*.

> **Errors:**
> | | |
> |---|---|
> | **EAGAIN** | Insufficient resources (`PTHREAD_KEYS_MAX` exceeded?) |
> | **ENOMEM** | Insufficient memory exists to create the *key*. |

`pthread_key_delete`

```
int pthread_key_delete(pthread_key_t key);
```

> This deletes a thread-specific data key. It is the responsibility of the application to free any storage or perform any cleanup actions for data structures related to the deleted key. No destructor functions are invoked by `pthread_key_delete()`.

> **References:**   Chapter 8, *TSD*.

> **Errors:**
> | | |
> |---|---|
> | EINVAL | The *key* value is invalid. |

> **Comment:**   This seems like a good function *not* to use.

Semaphores

---

sem_t sem;   _POSIX_SEMAPHORES

This is the semaphore type. It must be initialized dynamically. (Do not confuse these *unnamed* semaphores with system V semaphores!) There are two varients of semaphores, the named semaphores (which have system-wide names, accessible by any process, and are initialized with sem_open()) and the unnamed semaphores (which are what we've described, they do not have names and must be accessed only by direct reference).

---

sem_init   _POSIX_SEMAPHORES

        int sem_init(sem_t *sem, int pshared, unsigned int value);

sem_init() initializes the semaphore to *value*. If *pshared* is non-zero, then the semaphore will be sharable among processes.

References: Chapter 6, *Synchronization*.

errno:
> **EINVAL**   *value* exceeds SEM_VALUE_MAX.
> **ENOSPC**   Resource exhausted (SEM_NSEMS_MAX exceeded?)
> **ENOSYS**   Not supported by this implementation.
> **EPERM**   No privileges to initialize the semaphore.

Comment: Obviously a shared mutex must be in shared memory!

---

sem_destroy   _POSIX_SEMAPHORES

        int sem_destroy(sem_t *sem);

This destroys the semaphore. The memory the programmer allocated for the object is not freed (but any memory sem_init() allocated will be freed).

References: Chapter 6, *Synchronization*.

errno:

EINVAL	*sem* is not a valid semaphore.
ENOSYS	Not supported by this implementation.
EBUSY	Other processes or threads blocked on *sem*.

---

sem_post   _POSIX_SEMAPHORES

```
int sem_post(sem_t *sem);
```

This function increments the value of the semaphore. If other processes or threads were waiting for the semaphore, then one of them will be woken up. It is signal-safe and may be invoked from a signal handler.

References: Chapter 6, *Synchronization*.

errno:

EINVAL	*sem* does not refer to a valid semaphore.
ENOTSUP	Not supported by this implementation.

---

sem_wait   _POSIX_SEMAPHORES

```
int sem_trywait(sem_t *sem);
int sem_wait(sem_t *sem);
```

This decrements the value of *sem* by one. If the semaphore's value is zero, `sem_wait()` blocks, waiting for the semaphore to be incremented by another process or thread, while `sem_trywait()` will return immediately. `sem_wait()` can be interrupted by a signal, which will result in its premature return without decrementing the value.

References: Chapter 6, *Synchronization*.

errno:

EINVAL	*sem* does not refer to a valid semaphore.
EINTR	Interrupted by a signal.
ENOSYS	Not supported by this implementation.
EDEADLK	A deadlock condition was detected.
EAGAIN	The value of *sem* was zero when `sem_trywait()` was called. (Bug in Solaris 2.5 which returns **EBUSY**.)

---

sem_getvalue _POSIX_SEMAPHORES

```
int sem_getvalue(sem_t *sem, int *sval);
```

This sets *sval* to the current value of the semaphore. (The value may change before you get to use it of course, making this function difficult to use.)

References: Chapter 6, *Synchronization*.

errno:

EINVAL	*sem* does not refer to a valid semaphore.
ENOSYS	Not supported by this implementation.

---

sem_open _POSIX_SEMAPHORES

```
sem_t *sem_open(char *name, int oflag,...);
```

This returns a pointer to the semaphore *name*. All processes which call this on the same name will get the same semaphore pointer. It may be used as a normal semaphore, save that it must be closed with either sem_close() or sem_unlink(), not sem_destroy().

If *oflag* is O_CREAT a new kernel object will be created if *name* doesn't exist. If *oflag* is O_CREAT | O_EXCL, the call will fail if *name* does exist.

References: None.

errno:

EACESS	No permission to access/create semaphore.
EEXIST	O_EXCL is set, but *name* already exists.
EINTR	Interrupted by a signal.
EINVAL	Not supported.
EMFILE	Too many semaphores/files in process.
ENAMETOOLONG	(no room to describe error here!)
ENFILE	Too many semaphores in system.
ENOENT	O_CREAT not set and *name* doesn't exist.
ENOSPC	No space for new semaphore.
ENOSYS	Not supported by this implementation.

Comment: For named semaphores only!

---

sem_close   _POSIX_SEMAPHORES

```
int sem_close(sem_t *sem);
```

> This closes the named semaphore for this process. If the semaphore has been unlinked and this is the final referrant to it, the semaphore will be deleted from the system.

References: None.

errno:
> EINVAL   *sem* is not a semaphore.
> ENOSYS   Not supported by this implementation.

Comment: For named semaphores only!

---

sem_unlink   _POSIX_SEMAPHORES

```
int sem_unlink(char *name);
```

> This removes *name* from the system. Any future calls to sem_open(*name*) will return a different semaphore. If this is the only referrant to the semaphore, it shall be destroyed.

References: None.

errno:
> EACESS   No permission to access/create semaphore.
> ENAMETOOLONG (no room to describe error here!)
> ENOENT   *name* doesn't exist.
> ENOSYS   Not supported by this implementation.

Comment: For named semaphores only!

Signal Functions

pthread_kill

```
int pthread_kill(pthread_t thread, int signal);
```

This sends the *signal*, to *thread*. If *signal* is zero, then error checking is performed but no signal is actually sent; this can be used to check if *thread* exists.

References: *Signals in UNIX* on page 158.

Errors:

ESRCH	*thread* does not exist (already exited?).
EINVAL	The value of *signal* is invalid.

pthread_sigmask

```
int pthread_sigmask(int how, const sigset_t *set, sigset_t *oset);
```

This examines and/or changes the calling thread's signal mask. If the value of the argument *set* is not NULL, then it points to a set of signals to be used to change the currently blocked set. The value of the argument *how* determines the manner in which the set is changed. *how* may have one of the following values:

SIG_BLOCK The signals in set are added to the current signal mask.

SIG_UNBLOCK   The signals in set are deleted from the current signal mask.

SIG_SETMASKThe current signal mask is replaced by set.

If the value of *oset* is not NULL, then it points to the space where the previous signal mask is stored. If the value of *set* is NULL, the value of *how* is not significant and the thread's signal mask is unchanged. If a pending signal is unblocked, it will be delivered before this returns.

References: *Signals in UNIX* on page 158.

Errors:

EINVAL	*set* is not NULL and *how* is not defined.
EFAULT	*set* or *oset* is not a valid address.

sigwait

```
int sigwait(const sigset_t *set, int *signal);
```

> Wait for one of the signals in *set* to be sent. Returns with the signal in *signal*.

> **References:**   *Don't Use Signal Handlers!* on page 163.

> **errno:**
>> EINVAL   *set* contains an invalid signal.

sigtimedwait   _POSIX_REALTIME_SIGNALS

```
int sigtimedwait(const sigset_t *set, siginfo_t *info, const struct
    timespec *timeout);
```

> Wait for one of the signals in *set* to be sent. Returns with the signal in the si_signo member of *info* and the cause in the si_code member. Any queued value is returned in the si_value member. If *timeout* passes, it will return with EAGAIN.

> **References:**   *Don't Use Signal Handlers!* on page 163.

> **errno:**
>> EINVAL   *set* contains an invalid signal or bad timeout.
>> **EAGAIN**   The timeout passed.
>> **ENOSYS**   Not supported.

sigwaitinfo   _POSIX_REALTIME_SIGNALS

```
int sigwaitinfo(const sigset_t *set, siginfo_t *info);
```

> This is the same as sigtimedwait without the timeout.

> **References:**   *Don't Use Signal Handlers!* on page 163.

> **errno:**
>> EINVAL   *set* contains an invalid signal.
>> **ENOSYS**   Realtime signals are not supported.
>> **EINTR**   Interrupted by a signal.

Stdio

flockfile

```
int flockfile(FILE *file);
```

> This locks a recursive mutex associated with *file*, sleeping if another thread owns it.

> **Comment:** Use this to ensure that a *series* of writes occur in sequence.

ftrylockfile

```
int ftrylockfile(FILE *file);
```

> This locks a recursive mutex associated with *file*, or returns nonzero to indicate the lock is currently held by another thread.

funlockfile

```
int funlockfile(FILE *file);
```

> This unlocks a recursive mutex associated with *file*. If the recursive count was greater than one, it is simply decremented.

getc_unlocked

```
int getc_unlocked(FILE *file);
```

> This returns a single character from *file*. It is not thread-safe, but it is fast.

> **References:** *Are Libraries Safe?* on page 194.

> **Comment:** Use this in place of getc() when you know only one thread will be accessing *file*, or is locked with flockfile().

getchar_unlocked

```
int getchar_unlocked(FILE *file);
```

> This returns a single character from *file*. It is not thread-safe, but it is fast.

References: *Are Libraries Safe?* on page 194.

Comment: See getc_unlocked().

---

putc_unlocked

```
int putc_unlocked(FILE *file);
```

This places a single character into *file*. It is not thread-safe, but it is fast.

References: *Are Libraries Safe?* on page 194.

Comment: See getc_unlocked().

---

putchar_unlocked

```
int putchar_unlocked(FILE *file);
```

This places a single character into *file*. It is not thread-safe, but it is fast.

References: *Are Libraries Safe?* on page 194.

Comment: See getc_unlocked().

Glossary

API

The set of function calls in a library, along with their arguments and their semantics. APIs are published so programmers can always know which interface a vendor supports.

asynchronous signal

A signal that is sent to a process independently of what the process happens to be doing. An asynchronous signal can arrive at any time whatsoever, with no relation to what the program happens to be doing (cf: synchronous signal).

async I/O

An abbreviation for *Asynchronous Input/Output*—Normally, I/O calls block in the kernel while waiting for data to come off of a disk, a tape, or some other "slow" device. But async I/O calls are designed not to block. Such calls return immediately, so the user can continue to work. Whenever the data comes off the disk, the process will be sent a signal to let it know the call has completed.

atomic operation

An operation that is guaranteed to take place "at a single time." No other operation can do anything in the middle of an atomic operation that would change the result.

blocking system call

A system call that blocks in the kernel while it waits for something to happen. Disk reads and reading from a terminal are typically blocking calls.

cache memory

A section of very fast (and expensive) memory that is located very close to the CPU. It is an extra layer in the storage hierarchy and helps "well-behaved" programs run much faster.

CDE

An abbreviation for *Common Desktop Environment*—The specification for the look and feel that the major UNIX vendors have adopted. CDE includes a set of desktop tools.

CDE is the major result of the Cose agreement. It is a set of tools and window toolkits (Motif 1.2.3), along with supporting cross-process communications software (ToolTalk®), which will form the basis of the window offerings of all major UNIX vendors. Each vendor will productize CDE in its own fashion, and ultimately maintain separate source bases, doing its own value-add and its own bug fixing.

coarse-grained locking

See *fine-grained locking*.

context switch

The process of removing one process (or LWP or thread) from a CPU and moving another one on.

critical section

A section of code that must not be interrupted. If it doesn't complete atomically, then some data or resource may be left in an inconsistent state.

daemon

A process or a thread that works in the background. The pager is a daemon process in UNIX.

DCE

An abbreviation for *Distributed Computing Environment*—A set of functions deemed sufficient to write network programs. It was settled upon and implemented by the original OSF (Open Software Foundation). DCE is the environment of choice of a number of vendors including DEC and HP, while Sun has stayed with ONC+™. As part of the Cose agreement, all of the vendors will support both DCE and ONC+.

deadlock

A situation in which two things are stuck, each waiting for the other to do something first. More things can be stuck in a ring, waiting for each other, and even one thing could be stuck, waiting for itself.

device driver

A program that controls a physical device. The driver is always run as part of the kernel, with full kernel permissions. Device drivers may be threaded, but they would use the kernel threads library, not the library discussed in this book.

dynamic library

A library of routines that a user program can load into core "dynamically." That is, the library is not linked in as part of the user's executable image but is loaded only when the user program is run.

errno

An integer variable that is defined for all ANSI C programs (PCs running DOS as well as workstations running UNIX). It is the place where the operating system puts the return status for system calls when they return error codes.

external cache

Cache memory that is not physically located on the same chip as the CPU. External cache (aka "E$") is slower than internal cache (typically around five cycles versus one) but faster than main memory (upwards of 100 cycles, depending upon architecture).

FIFO

An abbreviation for *first in, first out*—A kind of a queue. Contrast to *last in, first out*, which is a stack.

file descriptor

An element in the process structure that describes the state of a file in use by that process. The actual file descriptor is in kernel space, but the user program also has a file descriptor that refers to this kernel structure.

fine-grained locking

The concept of putting lots of locks around tiny fragments of code. It's good because it means that there's less contention for the individual locks. It's bad because it means that the program must spend a lot of time obtaining locks. Coarse-grained locking is the opposite concept and has exactly the opposite qualities.

internal cache

Cache memory (aka I$) that is located on the same chip as the CPU, and, hence, is very fast.

interrupt

An external signal that interrupts the CPU. Typically, when an external device wants to get the CPU's attention, it asserts a voltage level on one of the CPU pins. This causes the CPU to stop what it's doing and run an interrupt handler.

interrupt handler

A section of code in the kernel that is called when an interrupt comes in. Different interrupts will run different handlers.

kernel mode

A mode of operation for a CPU in which all instructions are allowed (cf: user mode).

kernel space

The portion of memory that the kernel uses for itself. User programs cannot access it (cf: user space).

kernel stack

A stack in kernel space that the kernel uses when running system calls on behalf of a user program. All LWPs must have a kernel stack.

kernel threads

Threads that are used to write the operating system ("the kernel"). The various kernel threads libraries may be similar to the user threads library (e.g., Solaris), or may be totally different (e.g., Digital UNIX).

LADDIS

A standardized set of calls used to benchmark NFS performance. It was created by and is monitored by SPEC.

library

A collection of routines that many different programs may wish to use. Similar routines are grouped together into a single file and called a library.

library call

One of the routines in a library.

LWP

An abbreviation for *LightWeight Process*—A kernel schedulable entity.

memory management unit

See *MMU*.

memory-mapped file

A file that has been "mapped" into core. This is just like loading the file into core, except that any changes will be written back to the file itself. Because of this, that area of memory does not need any "backing store" for paging. It is also much faster than doing reads and writes because the kernel does not need to copy the kernel buffer.

MMU

An abbreviation for *Memory Management Unit*—The part of the computer that figures out which physical page of memory corresponds to which virtual page and takes care of keeping everything straight.

Motif

A description of what windows should look like, how mouse buttons work, etc. Motif is the GUI that is the basis for CDE. The word Motif is also used as the name of the libraries that implement the Motif look and feel.

multitasking OS

An operating system that can run one process for a while, then switch to another one, return to the first, etc. UNIX, VMS, MVS, TOPS, etc., are all multitasking systems. DOS and Microsoft® Windows™ are single-tasking operating systems. (Although MS-Windows™ can have more than one program active on the desktop, it does not do any kind of preemptive context-switching between them.)

NFS

> An abbreviation for *Network File System*—A kernel program that makes it possible to access files across the network without the user ever knowing that the network was involved.

page fault

> The process of bringing in a page from disk when it is not memory-resident. When a program accesses a word in virtual memory, the MMU must translate that virtual address into a physical one. If that block of memory is currently out on disk, the MMU must load that page in.

page table

> A table used by the MMU to show which virtual pages map to which physical pages.

POSIX

> An acronym for Portable Operating System Interface. This refers to a set of committees in the IEEE that are concerned with creating an API that can be common to all UNIX systems. There is a committee in POSIX that is concerned with creating a standard for writing multithreaded programs.

pre-emption

> The act of forcing a thread to stop running.

pre-emptive scheduling

> Scheduling that uses preemption. Time-slicing is pre-emptive, but preemption does not imply time-slicing.

process

> A running program and all the state associated with it.

process structure

> A kernel structure that describes all of the relevant aspects of a process.

program counter

> A register in the CPU that defines which instruction will be executed next.

race condition

> A situation in which the outcome of a program depends upon the luck of the draw—which thread happens to run first.

realtime
> Anything that is timed by a wall clock. Typically this is used by external devices that require servicing within some period of time, such as raster printers and aircraft autopilots. Realtime does not mean any particular amount of time, but is almost always used to refer to sub 100 millisecond (and often sub 1 millisecond) response time.

Reentrant
> A function is reentrant when it is possible for it to be called at the same time by more than one thread. This implies that any global state be protected by mutexes. Note that this term is not used uniformly and is sometimes used to mean either recursive or signal-safe. These three issues are orthogonal.

shared memory
> Memory that is shared by more than one process. Any process may write into this memory, and the others will see the change.

SIGLWP
> A signal that is implemented in Solaris and used to preempt a thread.

signal
> A mechanism that UNIX systems use to allow a process to be notified of some event, typically asynchronous and external. It is a software analog to hardware interrupts.

signal mask
> A mask that tells the kernel (or threads library) which signals will be accepted and which must be put onto a "pending" queue.

SIGSEGV
> A signal that is generated by UNIX systems when a user program attempts to access an address that it has not mapped into its address space.

SIGWAITING
> A signal that is implemented in Solaris and used to tell a threaded process that it should consider creating a new LWP.

SPEC
> An organization that creates benchmark programs and monitors their use.

store buffer

A buffer in a CPU that caches writes to main memory, allowing the CPU to run without waiting for main memory. It is a special case of cache memory.

SVR4

An abbreviation for *System Five, Release 4*—The merger of several different flavors of UNIX that was done by Sun and AT&T. SPEC 1170 merges SVR4, POSIX, and BSD—the main UNIX "flavors"—to specify a common base for all future UNIX implementations.

synchronous signal

A signal that is sent to a process "synchronously." This means that it is the direct result of something that process did, such as dividing by zero. Should a program do a divide-by-zero, the CPU will immediately trap into a kernel routine, which in turn will send a signal to the process (cf: asynchronous signal).

system call

A function that sets up its arguments, then traps into the kernel in order to have the kernel do something for it. This is the only means a user program has for communication with the kernel.

time-sliced scheduling

An algorithm that allocates a set amount of time for a process (or LWP or thread) to run before it is pre-empted from the CPU and another one is given time to run.

trap

An instruction that causes the CPU to stop what it is doing and jump to a special routine in the kernel (cf: system call).

user mode

An operating mode for a CPU in which certain instructions are not allowed. A user program runs in user mode (cf: kernel mode).

user space

That area of memory devoted to user programs. The kernel sets up this space but generally never looks inside (cf: kernel space).

virtual memory

The memory space that a program thinks it is using. It is mapped into physical memory by the MMU. Virtual memory allows a program to behave as if it had 100 Mbytes, even though the system only has 32 Mbytes.

XView

A library of routines that draws and operates Openlook GUI components on a screen. It is based on the SunView™ library of the mid-80s and has been superseded by CDE Motif.

Index